2nd Edition

W9-BAO-177

Praxis

A Brief Rhetoric

Carol Lea Clark

University of Texas | El Paso

also included:

Signs | A Grammar Handbook

by Allison D. Smith

FOUNTAINHEAD PRESS

cover window image: © Can Stock Photo Inc. / thesupe87

Design by Susan Moore
Editorial Consultant: Gina Huck Siegert, Imaginative Solutions, Inc.
Editorial Consultant: Ann Sass

Books may be purchased for educational purposes.

For information, please call or write:

1-800-586-0330
Fountainhead Press
Southlake, TX 76092

Web site: www.fountainheadpress.com
E-mail: customerservice@fountainheadpress.com

ISBN: 978-1-59871-618-4

Printed in the United States of America

FOUNTAINHEAD PRESS V SERIES

Praxis: A Brief Rhetoric can be used as a standalone text or in conjunction with the *Fountainhead Press V Series*. The *V Series* is a new collection of single-topic readers that take a unique look at some of today's most pressing issues. Designed to give writing students a more nuanced introduction to public discourse—on the environment, on food, and on digital life, to name a few of the topics—the books feature writing, research, and invention prompts that can be adapted to nearly any kind of college writing class. Each *V Series* textbook focuses on a single issue and includes multi-genre and multimodal readings and assignments that move the discourse beyond the most familiar patterns of debate—patterns usually fettered by entrenched positions and often obsessed with "winning."

The ultimate goal of the series is to help writing students—who tend to hover on the periphery of public discourse—think, explore, find their voices, and skillfully compose texts in a variety of media and genres. Not only do the books help students think about compelling issues and how they might address them, they also give students the practice they need to develop their research, rhetorical, and writing skills. Together, the readings, prompts, and longer assignments show students how to add their voices to the conversations about these issues in meaningful and productive ways.

The *V Series* uses the term "composition" in its broadest sense. Of course, the textbooks provide students plenty of opportunities to write, but they also include assignments that take students beyond the page. Books in the series encourage students to explore other modes of communication by prompting them to design websites, produce videos, posters, and presentations; conduct primary and secondary research; and develop projects with community partners that might incorporate any number of these skills. Ultimately, we have designed the *Fountainhead Press V Series* to work for teachers and students. With their carefully chosen readings, built-in flexibility, and sound rhetorical grounding, the *V Series* books are a dynamic and user-friendly addition to any writing class.

Current Books in the Series

978-1-59871-415-9

978-1-59871-431-9

978-1-59871-457-9

978-1-59871-472-9

978-1-59871-480-7

Coming Soon

Monsters, *Tolerance*, *Terror*, *Beauty*, *Sports*, *Music*, and *Death*

Carol Lea Clark would like to thank Craig Wynne,
her research assistant, for his invaluable help with
this second edition of *Praxis*.

Preface

Praxis is an appropriate name for this composition textbook because the goal of the composition classroom—and this text—is to enable the student to move from thinking about a topic to the action of creating an effective, as well as an ethical, argument for a particular rhetorical situation. This goal echoes the meaning of the Greek word *praxis*, which can be translated as "process," "practice," or "experience." However, the great Greek rhetorician Aristotle used the term in a special way, to specify practical reasoning, for which the goal was action, rather than theorizing. Furthermore, to ancient Greek rhetoricians, *praxis* had the connotation of moral and ethical actions that enhanced the individual's sense of well-being in life.

The content of this expanded and full-color new edition of *Praxis* is a response to the feedback from many composition instructors who made suggestions such as adding stasis theory, more interactive assignments, and additional readings. Moreover, all exercises are labeled with the same icons as the *Fountainhead Press V Series* readers.

Praxis: A Brief Rhetoric 2e takes basic concepts from the rich history of rhetoric—including *kairos, ethos, pathos*, and *logos*—and demonstrates how students can use these concepts together as a critical framework for analyzing the world around them. This framework enables students to become critical consumers of the flood of persuasive media—including books, newspaper articles, television programs, product reviews, social networks, and advertisements—that compete for their attention.

Moreover, *Praxis* encourages students to employ this rhetorical framework of concepts to the creation of their own texts—essays, yes, but also commonplace books, blogs, op-ed arguments, instructions, and a wide variety of other types of writing. Each chapter features readings, activities, and assignments—some serious and thought provoking, and others creativity-inspiring and *fun*.

This textbook is also written for instructors who have essentially the same practical goals as did Aristotle and other rhetors who taught in ancient Greece and Rome. They want to assist their students in developing skills that will enable them to be critical thinkers and critical writers. To achieve these goals, instructors must focus on several distinct but interconnected skills—reading critically; researching subjects formally and informally; understanding audience expectations; utilizing the structure of language to organize and to communicate information for a specific purpose; persuading readers through appropriate use of ethos, pathos, and logos; and revising to improve the effectiveness of a draft. The goal of *Praxis* is to move the student from theory to practical reason to action.

Chapter Highlights

Chapter 1 Practicing Rhetoric

Defines rhetoric and employs classical rhetorical concepts to introduce students to persuasive argument. Introduces visual rhetoric, commonplace books, and blogging.

Chapter 2 Responding Rhetorically

Demonstrates the connection between rhetoric and critical thinking. Introduces the rhetorical triangle, a checklist for rhetorical argument, and techniques for close reading. New assignments include composing a lexicon, considering song lyrics as an argument, and interpreting advertisements.

Chapter 3 Analyzing Rhetorically

Discusses how understanding the *kairos* of an argument enhances critical analysis and provides examples of arguments based on *ethos*, *pathos*, and *logos*. Explains audience analysis, deductive and inductive arguments, and logical fallacies. Assignments include writing a letter to the editor, creating a professional Facebook page, and writing a memo to explain the student's own collage expressing pathos.

Chapter 4 Inventing Rhetorically

Introduces Aristotle's artistic and inartistic proofs and explains how to use the discovery of artistic proofs as an invention strategy. Discusses the similarities and differences between ancient invention techniques and contemporary prewriting. Demonstrates how to use stasis theory to analyze an issue and to construct an effective argument. Includes three related readings that can be used to write a stasis-theory based mini-research paper. Other assignments include analyzing rhetorical techniques in a television courtroom drama, using stasis theory to develop a persuasive argument about a public debate, writing a product review, and composing a rhetorical analysis.

Chapter 5 Writing Rhetorically

Explains how writing allows students to enter the academic conversation. Demonstrates the similarities and differences between ancient and contemporary formats for compositions. Discusses writing basics such as constructing a thesis statement, composing an introduction, weaving in material from sources, and answering opposing arguments. Introduces page design concepts. Assignments include writing an argument-based research paper, a film review, and an op-ed argument.

Chapter 6 Revising Rhetorically

Describes the revision process, which begins with careful rereading, and includes procedures for peer editing. Suggests several ways to consider the qualities of effective writing, such as "William Safire's Rules for Writing" and "Grammar Girl's Top Ten Grammar Myths," as well as more standard criteria. Provides several sample student essays for peer editing.

Chapter 7 Researching Rhetorically

Introduces the research process as developing what Aristotle called inartistic proofs. Describes the difference between primary and secondary research. Assignments include writing a profile of a person, constructing an annotated bibliography, evaluating a website, and avoiding plagiarism.

Appendix

Provides a concise guide to APA and MLA documentation styles.

In summary, the new full-color *Praxis: A Brief Rhetoric 2e*, with its enhanced interactive exercises, celebrates the ancient heritage of the composition classroom and its ability to address the needs of today's students who live in a media-enhanced, technology-complex world.

Table of Contents

5 WRITING RHETORICALLY   145

Signs
A Grammar Handbook
by Allison D. Smith

PRACTICING RHETORIC

Praxis in Action

Why Rhetoric Is Important in My Writing by Elizabeth Jimenez

Rhetoric is an intangible power that has the ability to motivate and manipulate. If I master rhetoric, I know I possess the ability to move my audience toward my goal.

I communicate effectively when I gain the confidence of the audience. Influencing my class and professor is my number one goal and is done so by my ethos. My use of rhetoric is validated by my credibility in the subject I disseminate. I must possess credibility if I am to be a reputable source of information.

Once I have gained the attention of the audience, I obtain logos when I clearly and logically disseminate my thoughts. I accomplish my purpose when I prove my statements. This is done by substantiating my thoughts with supporting evidence. Many contributing factors that come into play have an influence on my argument, such as bias. If my argument is biased, this can strongly detract from my goal.

Persuasive rhetoric is not necessarily accomplished when I use too much emotion. I find if I overuse pathos, the general idea gets lost. If I want my idea to be well received, it is important for me to communicate with levelheadedness.

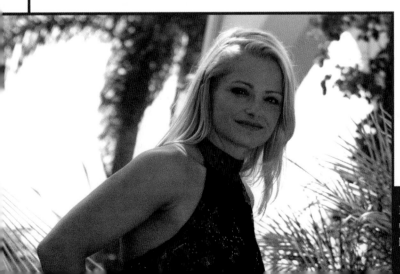

These elements help me to establish effective rhetoric, which is crucial as I write for different audiences in college. Rhetoric will open doors throughout my college career as I discover new ways of conveying information and opinions.

Elizabeth Jimenez writes that understanding rhetoric gives her the power to persuade an audience.

Through *Praxis*, Theory Becomes Action

The word **praxis** can be translated as "process" or "practice." Aristotle, the great Greek rhetorician, employed the term in a special way to mean practical reasoning, for which the goal was action. To be practical in the Aristotelian sense is a little different from what being practical means today. It indicates the ability to apply abstract theory to concrete situations and thus, to move from theory to action. Moreover, praxis embodies a creative element that raises it above the mundane or merely pragmatic. Therefore, "practicing rhetoric" is not practice in the sense of rehearsal. Rather, it is performing, or applying, or acting out rhetoric—taking theory and turning it into action.

So, if we understand praxis or the "practicing" part of "practicing rhetoric," what does the "rhetoric" part of the chapter title mean? In common usage, the word *argument* has a narrow definition that emphasizes heated or angry exchanges of clashing and often irreconcilable viewpoints. Moreover, sides in such arguments are limited to black and white opposites and include no shades of gray. If one person is right, then the other must be wrong.

In academia, in contrast, we argue because it causes us to examine critically our own as well as others' ideas. Argument compels us to consider conflicting claims, to evaluate evidence, and to clarify our thoughts. We know that even wise, well-intentioned people don't always agree, so we consider others' ideas respectfully. After one person presents an argument, either orally or in writing, others respond with arguments that support, modify, or contradict the original one. Then, in turn, more individuals counter with their own versions, and thus, the interchange becomes a conversation.

Academic arguments can be divided into several different categories, depending upon the extent of the writer's desire to persuade and the scope of the conversational exchange.

1. **One type of argument simply makes a point about the topic.** For example, later in this chapter you will read an article titled, "San Ysidro Shooting Survivor Lives His Dream of Being a Cop." In the article, the author describes the wounds inflicted on a young man during the McDonald's Massacre in San Ysidro in 1984 and then explains how and why this young man later became a cop. No one is likely to disagree with the writer's line of reasoning, at least not if the author offers sufficient evidence to back up the original statement that, for this man, being a cop is his dream. This article is a profile, a type of argument more often seen in magazines and newspapers than in journals.

2. A second type of argument involves a controversial issue, and the writer's aim is to persuade the audience to change its stance on the matter. The ideal result, for the writer, would be that members of the audience alter their positions to coincide with the writer's viewpoint. In this second type of argument, it is essential that the writer offer the complete structure of thesis, evidence, possible opposition viewpoints which are discussed and countered, and a conclusion. "The Sleepover Question," another reading in this chapter, presents this kind of argument. The author, who has conducted research in both America and Holland, argues the controversial position that if American parents would adopt more liberal attitudes toward their children's sexuality, like the parents in Holland, "the transition into adulthood need not be so painful for parents or children." A reading in Chapter 3, "Why Executions Should Be Televised," offers a more extreme version of this type of argument. Either executions are televised or they aren't, and the writer advocates that they should be.

3. A third type of argument emphasizes multiple perspectives and viewpoints and tries to find common ground that participants can agree upon. In Chapter 4, several readings are collected in a casebook called "The $300 House." The *Harvard Business Review* initiated a design competition intended to spark inclusive argument with the aim of gathering ideas about how to build inexpensive but adequate homes for the poor in the world's slums. "Hands Off Our Houses," one response to the competition that appears in the casebook, argues, for example, that bringing $300 houses into the slums of Mumbai is not the answer to the housing problem. In contrast, other responses posted on a website associated with the competition suggest ways the idea of the $300 house might work, while admitting enormous difficulties.

These three types of arguments represent points in a spectrum, and all persuasive texts may not neatly fit into one of the three categories. A crucial thing to remember, though, is that all arguments involve the presentation of a line of reasoning about a topic or an issue—a thesis, hypothesis, or claim—and the support of that reasoning with evidence.

Become Part of the Academic Conversation

As a student, you are expected to join academic conversations that are already in progress. How do you do that? How do you know what kind of response is appropriate? Have you ever entered a party where everyone is talking excitedly? Most likely, you paused near the doorway to get a sense of who was there and what they were discussing before you decided who to talk to and what to say. Or, have you become part of a Facebook group or a listserv discussion group? If so, you know it is a good idea to "lurk" for a while before asking questions or contributing a remark. Writing an academic paper involves a similar process. You read about a subject until you have a good grasp of the points authorities are debating. Then you find a way to integrate your own ideas about that subject with the ideas of others and create an informed contribution to the conversation.

For example, the following students' introductions to movie reviews demonstrate they not only understand the films and have interesting things to say about them; their writing also displays knowledge of what others have written about the films, whether the students agree with those evaluations or not.

- Roger Ebert claims that audience members who haven't seen the first two *Lord of the Rings* films (Peter Jackson, 2001, 2002) will likely "be adrift during the early passages of [the third] film's 200 minutes." But then again, Ebert continues, "to be adrift occasionally during this nine-hour saga comes with the territory" (par. 3). Ebert, though, misses one crucial fact regarding *Lord of the Rings: The Return of the King* (2003). This third installment opens with a flashback intended to familiarize new spectators about what happened in the previous two films. Within these five minutes, the audience discovers how Gollum (Andy Serkis) came to be corrupt through the destructive power of the Ring. The viewer, therefore, will not necessarily be "adrift," as Ebert claims, since the lighting, setting, and sound in the opening of *The Return of the King* show the lighter, more peaceful world before Gollum finds the ring, compared to the darker, more sinister world thereafter.

- "It's hard to resist a satire, even when it wobbles, that insists the most unbelievable parts are the most true" (*Rolling Stone* par. 1). This is Peter Travers's overarching view of Grant Heslov's satire, *The Men Who Stare at Goats* (2009). Travers is correct here; after all, Goats's opening title card, which reads, "More of this is real than you would believe," humorously teases the viewer that some of the film's most "unbelievable parts" will, in fact, offer the most truth. We experience this via Bill Wilson's (Ewan McGregor) interview of an ex "psy-ops" soldier, when Wilson's life spirals out of control, and all the other farfetched actions presenting "reality." But again, it is the film's opening—specifically, its setting, camera movements and angles, dialogue, effects, and ambient noise—that sets the foundation for an unbelievably realistic satire.[*]

In both of these introductions, the students quote reviews by professional film critics and respond to the critics' opinions. Moreover, the students continue their arguments by using the critics' ideas as springboards for their own arguments. These two short examples indicate these students have learned how to counter positions advocated by authorities without losing their own voices. If the rest of their essays continue as they have begun, the students will have written essays to which others can reply, thus continuing the conversation. Later in this textbook, you will have your own chance to enter the conversation of film reviews by reviewing a favorite movie of your own.

Collaborative Groups Help Students Enter the Academic Conversation

Likely, your writing class will include collaborative group work as part of the mix of activities, along with lecture, class discussion, and in-class writing. You may wonder why there is so much talk in a writing class, which is a good question. Use of collaborative groups is based on extensive research, which shows that students who work in small groups as part of their courses tend to learn more and retain the knowledge longer than students who are not asked to work in groups. Also, research shows students who participate in collaborative group work generally are more satisfied with the course. Groups give students a chance to apply knowledge they have learned and provide a change of pace from lectures or other class activities. There are several types of groups, and your class may include one or all of them:

- Informal, one-time pairs or groups. After presenting some material, your instructor may ask you to turn to the person next to you and discuss the topic or answer a question.

- Ongoing small classroom groups. Usually, these groups work together for a significant part of the semester, and your instructor may assign roles to members of the group such as recorder, facilitator, editor, and spokesperson. Often, the roles will rotate, so that everyone has a chance to try out each job. Your instructor may give you a job description for each role or train the class in the tasks for each role.

---

[*] Kelli Marshall. "Entering a Conversation, Teaching the Academic Essay," *Unmuzzled Thoughts about Teaching and Pop Culture*, October 23, 2010, http://kellimarshall.net/unmuzzledthoughts/teaching/academic-essay/. Accessed August 30, 2011.

- Task groups. These groups are formed to write a report, complete a project, or do some other task together. These groups meet several times, often outside of class. The products of these groups are usually graded, and your instructor will often require members to rate each other on their performance.

- Peer editing groups. When you have completed a draft of an essay or other text, your instructor may ask you to exchange papers in pairs or within small groups. You will be asked to read your classmate's paper carefully and make comments, either on a peer editing form or on the paper itself. Likewise, your classmate will read and make comments on your paper. Then, when you receive your paper back, you can make revisions based on your classmate's comments.

An added benefit to the use of collaborative groups in writing classes is that students can help each other figure out what the ongoing conversation is for a particular topic or issue before writing about it. Also, groups provide a forum where students can practice making comments that are part of that conversation.

Rhetoric and Argument

The structure of an argument—introduction (including a thesis), supporting evidence, counterarguments, and conclusion—will be familiar to you from previous English classes. What you may not realize is that ancient Greeks developed this argumentative structure out of necessity. Their democratic system of government required that citizens be able to speak persuasively in public, as there were no attorneys or professional politicians. Ancient Greeks called their persuasive strategies rhetoric, and rhetoric became the primary means of education of the elite youth in Athens.

Rhetoric, like argument, is a word that has both a popular meaning and an academic meaning. You have probably heard someone say of a politician's speech, "Oh, that's just rhetoric," meaning the politician's words are empty verbiage or hot air. The politician is attempting to sound impressive while saying nothing that has real meaning. Or perhaps the politician is making promises that listeners believe he or she has no intention of keeping. Politicians who engage in verbal deception often succeed only in acquiring the reputation of dishonesty.

In the field of rhetoric and composition today, rhetoric has a much different meaning. Though definitions vary somewhat from one practitioner to another, rhetoric generally means the study and use of persuasive communication (or argument), a meaning that traces its roots back to the original use of the term by ancient Greeks. Rhetoric, in the form of oratory, was essential to the Greeks, as they used it to resolve disputes in the law courts and to promote political action in the Assembly.

Are We All Greeks?

As Americans, we owe an immense debt to ancient Greek civilization. Our laws, our democratic form of government, our literature, and our art have their roots in ancient Athens. Earlier generations of Americans and Western Europeans, who often studied Latin and Greek, may have had a clearer understanding of the direct connections of our culture to Athens of the 4th and 5th centuries BCE. Indeed, the English poet Percy Bysshe Shelley famously said, "We are all Greeks" because of the essential influence of ancient Greek culture upon Western civilization. However, even translated into 21st century American English, the linkage is still there.

Something quite amazing happened in Athens, around 500 BCE. Instead of being invaded by a foreign country who appointed a puppet ruler or experiencing a coup in which a strong man seized power, the people peaceably chose to put in place a direct democracy. Attica was not the only city-state to have a democracy, but it was the most successful. During the golden age of Greece, from roughly 500 BCE to 300 BCE, art, architecture, and literature thrived.

Direct or radical democracy meant all male citizens of Attica over the age of 20 could vote in the Assembly, the policy-making body of the city-state. They did not elect senators or representatives as we do today. Each of these men *voted directly*. Moreover, they could settle differences with fellow citizens by suing in the law courts. Out of 250,000 to 300,000 residents in Attica, some 30,000 were citizens. Amazingly, it was not unusual for 10,000 of these eligible men to vote in the Assembly. The law courts had juries of 500 or more. Imagine trying to speak to an audience of 10,000 people without modern loudspeakers. Even with the wonderful acoustics in Greek theatres, it would have been a challenge.

Ordinary citizens were required to speak in the Assembly or the courts to promote laws or defend themselves from lawsuits, as there were no attorneys or professional politicians. Certainly, speaking before such large audiences necessitated special skills acquired only through extensive training and practice. Many sought out teachers to help them learn how to speak persuasively, and, indeed, training in rhetoric became the primary method of education for the elite young men of Athens. A few women were also educated in rhetoric, but they were in the minority.

The earliest teachers of verbal persuasive skills we now call rhetoric were Sophists who migrated from Sicily and other Greek states. Some of their viewpoints were curiously modern—for example, that knowledge is relative and that pure truth does not exist. However, they became known for teaching their pupils to persuade an audience to think whatever they wanted them to believe. Sophists such as Gorgias themselves often presented entertainment speeches during which they would argue, on the spur of the moment, on any topic raised by the audience, just to show they were able to construct effective arguments on any subject.

The term rhetoric comes from the Greek word *rhetorike*, which Plato coined as a criticism of the Sophists, claiming the Sophists' rhetoric could be employed to manipulate the masses for good or ill, and that rhetoricians used it irresponsibly. Ironically, Plato demonstrates excellent rhetorical techniques himself when he condemns rhetoric and argues that only the elite who are educated in philosophy are suited to rule, not the rhetoricians. Aristotle, Plato's student, took a more moderate viewpoint toward rhetoric. Indeed, he was the first philosopher to classify rhetoric as a tool for practical debate with general audiences. His book *On Rhetoric* (though it was probably lecture notes possibly combined with student responses, rather than a manuscript intended for publication) is the single most important text that establishes rhetoric as a system of persuasive communication.

Athens, even in its glory days, seethed with controversy and bickering over the many inefficiencies of democracy. Men trained in rhetoric executed two coups, the Tyranny of the Four Hundred in 411 BCE and the Tyranny of the Thirty in 404 BCE, neither of which was an improvement; after each coup, democracy returned. Moreover, Athenians fought wars with Persia (the Battle of Marathon in 490 BCE and the Battle of Thermopylae in 480 BCE) and Sparta (the Peloponnesian War in 431–404 BCE and the Corinthian War of 395–387 BCE). Finally, the armies of Philip II of Macedonia defeated Athens at the Battle of Chaeronea in 338 BCE, ending Athenian independence. Despite coups and wars, democracy remained in place in Athens for nearly 200 years.

If Americans might be called Greeks because our country is based on Greek traditions, this is not to say that rhetoric appears in all cultures. True, one might say that all civilizations have some sort of persuasive negotiation process; but profound differences exist between cultures in terms of what verbal strategies are persuasive. Indeed, disparity in expectations and the actions of individuals and groups from different traditions can be a cause of strife.

Rhetoric and Power

Aristotle defined rhetoric as "the faculty of discovering, in a given instance, the available means of persuasion," which we might paraphrase as the power to see the means of persuasion available in any given situation. Each part of this definition is important. Rhetoric is power; the person who is able to speak eloquently, choosing the most suitable arguments about a topic for a specific audience in a particular situation, is the person most likely to persuade. In both Greece and Rome, the primary use of rhetoric was oratory—persuasion through public speaking. However, the texts of many famous speeches were recorded and studied as models by students, and prominent rhetoricians wrote treatises and handbooks for teaching rhetoric. To Greeks and Romans, a person who could use rhetoric effectively was a person of influence and power because he could persuade his audience to action. The effective orator could win court cases; the effective orator could influence the passage or failure of laws; the effective orator could send a nation to war or negotiate peace.

Skill with rhetoric has conveyed power through the ages, though in our contemporary world, rhetoric is often displayed in written text such as a book, newspaper or magazine article, or scientific report, rather than presented as a speech. Persuasive communication also can be expressed visually, as an illustration that accompanies a text or a cartoon that conveys its own message. Indeed, in our highly visual society, with television, movies, video games, and the Internet, images can often persuade more powerfully than words alone.

Using rhetoric effectively means being able to interpret the rhetoric we are presented with in our everyday lives. Knowledge of persuasive communication or rhetoric empowers us to present our views and persuade others to modify their ideas. Through changes in ideas, rhetoric leads to action. Through changes in actions, rhetoric affects society.

Selected Definitions of Rhetoric

Aristotle, 350 BCE—*Rhetoric is "the faculty of discovering, in a given instance, the available means of persuasion."*

Cicero, 90 BCE—*Rhetoric is "speech designed to persuade" and "eloquence based on the rules of art."*

Quintilian, 95 CE—*Rhetoric is "the science of speaking well."*

Augustine of Hippo, ca. 426 CE—*Rhetoric is "the art of persuading people to accept something, whether it is true or false."*

Anonymous, ca. 1490–1495—*Rhetoric is "the science which refreshes the hungry, renders the mute articulate, makes the blind see, and teaches one to avoid every lingual ineptitude."*

Heinrich Cornelius Agrippa, 1531—*"To confess the truth, it is generally granted that the entire discipline of rhetoric from start to finish is nothing other than an art of flattery, adulation, and, as some say more audaciously, lying, in that, if it cannot persuade others through the truth of the case, it does so by means of deceitful speech."*

Hoyt Hudson, 1923—*"In this sense, plainly, the man who speaks most persuasively uses the most, or certainly the best, rhetoric; and the man whom we censure for inflation of style and strained effects is suffering not from too much rhetoric, but from a lack of it."*

I. A. Richards, 1936—*"Rhetoric, I shall urge, should be a study of misunderstanding and its remedies."*

Sister Miriam Joseph, 1937—*Rhetoric is "the art of communicating thought from one mind to another, the adaptation of language to circumstance."*

Kenneth Burke, 1950—*"[T]he basic function of rhetoric [is] the use of words by human agents to form attitudes or to induce actions in other human agents."*

Gerard A. Hauser, 2002—*"Rhetoric, as an area of study, is concerned with how humans use symbols, especially language, to reach agreement that permits coordinated effort of some sort."*

Activity 1.1 **Historical Usage of the Word "Rhetoric"**

Read through the list of historical definitions of the word "rhetoric" on the previous page, and choose one that you find interesting. In a discussion, compare your chosen definition with those of your classmates.

Activity 1.2 **Contemporary Usage of the Word "Rhetoric"**

Find at least two recent but different examples involving use of the word "rhetoric." For example, search your local newspaper for an example of how the word "rhetoric" is being used. A search of the *Dallas Morning News* for the word "rhetoric" led to a story about citizen efforts to clean up a neglected area of town: "He now hopes for help to finally fill the gap between rhetoric and reality." Or ask a friend, fellow employee, or a family member to tell you what the word "rhetoric" means and write down what they say. Discuss your examples in your small group and present the best ones to the class.

Visual Map of Meanings for the Word "Rhetoric"

The word map for the word "rhetoric" shown on page 12 has branches for different meanings of the word, with some branches splitting again to display subtle subsets of connotation. It was created by a website, Visual Thesaurus (www.visualthesaurus.com), which computes visual word maps for any word inputted in its search box. The idea is that words lead to branches that lead to more words, inspiring users to think of language in new ways.

At the Visual Thesaurus site, if you place your cursor over one of the circles connecting the branches, a small box will pop up that defines that connection. One of these connection boxes is visible. Notice it says, "using language effectively to please or persuade." This is the branch of the visual map that is closest to the meaning of "rhetoric" as used in this book. The other branches illustrate other contemporary uses of the word.

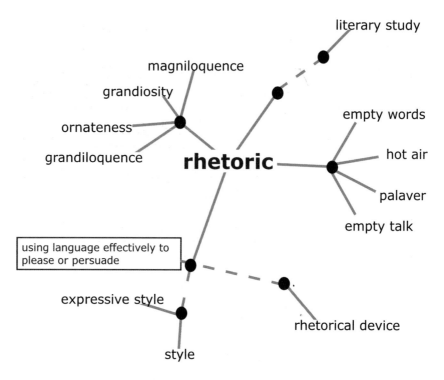

Activity 1.3 Explore the Visual Map of the Word "Rhetoric"

In your small group, choose one of the five branches of words in the visual map of the word "rhetoric." Go to one or more good dictionaries and explore the meanings of the words in that branch. A good place to start would be the *Oxford English Dictionary*, which your college library may offer online. The *OED* offers intricate analyses of the histories of word meanings. Report to the class what you find out about the words on your particular branch.

Rhetorical Argument

Often, in our culture, the word "argument" is taken to mean a disagreement or even a fight, with raised voices, rash words, and hurt feelings. We have the perception of an argument as something that has victory and defeat, winners and losers. Argument, in the sense of a **rhetorical argument**, however, means the carefully crafted presentation of a viewpoint or position on a topic and the giving of thoughts, ideas, and opinions along with reasons for their support. The persuasive strength of an argument rests upon the rhetorical skills of the rhetor (the speaker or the writer) in utilizing the tools of language to persuade a particular audience.

Aristotle identified three appeals or three ways to persuade an audience, and we are still using these today, though often without using the Greek terms to identify the means of persuasion:

Ethos—The rhetor convinces an audience by means of his character or credibility. In oratory, the speaker projects an air of confidence and authority. In writing, ethos is conveyed by the qualifications of the writer or the authorities that are cited and also by the quality of the writing.

Pathos—The rhetor persuades by playing upon the listener's (or reader's) emotions. He or she may refer to children, death, disaster, injustice, or other topics that arouse pity, fear, or other emotions.

Logos—The rhetor persuades by the use of reasoning and evidence. Arguments based on logos employ deductive or inductive reasoning.

Although a good argument will contain at least traces of all three appeals, skilled rhetors analyze their audiences to determine which of the three would be most persuasive to that particular audience. Then, they construct arguments that emphasize that particular appeal.

In addition, a knowledgeable rhetor considers the time, place, audience, topic, and other aspects of the occasion for writing or speaking to determine the **kairos**, or opportune moment of the composition. This factor or critical moment both provides and limits opportunities for appeals suitable to that moment. For example, someone giving a commencement address has certain opportunities and constraints. Likewise, an attorney writing a last-minute appeal for someone on death row has a very different set of options.

The editorial below addresses the shooting attack on Arizona Congresswoman Gabrielle Giffords that killed six and left Giffords and others seriously wounded. The text, published on *Time* magazine's website shortly after the attack, addresses the kairos of the situation—a United States Congresswoman has been shot, certainly an exceptional moment in many ways. The editorial demonstrates several important things to remember in understanding rhetoric and its use in American society. The author, Nathan Thornburgh, addresses the controversy about whether "overheated rhetoric" (exaggerated pathos) had inspired the shooting, an important question considering the often-inflammatory language of political rhetoric in the United States. However, his text is not filled with rash or harsh words that could further inflame the controversy. Though the text is an opinion piece, taking a position regarding this controversy and offering evidence to support his opinion, it is not itself "overheated rhetoric." As you read the text, think about whether he emphasizes ethos, pathos, or logos. You may or may not agree with his position. Rhetorical language is never neutral; its purpose is to persuade an audience to share the author's opinion. Good arguments, though, do not use "overheated rhetoric," false evidence, or logical fallacies to win over an audience.

Reading 1.1

Violent Rhetoric and Arizona Politics
by Nathan Thornburgh

This editorial by Nathan Thornburgh was originally printed in *Time* shortly after the shooting of Arizona Congresswoman Gabrielle Giffords.

Sometimes, rumors of violence beget actual violence. Saturday's mass shooting at a Safeway on North Oracle Road in Tucson, which killed six and left Democratic Congresswoman Gabrielle Giffords and others gravely wounded, may well be one of those occasions.

It's impossible to know this early what the motivations for the attack were. Was the alleged shooter—who has been identified as 22-year-old Tucsonan

Jared Loughner—angry about immigration? Or perhaps another hot-button issue? YouTube videos ascribed to him bore the mark of mental illness—they were conspiratorial, unintelligible, espousing no particular cause—but no matter his mental state, his crime took place in an overheated political environment. Last March, at the height of the health care reform battle, Giffords's office was vandalized. She mentioned in an MSNBC interview that a Sarah Palin graphic had depicted her district in the crosshairs of a gun sight. "They've got to realize there are consequences to that," she said. "The rhetoric is incredibly heated." The corner next to her office had also become, she said, a popular spot for Tea Party protests.

As Pima County Sheriff Clarence Dupnik put it in an extraordinary and melancholic press conference after the shooting, "we have become the Mecca for prejudice and bigotry." He added that he's "not aware of any public officials who are not receiving threats."

Another shooting victim, a federal judge named John Roll, had been placed under 24-hour security in 2009 after ruling in favor of illegal immigrants in a high-profile case. It's unclear why he was at the supermarket event. But for almost a year now, Arizona's leaders have been grappling with anti-immigration sentiments, inflamed by reports of crossborder violence. National media attention, with its attendant voices of hysteria, only added to the churn. Pundits spoke gravely about a wave of violence, born in Mexico and now flooding Arizona. Arizona's two most famous politicians fueled the fury. Republican Senator John McCain, facing an unexpected reelection challenge from the right, ran a campaign obsessed with crossborder crime. And GOP Governor Jan Brewer, who invited the national spotlight by championing strict anti-illegal immigrant legislation, talked of beheadings in the desert.

The only problem with all this talk about a massive crossborder crime wave is that it wasn't true. Phoenix had not become one of the world's kidnapping capitals. Crime rates in Arizona had been steady or even fallen in some areas. There had been no beheadings in the desert. There were plenty of deaths there, but they were pathetic and meek tragedies: impoverished border-crossers, abandoned by their heartless guides, dying of exposure and dehydration.

But the idea of a state under siege took hold. When I was on the border last year reporting on the murder of rancher Rob Krentz, I talked to many who sincerely believed that they were under attack. Krentz's murder was a terrible event, but it was an isolated event. The relatively small number of home invasions, holdups and other crimes deeply disturbed border communities, but only because they had been living in such calm for so long. Their crime rates still don't match most cities in the states.

The supermarket meet-and-greet where Giffords was shot was actually a testimony to just how safe southern Arizona is. As a press release from her office last week put it, "'Congress on Your Corner' allows residents of Arizona's 8th Congressional District to meet their congresswoman one-on-one and discuss with her any issue, concern or problem involving the federal government." Not exactly the kind of event a politician would hold in a war zone.

It's true that Giffords was not a fan of the state's anti-immigration bill SB1070, but there were higher-profile opponents, such as her fellow Congressional Representative in Tucson, Raul Grijalva. Yet the idea that Arizona is under attack has been pushed hard enough that it's very possible that the coward who shot her (in the head, according to a Tucson paper) believed that the 40-year-old Democrat, who had been tarred by some as soft on immigration because she didn't support SB1070, was contributing to larger-scale violence against Arizonans.

If that is the case, it would only add to the tragedy. The fact is, that among all the overwrought promises and all the panic I heard last summer in Arizona, I found that Giffords was one of the few politicians offering concrete law enforcement steps that would actually work against the drug cartels and other smugglers. It's not just that she fought for more money and police for border protection, although she did that. She co-sponsored legislation last year with a California Republican that aimed to give law enforcement important new tools in cracking down on the cash cards that were a favored method of money-laundering. It was one of the many sensible, pragmatic ideas she had for cracking down on crime.

Whatever dark fantasies drove someone to try to take her life, Giffords is a sensible politician who was likely shot because she dealt with Arizona's reality, not its rumors.

Activity 1.4 **Write a Summary of "Violent Rhetoric and Arizona Politics"**

Summarizing is an excellent technique to use when preparing for an exam or doing research for an essay. It allows you to discern the main points of a text and how they fit together. With a classmate, review the editorial by Thornburgh. Read the article together carefully, and list the main points individually. After you've listed the main points, put them into paragraph form.

Caution: Beware of the temptation to add your own analysis of what the text is saying. For example, if you are summarizing a scientist's article on global warming, you need to be careful not to reveal your personal opinion about whether or not global warming is occurring or whether or not human actions are to blame. In this assignment, you summarize only. You do not argue or analyze.

When you're finished, compare your summary with that of your partner.

Activity 1.5 **Analyzing "Violent Rhetoric and Arizona Politics"**

1. What does Nathan Thornburgh mean when he uses the term "overheated rhetoric"?

2. What is the argument that Thornburgh is making about the cause of the attack on Representative Giffords?

3. What evidence does Thornburgh offer to support his argument?

4. Does Thornburgh make his case? Is he convincing? Why or why not?

Reading 1.2

The Sleepover Question

by Amy Schalet

This text by Amy Schalet was first published in *The New York Times*. "The Sleepover Question" hazards an argument that many Americans—or at least American parents—may find controversial. Backed by her credentials as a professor of sociology, she cites research from 130 interviews, both in the United States and the Netherlands, and tackles the issue of whether or not American parents should allow their adolescent children to have sex in the family home. Pay particular attention, for she shows how to argue a subject that is not only controversial but often ignored.

NOT under my roof. That's the attitude most American parents have toward teenagers and their sex lives. Squeamishness and concern describe most parents' approach to their offspring's carnality. We don't want them doing it—whatever "it" is!—in our homes. Not surprisingly, teenage sex is a source of conflict in many American families.

Would Americans increase peace in family life and strengthen family bonds if they adopted more accepting attitudes about sex and what's allowable under the family roof? I've interviewed 130 people, all white, middle class and not particularly religious, as part of a study of teenage sex and family life here and in the Netherlands. My look into cultural differences suggests family life might be much improved, for all, if Americans had more open ideas about teenage sex. The question of who sleeps where when a teenager brings a boyfriend or girlfriend home for the night fits within the larger world of culturally divergent ideas about teenage sex, lust and capacity for love.

Kimberly and Natalie dramatize the cultural differences in the way young women experience their sexuality. (I have changed their names to protect confidentiality.) Kimberly, a 16-year-old American, never received sex education at home. "God, no! No, no! That's not going to happen," she told me. She'd like to tell her parents that she and her boyfriend are having sex, but she believes it is easier for her parents not to know because the truth would "shatter" their image of her as their "little princess."

Natalie, who is also 16 but Dutch, didn't tell her parents immediately when she first had intercourse with her boyfriend of three months. But, soon after, she says, she was so happy, she wanted to share the good news. Initially her father was upset and worried about his daughter and his honor. "Talk to him," his wife advised Natalie; after she did, her father made peace with the change. Essentially Natalie and her family negotiated a life change together and figured out, as a family, how to adjust to changed circumstance.

Respecting what she understood as her family's "don't ask, don't tell" policy, Kimberly only slept with her boyfriend at his house, when no one was home. She enjoyed being close to her boyfriend but did not like having to keep an important part of her life secret from her parents. In contrast, Natalie and her boyfriend enjoyed time and a new closeness with her family; the fact that her parents knew and approved of her boyfriend seemed a source of pleasure.

The difference in their experiences stems from divergent cultural ideas about sex and what responsible parents ought to do about it. Here, we see teenagers as helpless victims beset by raging hormones and believe parents should protect them from urges they cannot control. Matters aren't helped by the stereotype that all boys want the same thing, and all girls want love and cuddling. This compounds the burden on parents to steer teenage children away from relationships that will do more harm than good.

The Dutch parents I interviewed regard teenagers, girls and boys, as capable of falling in love, and of reasonably assessing their own readiness for sex. Dutch parents like Natalie's talk to their children about sex and its unintended consequences and urge them to use contraceptives and practice safe sex.

Cultural differences about teenage sex are more complicated than clichéd images of puritanical Americans and permissive Europeans. Normalizing ideas about teenage sex in fact allows the Dutch to exert *more* control over their children. Most of the parents I interviewed actively discouraged promiscuous behavior. And Dutch teenagers often reinforced what we see as 1950s-style mores: eager to win approval, they bring up their partners in conversation, introduce them to their parents and help them make favorable impressions.

Some Dutch teenagers went so far as to express their ideas about sex and love in self-consciously traditional terms; one Dutch boy said the advantage of spending the night with a partner was that it was "Like Mom and Dad, like when you're married, you also wake up next to the person you love."

Normalizing teenage sex under the family roof opens the way for more responsible sex education. In a national survey, 7 of 10 Dutch girls reported that by the time they were 16, their parents had talked to them about pregnancy and contraception. It seems these conversations helped teenagers prepare, responsibly, for active sex lives: 6 of 10 Dutch girls said they were on the pill when they first had intercourse. Widespread use of oral contraceptives contributes to low teenage pregnancy rates — more than 4 times lower in the Netherlands than in the United States.

Obviously sleepovers aren't a direct route to family happiness. But even the most traditional parents can appreciate the virtue of having their children be comfortable bringing a girlfriend or boyfriend home, rather than have them sneak around.

Unlike the American teenagers I interviewed, who said they felt they had to split their burgeoning sexual selves from their family roles, the Dutch teens had a chance to integrate different parts of themselves into their family life. When children feel safe enough to tell parents what they are doing and feeling, presumably it's that much easier for them to ask for help. This allows parents to have more influence, to control through connection.

Sexual maturation is awkward and difficult. The Dutch experience suggests that it is possible for families to stay connected when teenagers start having sex, and that if they do, the transition into adulthood need not be so painful for parents or children.

Explore

Activity 1.6 Analyze "The Sleepover Question"

1. What do you think about the "not under my roof" approach to a parent controlling a teen's sexuality versus the Dutch approach of allowing a teen's partner to sleep over? Discuss in your small group.

2. How do stereotypes play against the argument for a more open approach to teen sex in America? How much of parents' discomfort with their teen potentially having sex is guided by how their parents treated the subject when they were teens?

3. "The Sleepover Question" emphasizes logos. Can you paraphrase the logic of the argument? How does emotion (pathos) play a role in resistance to this argument?

4. In the article, the writer discusses the link between the use of oral contraceptives and lower teen pregnancy rates but does not mention the risk of STDs or condom use. Is it irresponsible of the author not to discuss the risk of STDs and sex, especially when she is willing to discuss teen pregnancy? Does it feel like an incomplete argument without discussing STDs?

5. If you were going to write a letter to the editor about this article, what would you say?

Why Study Rhetoric?

Rhetoric, or persuasive communication, happens all around us every day, in conversation at the grocery store, in blogs, on television, and in the classroom. We Americans constantly air our opinions about almost everything. Sometimes it is to convince others to share our opinions, sometimes the reason is to engage in a dialogue that will help us understand the world around us, and sometimes it is to persuade others to action.

Argument is essential to human interaction and to society, for it is through the interplay of ideas in argument that we discover answers to problems, try out new ideas, shape scientific experiments, communicate with family members, recruit others to join a team, and work out any of the multitude of human interactions essential for society to function. When issues are complex, arguments do not result in immediate persuasion of the audience; rather, argument is part of an ongoing conversation between concerned parties who seek resolution, rather than speedy answers.

Rhetoric provides a useful framework for looking at the world, as well as for evaluating and initiating communications. In the modern world, writing and communicating persuasively is a necessary skill. Those who can present effective arguments in writing are, in the business world, often the ones who are promoted. In addition, those who are able to evaluate the arguments presented to them, whether by politicians, advertisers, or even family members, are less likely to be swayed by logical fallacies or ill-supported research.

Also, writing rhetorically is a tool with sometimes surprising uses. Research shows that, as students, we are more likely to remember material we have written about rather than simply memorized. Also, through the process of writing, writers often find that they initiate ideas and connections between ideas that they might not otherwise have found. Thus, writing may lead to new discoveries.

Rhetoric is a part of our everyday lives. When we're in a conversation with someone, we use rhetoric on a conscious or subconscious level. If you go to class wearing the T-shirt of your favorite musician or band, you're ultimately sending a rhetorical message identifying you as a fan of that artist or group.

If you've ever written a profile on a dating site, you've used rhetorical principles to convince an audience of potential partners to contact you or to write you back if you have chosen to make the first contact. You build ethos by talking about yourself in order to build credibility among potential partners, and you establish pathos when you talk about an interest that is shared by a potential mate.

Being able to use the tools of rhetoric effectively gives you the power to control your communication—both incoming and outgoing—and to affect your environment in a positive way.

Reading 1.3

San Ysidro Shooting Survivor Lives His Dream of Being a Cop

by Janine Zuniga

In this feature story from the *San Diego Union-Tribune*, Janine Zuniga describes vividly how Alberto Leos, then a 17-year-old cook and high school football star, was shot and left for dead during James Oliver Huberty's rampage at a San Ysidro McDonald's in 1984. The 21 dead and 19 wounded made the massacre the worst one-day shooting by a single individual in United States history at the time. But Leos's story did not end there. The young man under-went surgeries and completed rehabilitation, going on to become a policeman. Notice how the author makes use of both ethos and pathos in writing this profile.

The shots fired at point-blank range pierced both arms, his right leg, stomach and chest, and Alberto Leos crumpled to the kitchen floor next to three co-workers at a San Ysidro McDonald's. Even with his injuries, the 17-year-old cook, three weeks into his first job, knew the others were dead. He could tell by the lifeless positions of their bodies.

During a harrowing 77 minutes 20 years ago today, Leos, a high school football star, watched in helpless horror as a heavily armed James Oliver Huberty "executed, killed families, babies, my manager."

In all, 21 people were killed and 19 wounded in what was, up to that time, the worst one-day massacre by a single gunman in U.S. history. "All I remember is saying a prayer," Leos said. "I prayed to see my family one more time . . . before I died."

The McDonald's Massacre, as it came to be called, has faded for many San Diegans during the past two decades, but for those such as Leos who survived, it became the defining moment of their lives.

Leos's recovery included three months in the hospital, where he underwent five surgeries to remove the bullets and repair damage. He spent two years in therapy, for both physical and emotional injuries.

Despite painful rehabilitation, scars and memories, Leos became even more determined to fulfill his childhood dream of becoming a police officer. He has been a cop for 17 years.

After stints with the National City and Chula Vista police departments, Leos is now a San Diego police sergeant working the Southern Division, which includes routine patrols of San Ysidro.

"I was born to do this work," said Leos, who is married and lives in Chula Vista. "I was born to be in this profession. That's how I feel."

Leos said that while growing up in Cudahy, a city southeast of Los Angeles, the only time he saw deputies was when they were taking someone to jail. But that image changed one day when an L.A. County sheriff's deputy visited his third-grade classroom.

"To see him in the school setting, I was in awe—his uniform, his nice, shiny badge," Leos said. "He told us they were there to help people, to help those who can't help themselves. I told myself that when I was older, I wanted to do that."

But Leos's parents quickly and, for a decade, successfully discouraged him from pursuing the dream, saying it was too dangerous a career for their only son. Their opposition vanished on the day he almost lost his life.

"When I was shot and my friends and co-workers were killed, my parents were very, very supportive of me doing whatever I wanted," Leos said. "I guess they felt I had a second chance."

The short sleeves of Leos's dark-blue uniform can't hide the scars on his arms, but he doesn't often share the details of that day. The 5-foot-8, clean-shaven officer is soft-spoken and somewhat formal.

Photo by Howard Lipin / Union-Tribune

San Diego police sergeant, Alberto Leos, preparing to go out on patrol recently, overcame five surgeries and two years of painful therapy after the McDonald's Massacre to fulfill his childhood dream of becoming a police officer.

"Even as a young, young man, I could tell he was a serious kind of person, not in a sober sense, but in that he had a job and wanted to help his folks, that he was a good kid," said Andrea Skorepa, who as an employee of the local social-services agency Casa Familiar helped administer a $1.4 million fund for survivors and those injured in the McDonald's Massacre.

Skorepa, who has remained friends with the officer, said some who lived through it, such as Leos, have accomplished their goals, while others have succumbed to the tragedy.

"For the people who survived, that day was the beginning of a new life for them," Skorepa said. "What they have done with their lives becomes the important story. He doesn't live as a victim. He's not gone that way."

He tries to get assigned to San Ysidro when he can, because he wants to give back to the community and to Casa Familiar. The agency not only helped with the fund but helped get his family through a very tough time.

"That's when I learned about community service and how much it's needed," Leos said.

Said Skorepa, now executive director of Casa Familiar, "I think it gives you a different perspective, if you've come that close to losing your life and are somehow spared, on how to live your life."

In all his years in law enforcement, Leos has never fired his weapon at anyone. He's sure he will if he has to, but his instincts, which he has learned to trust, help guide him more calmly through tense situations.

Now, if a situation doesn't feel right, he will take a few steps back and think it through. Back on that unforgettable day, Leos said something told him not to go to work, but he didn't listen to his gut.

"I woke up with this feeling that I shouldn't go in," said Leos, who will turn 38 next month. "My friends were going to the beach and invited me to go. But it was the first job I ever had, and I talked myself out of it."

Collaborate

Activity 1.7 **Consider a Profile**

1. In your small group, decide what argument Janine Zuniga is making in this profile of the San Ysidro massacre survivor.

2. Describe what you think are the best specific details the writer includes, either of the shooting or of Leos's subsequent recovery and career as a policeman. How do these details contribute to the story?

3. A profile generally emphasizes the ethos of the subject. In this profile, how does the author do that? How does the author also make use of pathos?

4. As the readers, what conclusion are you left with after you read the article? Is this the impression that the writer wanted you to have, do you think?

Memories of McDonald's Rhetorical Actions 20 Years Later

In 2004, twenty years after the massacre, a memorial service was held at the site, and the media ran stories about the anniversary. Many people contributed to a blog associated with the anniversary story in the local newspaper:

Shortly after the shooting that injured Alberto Leos, wounded 18 others, and killed 21 people (see the reading on page 22), a committee in San Ysidro, California, collected 1,400 signatures asking that the McDonald's be razed and a memorial park built. Although McDonald's was in no way responsible for the attack, it responded to the committee's rhetorical appeal. Bob Kaiser, director of media relations for McDonald's, said, "The concern is for the people, not simply business" and reported that the company's decision whether to reopen the restaurant was being held in abeyance. Later, the company tore down the restaurant and donated the land to the city. After debating what to do with the land, the city used it to build a community college.

Jennifer wrote: "I live in La Jolla, exactly twenty five miles north of the former McDonald's where this tragedy took place some twenty plus years ago. The site is now the home of Southwestern College, but I have seen the memorial and am always filled with sadness when I go there. They have done a wonderful job on the memorial which is just in front of the former McDonald's building which you can tell was once the eatery, but has been painted grey, though the general shape of the building is still there. I am especially touched by the comments in this story and it is great that the memory of what happened not so long ago in our city is kept alive. ALL those that survived or not on that very sad day, were heroes, but their memories will never be in vain and we, as the citizens of this beautiful city will always be proud of their bravery and courage."

Leonor wrote: "I was seven at the time and I lived half a block from McDonald's. I saw bullets flying in the air and I remember police officers not letting us go to our house. They told us to get down in our car and not move. It was scary because we did not know what was going on. We were going to eat at McDonald's but my grandma invited us to her house. I still live in San Ysidro and I graduated from Southwestern College and I see the area everyday. It's not easy to forget what I do remember."

Armida wrote: "I remember that day. I was there. I had just turned 17. This was my first job. I lost my cousin and two friends because they threw a coffee pot at him to save this guy who became a cop. I saved a co-worker. I never told anybody or wrote about this day till now."

Sergio wrote: "I still remember this event. I'm now 33 years old and I was 9 years old. I still remember the gun shots, many of them. I grew up about 3 blocks away. I remember the countless police officers blocking the streets of Sunset Lane, which was my street. Two of my friends were murdered. I could have been there. My best friend died that day. This has been a funeral I will always remember. I just like to share a tiny bit on that day in the summer of July."

Joe Bloggs wrote: "I remember this happening. I was only about 12 years old at the time and living in Australia, but it is something I never forget about. Why America is so obsessed with guns I will never understand. Nobody except the police and army should have access to firearms. The private ownership of guns should be illegal and there should be gun amnesty days where guns can be handed in to be crushed. This is going to happen time and time again, people, unless you stand up and say no to gun ownership."

The blog entries show the impact of the event, even 20 years later. Notice that there are no negative comments about the McDonald's, nor about what the community decided to do with the land. Nothing McDonald's could have done would have erased the pain of the event, but its rhetorical actions, in both word and deed, did not add to the trauma of the event. McDonald's response to the citizens' request to tear down the building and donate the land to the city continues to be praised 20 years later.

Collaborate Activity 1.8 **Blogging and Responding to Blogging**

In your group, discuss the blog entries above about the San Ysidro shooting. Which blog entry attracts your attention the most? What do you think was the author's rhetorical purpose?

Write your own blog entry in response to the McDonald's story. What would you say to the citizens who remember the event? What would you say to the people at McDonald's who made the decision to tear down the building and donate the land to the city?

Do you blog? Why? Do you check your blog frequently? How do you feel if there are responses to your comments? How do you feel if there are no responses to your comments? Does it matter if the response is positive or negative?

Activity 1.9 Write about Everyday Arguments

Read your local newspaper or news magazines such as *Time* or *Newsweek* or search the Internet and bring to class a copy of a recent text or visual image that makes an argument about an issue. You might find, for example, an editorial in your local newspaper about recycling efforts in your community or a blog entry about parenting practices. Be sure, however, that the text or image takes a position on the issue. Write a paragraph of approximately 100 to 150 words describing the argument to your classmates and your reaction to it.

Encountering Visual Rhetoric

Why is a visual so powerful? Colors, shapes, and symbols impact viewers in ways text alone cannot. Many images present arguments and, because they are visual, they communicate more quickly and, sometimes, more powerfully than words.

The images on the next page are covers from *GQ* magazine. On the left, Sacha Baron Cohen, in the Bruno character, graces the humor edition of the magazine in a pose echoing that of Jennifer Aniston, on the right, which was printed on a cover a few months previously. What do you think when you see a man positioned in a way that is typical for a scantily dressed (or nude) female? Is it funny? Many think so, but not everyone. A posting on a blog called thesocietypages.org says of Cohen, "The contrast between the meaning of the pose (sexy and feminine) with the fact that he's male draws attention to how powerfully gendered the pose is… women look sexy when they pose like this, men look stupid when they do."

A photo's ability to persuade can be significant, whether it is a news photo or an advertisement. However, not everyone interprets images the same way, especially when they evoke stereotypes of gender, race, or religion.

© GQ Magazine

Compare these two cover photos from *GQ* magazine. Though the poses are similar, because the figure on the left is a man and the one on the right is a woman, they evoke very different responses from readers. Some see the photo on the left as paying humorous tribute to the one on the right. Others interpret both images as exploiting feminine gender stereotypes.

Activity 1.10   Write a Caption for a Photo or a Pair of Photos

Choose a news photo or advertisement from a newspaper, magazine, or the Internet that presents an argument. Alternatively, compare two news photos or advertisements. Copy or paste the photo or photos on a piece of paper and write a caption that expresses the argument(s) you see in the photo.

Rhetorical Arguments Stand the Test of Time

Abraham Lincoln's Gettysburg Address is the short speech that the president delivered at the site of the battle of Gettysburg where, four months previously, the Union Army defeated Confederate forces. His was not the only talk that day at the dedication of the Soldiers' National Cemetery, but it is the only one remembered. In just over two minutes, he was able to reframe the Civil War not just as a victory for the North but as a "new birth of freedom" for all

Americans. Now, during the 150th anniversary of the Civil War, is a good time to remember Lincoln's rhetoric—in terms of both the content and the style of his speech.

Reading 1.5

Text of the Gettysburg Address

Four score and seven years ago our fathers brought forth on this continent, a new nation, conceived in Liberty, and dedicated to the proposition that all men are created equal.

Now we are engaged in a great civil war, testing whether that nation, or any nation so conceived and so dedicated, can long endure. We are met on a great battlefield of that war. We have come to dedicate a portion of that field, as a final resting place for those who here gave their lives that that nation might live. It is altogether fitting and proper that we should do this.

But, in a larger sense, we cannot dedicate—we cannot consecrate—we cannot hallow—this ground. The brave men, living and dead, who struggled here, have consecrated it, far above our poor power to add or detract. The world will little note, nor long remember what we say here, but it can never forget what they did here. It is for us the living, rather, to be dedicated here to the unfinished work which they who fought here have thus far so nobly advanced. It is rather for us to be here dedicated to the great task remaining before us—that from these honored dead we take increased devotion to that cause for which they gave the last full measure of devotion—that we here highly resolve that these dead shall not have died in vain—that this nation, under God, shall have a new birth of freedom—and that government of the people, by the people, for the people, shall not perish from the earth.

Though no actual recording exists of Lincoln giving the speech, you can listen to it if you search on the Internet for "recording of Gettysburg Address." Listen to the speech, noting the phrase "Four score and seven years ago," which is so famous that Americans know instantly, when it is quoted by orators or writers, that it is a reference to Lincoln. Consider what arguments the president makes in his speech. Think about their relevance today.

Activity 1.11 **Paraphrase the Gettysburg Address**

Rephrase each sentence of the Gettysburg Address, one by one, in your own words, putting it in 21st century wording rather than Lincoln's ceremonial, 19th century phrasing. In a paraphrase, the text does not become shorter; it is recreated in different words. This is a useful technique in helping you understand a text. It is also helpful when you are writing an analysis of a text because you can use your paraphrase rather than long, block quotes. Remember, though, when you are writing an essay, you must cite a paraphrase in the text and also include it in your list of references.

Activity 1.12 **Keep a Commonplace Book**

Ancient rhetoricians performed speeches with little warning, often to advertise their services as teachers of rhetoric. Thus, they frequently memorized arguments about specific topics that could be adapted to the audience and situation on a moment's notice. They called these memorized arguments "commonplaces." Commonplace books are an outgrowth of the Greek concept of commonplaces, but they are a little different. They became popular in the Middle Ages as notebooks in which individuals would write down quotes or ideas about a particular topic.

For thousands of years, people have been keeping commonplace books, a kind of journal or diary in which the author includes quotes, drawings, and images.

These notations might later be used to generate an idea for a composition. In more modern times, people have created commonplace books in the form of scrapbooks in which they collect quotes as well as drawings and clippings. Thus, they become a record of a person's intellectual life and can be saved for later reference.

For this class, take a notebook, perhaps one with a colorful or interesting cover, and keep notes, quotes, vocabulary words, and clippings related to the topics discussed in class. As your instructor directs, this commonplace book may be graded as evidence of class participation or it may be a private journal. Take a look at the commonplace books shown here for ideas. Be creative and enjoy adapting this ancient journal form to record ideas that interest you.

Activity 1.13 **Create Your Own Blog**

Create a home page for a professional blog using a site like Blogger, WordPress, or Live Journal. Blogger is the easiest to use, but the others have more flexible options. Read the help screens for instructions on how to create your blog. Your design choices should reflect your personality. Keep in mind, though, that you are building an "academic self," so all the topics you write about should be of an academic nature and in an academic tone. Some students decide to have two blogs, one for their friends and one for professional networking, so you may want to do this, especially if you already have a blog.

End of the Year... My Favorite Memory
May 15, 2011

Exactly one week ago, I was at my graduation ceremony receiving my college degree. Normally, graduating would be the last thing a student would do before summer vacation however I am still at CMC working away. You see, me and my RA crew had to stay in the residence halls for a few days after graduation to close down the building. Although they left 2 days ago, I am still here working on a special project. Sitting in an empty 250 bedroom mansion has given me a lot of time to think about my year. With all this reminiscing, I tried to think of my favorite memory of 2nd semester. It was difficult to choose but my 2nd semester Sky Club trip was my favorite memory of all.

For our 2nd semester Sky Club trip, we went to the McDonald Observatory in Fort David Texas. This was the 2nd trip we took and it was my favorite. We embarked out on April Fools Day (no joke) and headed south towards Texas. It was nice because we took two 11 man vans and only had 14 people on the trip so the drive was very comfortable.

We stopped in several spots throughout the day and finally 15 hours later we arrived in the famous town of Fort Davis! We were all shocked to actually be in Texas because our amusement for the entire ski season in Steamboat was making fun of Texan tourists. Since we were now tourists in Texas, we began acting like tourists. Immediately we busted out cameras and took pictures of anything and everything we could see.

During this class, you'll use the blog to explore different aspects of each chapter in the textbook (and other topics that your instructor directs). You can also blog about other topics related to your writing this semester, and you can link to other blogs that you think your readers would find of interest.

After you have created the look of your blog, write a first entry that introduces you to your readers. You might include your major, your college, and something interesting that might attract readers to your blog.

2
RESPONDING RHETORICALLY

Praxis in Action

Why I Annotate Readings by Lauren Connolly

comment

Annotating a reading gives me the ability to participate in a conversation with the author of the text in order to develop my ideas for writing and understanding the information presented. My annotation style uses two methods: one is with a pencil and the other is with a highlighter.

As with a conversation, my side comments may be to protest the author's ideas or to make connections with other things in my life, other readings for the class, or my other classes. By making notes, I am actively participating in the conversation, opposed to passively taking in the information presented, and it gives me an opportunity to create something meaningful from the text. Using the highlighter sparingly, I only mark a word or phrase, in order to point out specific ideas or words that I want to reference, understand, or quote in my writing at a later point in time. The meaningful interaction is when, using a pencil, I write comments in the margins in response to these highlights. These comments are frequently a part of my prewriting stage, as I use my marginal comments directly in my early written drafts. Annotating allows me to respond, clarify, and develop my ideas about what I have learned, enabling me to use the ideas later in both my writing and research.

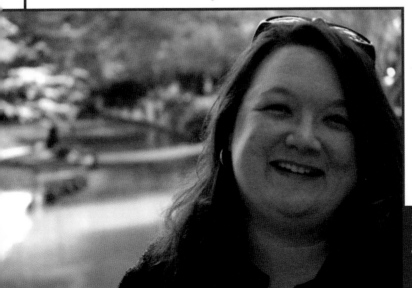

Lauren Connolly likes to annotate readings because it allows her to have a conversation with the writer.

33

Thinking Critically, Reading Rhetorically

In contemporary times we study texts to encourage students to develop critical thinking, a skill which is essential for understanding the scientific method and for making effective judgments in the workplace and in civil life. This student-centered emphasis would have seemed strange to ancient Greek and Roman rhetoricians and their students. They believed that a rhetor's skill was best developed by honoring the skills of those who excelled in the past. Therefore, a large part of the educational process involved having students study the texts of well-regarded speeches, memorize and recite them, and model new compositions based on their approaches to topics and language style. As Isocrates explained:

> Since language is of such a nature that it is possible to discourse on the same subject matter in many different ways—to represent the great as lowly or invest the little with grandeur, to recount the things of old in a new manner or set forth events of recent date in an old fashion—it follows that one must not shun the subjects upon which others have composed before, but must try to compose better than they . . . (Panegyricus).

Thus, students in ancient Greece or Rome would have been presented with a text, often read aloud by a teacher, and they would be asked to transcribe or copy it down with the idea that they would internalize the skills of the master rhetor who had originally given the speech. Then, they would be asked to write about the same subject in a way that built upon what they had learned from the master text but incorporated their own personal attitudes or perspectives.

Today, rather than being asked to model new compositions based upon the techniques of classic texts, students are asked to read texts carefully and then to engage in critical thinking and discussion about those texts.

Critical thinking involves considering issues thoughtfully and independently. Critical thinkers do not believe facts or opinions just because they are published—whether it is in newspapers, textbooks, on television, or on the Internet. Nor do they focus upon just understanding or memorizing information, as in facts and figures. Critical thinkers examine the reasoning of the information in front of them, looking for premises and considering the inferences drawn from those premises. They are able to think for themselves, making logical connections between ideas, seeing cause and effect relationships, and using information to solve problems.

Reading rhetorically makes use of critical thinking skills, but it also involves looking at texts as arguments and evaluating them for validity, adequacy of evidence, and presence of bias. Moreover, reading rhetorically involves having a knowledge of rhetoric and specialized Greek terms such as logos, pathos, ethos, and kairos—words that were defined briefly in Chapter 1 and will be discussed more extensively in Chapter 3. Practice reading rhetorically as you read the following article on the Strauss-Kahn sexual assault case.

Reading 2.1

A wealthy public figure accused of sexual misconduct in a swanky hotel says that the charge is trumped up, that his alleged victim lacks credibility.

In their eagerness to bag a famous name, the defendant says, investigators have rushed to judgment. He says they have failed to carefully consider whether the woman who reported being accosted had a motive to lie.

That's what Dominque Strauss-Kahn says, through his attorneys.

And that's what lawyer A. Scott Bolden says. He represents Washington Redskins lineman Albert Haynesworth, awaiting trial on a misdemeanor charge that he indecently groped a waitress at the posh W Hotel in Washington.

"Let me tell you something about sex-crimes prosecutors," said Bolden, a former sex-crimes prosecutor. "They tend to be true believers. I mean, they've never met a victim they don't want to save or who they don't believe. . . . And when credibility issues arise, they tend to just want to explain them away."

As authorities Friday acknowledged doubts about the credibility of Strauss-Kahn's accuser in New York, and the rape case against the former head of the International Monetary Fund seemed in jeopardy, Bolden and other lawyers said the news highlights one of the thorniest issues in sex-crimes prosecutions:

In Sex-Crime Cases, Credibility a Thorny Issue
by Paul Duggan

In 2011, Dominique Strauss-Kahn, the head of the International Monetary Fund (IMF), was accused of sexual assault by a housekeeper at the Sofitel New York hotel. He pled not guilty. During the case, the victim's credibility was called into question, as she had reportedly lied to the police in her first statement about the case. The following article, by Paul Duggan, published in *The Washington Post*, talks about the credibility of alleged victims in sex-crime cases, and how, in the Strauss-Kahn case, it could affect the outcome. To begin a critical reading of an article, you want to read the entire piece first for content. Then, reread the introduction. How does the author attempt to capture the audience's attention? How does the author use the Lanigan case as a frame of reference?

Will jurors believe the alleged victim?

Sometimes the believability issue has nothing to do with the allegation itself. The witness may have a troubled past that could cast doubt on her testimony.

Harry O'Reilly, a retired New York City police detective who helped create the department's Special Victims Unit in the early 1970s—the unit that handled the Strauss-Kahn case—said investigators often deal with accusers who have less-than-savory backgrounds and who offer changing accounts of alleged assaults.

"It's quite common for there to be credibility issues," he said. He said detectives initially should focus only on whether the alleged crime occurred, and not be deterred by the woman's personal history, even if it involves dishonesty.

"If someone makes an allegation, we listen," he said. "And then we look for chinks in the story. And if the story begins to dissipate, then we go from there. But at the onset, we're not looking at things in her past that aren't relevant to the allegation."

Attorney Peter Greenspun, who defended Fairfax County teacher Sean Lanigan, acquitted this year of sexually molesting a 12-year-old female student, said authorities have to proceed in such cases with caution.

"These are the kinds of cases where the most care has to be exercised before anyone is charged, because of what allegations like this do to people," Greenspun said.

Jurors in the Fairfax trial later voiced outrage at the dearth of evidence against Lanigan, a married father of three whose life was shattered by the allegations.

"These are devastating charges," Greenspun said. "There's an assumption of guilt by the public, and reputations and life trajectories are destroyed."

In New York, prosecutors acknowledged that the hotel maid who accused Strauss-Kahn of raping her in his luxury suite May 14 later lied to investigators about her personal history and gave them inconsistent accounts of the moments after the alleged assault.

Strauss-Kahn, 62, who was arrested hours after the allegation and resigned from the IMF, was ordered released from home confinement in Manhattan on Friday. But the district attorney's office has not moved to dismiss the rape case.

"She said it happened, and he's sort of a pompous guy with a reputation ... for grabbing women, so they thought, well, of course, it must have happened," Greenspun said. He said police generally spend too little time investigating such cases before making arrests, especially when the suspects are prominent men.

Even if Strauss-Kahn's attorneys have information about his accuser that they could use in court to cast doubt on her veracity, prosecutors have a "moral obligation" to proceed with the case if they believe that the woman is being truthful, said lawyer Mai Fernandez, director of the National Center for Victims of Crime.

"You could have Attila the Hun come to you and say he's a victim, and the truth of the matter is, in this particular case, he may be," Fernandez said.

"You have to look first at the evidence that's directly related to the case at hand," she added. "The victim? Well, everybody has a past. None of us is without sin. There's always something that a defense lawyer can use to tarnish your reputation."

Kristina Korobov, a former prosecutor, agreed with Fernandez, but only to an extent.

"It's true that you can't just say to a victim, 'Well, you have a credibility problem, so too bad,' and then, based on that, you don't proceed with the case," Korobov said. "Because that just rewards offenders who choose victims with credibility problems."

In a case like Strauss-Kahn's, she said, prosecutors are probably weighing whether the woman's credibility is so badly damaged that a conviction would be highly unlikely.

"There were a number of victims in my lifetime who I legitimately believed had been victimized, but I didn't file a charge," said Korobov, now a senior attorney with the National Center for the Prosecution of Violence Against Women. "You've got to be very selective about what cases you bring, based on what you think you can prove."

Explore

Activity 2.1 **Analyze a Text**

In your small group, discuss the following questions and then report your group's opinion(s) to the class.

1. What is the problem that the author is concerned about in regard to prosecuting sex crimes?

2. What court cases does he mention? How was the victim's ethos involved?

3. How does the writer appeal to logos? To pathos?

4. If your group were writing a letter to the editor of the *Washington Post* commenting about this article, what might you say about the controversy the writer presents?

Rhetoric's Visual Heritage and Impact

The first televised presidential debate in September 1960 is a famous example of the power of visual rhetoric and a vivid illustration of the fact that visual elements must be considered when "reading" rhetorical situations. Radio listeners who could hear but not see the debate rated Vice President Richard Nixon as the winner over Senator John F. Kennedy—Nixon's arguments sounded more logical and were more clearly expressed. However, the television audience experienced a new element in the history of presidential debates: They could see the performances of the handsome and tan Senator Kennedy and the pasty-white and ill-looking Vice President Nixon, and they clearly preferred Kennedy. He *looked and acted presidential*, which overcame the drawbacks that had troubled his campaign previously—that he was relatively unknown, young, and Catholic. It overcame any advantage that Nixon may have had in presenting logical arguments and also by being an incumbent vice president. And unfortunately for Nixon, by 1960, 88 percent of Americans had televisions. "It's one of those unusual points on the timeline of history where you can say things changed very dramatically—in this case, in a single night," says Alan Schroeder, a media historian who authored the book, *Presidential Debates: Forty Years of High-Risk TV.*[*] Indeed, after the unexpected impact of the Kennedy-Nixon debates, presidential candidates were so apprehensive about competing on television that it was 16 years before candidates (President Gerald R. Ford and former Governor Jimmy

---

[*] Kayla Webley, "How the Nixon-Kennedy Debate Changed the World" *Breaking News, Analysis, Politics, Blogs, News Photos, Video, Tech Reviews,* September 23, 2010. http://www.time.com/time/nation/article/0,8599,2021078,00.html. Accessed July 30, 2011.

Carter) were again willing to risk presenting themselves side by side on television.

Why did the experience of seeing the two candidates, rather than hearing them or reading their speeches, make such a difference? The ancient Greeks and Romans who developed rhetoric would have understood the reason: It was what they called ethos, which can be translated only imperfectly as credibility. A person's ethos is determined partially by his or her reputation, but as Richard Nixon learned the hard way, it is conveyed even more powerfully by appearance, gestures, tone, and cadence of speech. It is important to remember that the standards and perceptions of Americans are heavily influenced by rhetoric as it was defined and implemented by the Greeks and Romans—first in oral presentations. Many of the attributes of rhetoric translate to written texts, but not all. Thus, when considering a text that was originally presented as a speech, reading rhetorically means thinking about visual rhetoric—the impact the speech would have had on an audience that was *watching and listening to the presentation.*

The first presidential debate between Vice President Richard Nixon and Senator John F. Kennedy illustrated the power of visual rhetoric.

Moreover, the impact of visual rhetoric involves more than speeches: It concerns television shows, films, photographs, paintings, advertisements, and even the typesetting layout of a text that has no illustrations. We will consider these types of visual rhetoric in more detail later in this chapter.

On page 41, we reprint President Barack Obama's speech announcing the death of Osama bin Laden. This speech is available widely on the Internet at such sites as AmericanRhetoric.com, NYTimes.com, and YouTube.com. If possible, watch the speech before you read the text, and as you do so think about the impact of the speech, including the president's verbal presentation and the setting at the White House, as well as the content of the speech. Think about the various audiences President Obama was speaking to—Americans and people around the world who might be watching at that moment, as well as a historic audience of people such as yourself who would be viewing the speech months or years later.

The Rhetorical Triangle

When reading a text or listening to a speech, keep in mind the three parts of the rhetorical triangle—writer, audience, and subject. Each of these can be framed as a question:

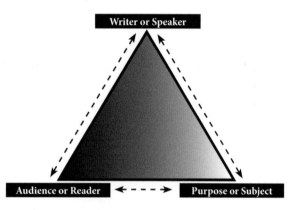

- Who is the writer? What is the impression the writer wants to make on the audience? What does the writer do to establish credibility (ethos)? How does the writer create common ground with the audience?

- Who is the intended audience? How would a logical appeal influence the audience? An ethical appeal? An emotional appeal? What does the audience anticipate in terms of organization and format of the presentation or paper? What is the extent of their knowledge about the subject, and do they have prejudices or preferences?

- What is the purpose of the communication? In the case of an argument, the purpose would be to persuade. Is that the case with this reading? Is it clear what the writer wants to persuade the audience to believe or to do? Is the request phrased in a logical manner?

Activity 2.2 **Apply the Rhetorical Triangle**

For each of the readings presented thus far in the textbook, identify the speaker, the audience, and the purpose. Then analyze how each of those elements affects the content of the reading.

1. "Violent Rhetoric and Arizona Politics" (Chapter 1, p. 14)

2. "The Sleepover Question" (Chapter 1, p. 18)

3. "San Ysidro Shooting Survivor Lives His Dream of Being a Cop" (Chapter 1, p. 22)

4. "In Sex-Crime Cases, Credibility a Thorny Issue" (Chapter 2, p. 35)

Reading 2.2

Good evening. Tonight, I can report to the American people and to the world that the United States has conducted an operation that killed Osama bin Laden, the leader of al Qaeda, and a terrorist who's responsible for the murder of thousands of innocent men, women, and children.

President Barack Obama on the Death of Osama bin Laden

President Barack Obama announced the death of Osama bin Laden.

It was nearly 10 years ago that a bright September day was darkened by the worst attack on the American people in our history. The images of 9/11 are seared into our national memory— hijacked planes cutting through a cloudless September sky; the Twin Towers collapsing to the ground; black smoke billowing up from the Pentagon; the wreckage of Flight 93 in Shanksville, Pennsylvania, where the actions of heroic citizens saved even more heartbreak and destruction.

And yet we know that the worst images are those that were unseen to the world. The empty seat at the dinner table. Children who were forced to grow up without their mother or their father. Parents who would never know the feeling of their child's embrace. Nearly 3,000 citizens taken from us, leaving a gaping hole in our hearts.

On September 11, 2001, in our time of grief, the American people came together. We offered our neighbors a hand, and we offered the wounded our blood. We reaffirmed our ties to each other, and our love of community and country. On that day, no matter where we came from, what God we prayed to, or what race or ethnicity we were, we were united as one American family.

We were also united in our resolve to protect our nation and to bring those who committed this vicious attack to justice. We quickly learned that the 9/11 attacks were carried out by al Qaeda—an organization headed by Osama bin Laden, which had openly declared war on the United States and was committed to killing innocents in our country and around the globe. And so we went to war against al Qaeda to protect our citizens, our friends, and our allies.

Over the last 10 years, thanks to the tireless and heroic work of our military and our counterterrorism professionals, we've made great strides in that effort. We've disrupted terrorist attacks and strengthened our homeland defense. In Afghanistan, we removed the Taliban government, which had given Bin Laden and al Qaeda safe haven and support. And around the globe, we worked with our friends and allies to capture or kill scores of al Qaeda terrorists, including several who were a part of the 9/11 plot.

Yet Osama bin Laden avoided capture and escaped across the Afghan border into Pakistan. Meanwhile, al Qaeda continued to operate from along that border and operate through its affiliates across the world. And so shortly after taking office, I directed Leon Panetta, the director of the CIA, to make the killing or capture of Bin Laden the top priority of our war against al Qaeda, even as we continued our broader efforts to disrupt, dismantle, and defeat his network.

Then, last August, after years of painstaking work by our intelligence community, I was briefed on a possible lead to Bin Laden. It was far from certain, and it took many months to run this thread to ground. I met repeatedly with my national security team as we developed more information about the possibility that we had located Bin Laden hiding within a compound deep inside of Pakistan. And finally, last week, I determined that we had enough intelligence to take action, and authorized an operation to get Osama bin Laden and bring him to justice.

Today, at my direction, the United States launched a targeted operation against that compound in Abbottabad, Pakistan. A small team of Americans carried out the operation with extraordinary courage and capability. No Americans were harmed. They took care to avoid civilian casualties. After a firefight, they killed Osama bin Laden and took custody of his body.

For over two decades, Bin Laden has been al Qaeda's leader and symbol, and has continued to plot attacks against our country and our friends and allies. The death of Bin Laden marks the most significant achievement to date in our nation's effort to defeat al Qaeda.

Yet his death does not mark the end of our effort. There's no doubt that al Qaeda will continue to pursue attacks against us. We must—and we will—remain vigilant at home and abroad.

As we do, we must also reaffirm that the United States is not—and never will be—at war with Islam. I've made clear, just as President Bush did shortly after 9/11, that our war is not against Islam. Bin Laden was not a Muslim leader; he was a mass murderer of Muslims. Indeed, al Qaeda has slaughtered scores of Muslims in many countries, including our own. So his demise should be welcomed by all who believe in peace and human dignity.

Over the years, I've repeatedly made clear that we would take action within Pakistan if we knew where Bin Laden was. That is what we've done. But it's important to note that our counterterrorism cooperation with Pakistan helped lead us to Bin Laden and the compound where he was hiding. Indeed, Bin Laden had declared war against Pakistan as well, and ordered attacks against the Pakistani people.

Tonight, I called President Zardari, and my team has also spoken with their Pakistani counterparts. They agree that this is a good and historic day for both of our nations. And going forward, it is essential that Pakistan continue to join us in the fight against al Qaeda and its affiliates.

The American people did not choose this fight. It came to our shores, and started with the senseless slaughter of our citizens. After nearly 10 years of service, struggle, and sacrifice, we know well the costs of war. These efforts weigh on me every time I, as Commander-in-Chief, have to sign a letter to a family that has lost a loved one, or look into the eyes of a service member who's been gravely wounded.

So Americans understand the costs of war. Yet as a country, we will never tolerate our security being threatened, nor stand idly by when our people have been killed. We will be relentless in defense of our citizens and our friends and allies. We will be true to the values that make us who we are. And on nights like this one, we can say to those families who have lost loved ones to al Qaeda's terror: Justice has been done.

Tonight, we give thanks to the countless intelligence and counterterrorism professionals who've worked tirelessly to achieve this outcome. The American people do not see their work, nor know their names. But tonight, they feel the satisfaction of their work and the result of their pursuit of justice.

We give thanks for the men who carried out this operation, for they exemplify the professionalism, patriotism, and unparalleled courage of those who serve our country. And they are part of a generation that has borne the heaviest share of the burden since that September day.

Finally, let me say to the families who lost loved ones on 9/11 that we have never forgotten your loss, nor wavered in our commitment to see that we do whatever it takes to prevent another attack on our shores.

And tonight, let us think back to the sense of unity that prevailed on 9/11. I know that it has, at times, frayed. Yet today's achievement is a testament to the greatness of our country and the determination of the American people.

The cause of securing our country is not complete. But tonight, we are once again reminded that America can do whatever we set our mind to. That is the story of our history, whether it's the pursuit of prosperity for our people, or the struggle for equality for all our citizens; our commitment to stand up for our values abroad, and our sacrifices to make the world a safer place.

Let us remember that we can do these things not just because of wealth or power, but because of who we are: one nation, under God, indivisible, with liberty and justice for all.

Thank you.

May God bless you.

And may God bless the United States of America.

Activity 2.3 **Evaluate the President's Speech**

After you have both watched President Obama's speech on the Internet and read the text, discuss these questions in your small group and then present the consensus of your group's answers to the class.

1. Discuss the president's presentation of the speech. Do you think the speech had a different impact on those who watched it on television versus those who heard it on the radio? What about those who neither saw nor heard it but rather read the speech?

2. How would you describe the president's tone, appearance, and mannerisms (all part of his ethos)? What about the location he chose for the speech and the timing just after news agencies had announced Bin Laden's death (the kairos)?

3. Summarize what the president says about the government's reasons for seeking Osama bin Laden and killing him. Does the president make a good argument for the necessity and importance of this act?

4. Notice that the president uses visual imagery in his speech. For example, in paragraph two, immediately after he announces his news, he refers to 9/11—"a bright September day was darkened by the worst attack on the American people in our history." What is the purpose of the visual descriptions in his speech?

5. Do you agree or disagree with what the president has to say? How so?

Activity 2.4 **Research Reactions to President Obama's Speech**

Using Google or another search engine, research the reactions to the president's speech announcing the death of Bin Laden.

1. In the days after the speech, what did the media report about the attack on Bin Laden's compound?

2. What were some American reactions to the speech and to the killing of Bin Laden?

3. What was the reaction around the world, both in Muslim and non-Muslim countries?

4. Did you learn anything during your research that surprised you? How so?

As your instructor directs, either discuss these questions in class or turn in written answers to the questions.

Reading 2.3

The Lexicon
by Charles McGrath

A *lexicon* is a synonym for dictionary, thesaurus, and wordlist. Charles McGrath, in his *New York Times* essay, "The Lexicon," examines the changes that 9/11 wrought in the English language. The attack on the World Trade Center, unlike other world-changing violent events, hasn't yet created many new words, he decides. Rather, it has brought already-existing words to our everyday vocabulary—such as jihad, T.S.A. shoe bomber, and sleeper cell. These not-so-pretty words are the lexicon of 9/11.

Ground zero, sleeper cells, progressive vertical collapse: The most resonant phrases of 9/11 are imbued with what might be called antipoetry, a resistance to prettification.

Unlike some other momentous events in our history—World War II, say, or the Vietnam War—the attacks that took place on Sept. 11, 2001, have not particularly changed or enriched our vocabulary. Sometimes these things take a while. It wasn't until the 1960s, for example, that the term "holocaust," which used to mean any large-scale massacre, took on the specific connotations it has today. For now, though, you could argue that the events of 9/11 still seem so unfathomable that they have actually impoverished the language a little, leaving us with a vacuous phrase like **war on terror**, which manages to empty both "war" and "terror" of much their meaning, or the creepy, Nazi-sounding **homeland**, which seems a far less pleasant place to live than just plain America.

We do know a lot of words now that we probably should have known before, like **jihad, Taliban, mujahedeen** and **Al Qaeda**. And some that we'd just as soon forget, like **T.S.A., security checkpoint, shoe bomber** and **progressive vertical collapse**. A term like **sleeper cell** probably sticks in our heads because it contains a tiny hint of embedded poetry, and for the same reason it's hard to forget those **72 black-eyed virgins** whom the terrorists believed they were on their way to meet. The "black-eyed" bit is a brilliant touch, even if it's probably a mistranslation.

But the most resonant phrases that have taken residence in our consciousness since that September morning are ones imbued with what might be called antipoetry, a resistance to metaphor or to prettification. **Ground zero**, for example—a term that originated with the Manhattan Project and was originally used in connection with nuclear explosions—seems particularly apt in this new context, with its sense of absolute finality, of a point that is both an end and a beginning and to which everything else refers.

And even **9/11** itself has a kind of rightness. No one says "September 11th" anymore as shorthand for that awful day. (To do so, a friend once joked, would be "so September 10th.") There's a pleasing, no-nonsense simplicity and precision to the expression—the same effect created by "24/7," only starker, and with none of the exaggeration. These four syllables are right at the end of language, where words turn into abstraction. Individually, they're just random, empty numbers, but yoked by that fateful slash they contain volumes. 9/11—everyone knows what that means, and to say any more would be pointless. Sometimes words fail.

Activity 2.5 **Develop a Lexicon**

Choose one of the following activities and create a lexicon as a group or individually:

1. Reread President Obama's speech about the death of Osama bin Laden. What words have become a more frequent part of the nation's vocabulary as a result of Bin Laden's actions? Al Qaeda and Taliban are two. Can you find others? Do an Internet search for Osama bin Laden, until you have five to seven words. Then write a 250 to 300 word essay, similar to McGrath's, in which you consider how Bin Laden's life and death have affected our country's vocabulary.

2. Do a search on the Internet for "new words." You will find lists of words and phrases that have been added to new editions of dictionaries. Examples may include such words as "aquascape," "soul patch," and "sandwich generation." Choose five to seven new words that are related to each other in some way. Create a lexicon of your own with a paragraph about each word that emphasizes the invention or recent history of the word. Give examples of each word's usage in blogs or other publications.

Ways of Reading Rhetorically

Reading theorist Louise Rosenblatt suggests a technique for analyzing written texts—particularly those with few visual cues other than words on paper or a computer screen. She says that we take the pattern of verbal signs left by the author and use them to recreate the text, not in the exact way the author perceived the text, but guided by it.

So, as we read, there is a constant stream of response to the text. However, Rosenblatt says that even as the reader is recreating the text, he or she is also reacting to it. Thus, there are two interacting streams of response involved as the person moves through the text. The reader, rather than being a passive receptor for the author's text, actually participates in the creative process during reading.

However, we read differently depending on the text and the occasion. For example, if you take a paperback novel on an airplane trip, you probably read simply for entertainment and to pass the time in the air. If you read *King Lear* for a literature class, you read for the plot, characterization, and other elements that you know will be discussed in class. If you read a chapter in your chemistry textbook before an exam, you are focusing on remembering concepts and details that might be on the test. Reading as a writer is another type of reading. You examine the text with an eye for the choices the writer made when crafting the text, such as whether the writer begins with a narrative introduction, a quote from a noted authority, or a startling statement. You notice, for example, what people are mentioned in the text, either as authorities or participants in activities.

Rosenblatt also makes a useful distinction between two main kinds of reading—aesthetic reading and efferent reading. In **aesthetic reading**, the reader is most interested in what happens "during the reading event, as he fixes his attention on the actual experience he is living through," according to Rosenblatt. Readers focus upon the ideas, images, and story of the text that evoke an aesthetic experience in the moment of reading. **Efferent readers**, in contrast, read to learn from the text, and, thus, according to Rosenblatt, "concentrate on the information, the concepts, the guides to action, that will be left with him when the reading is over."

Reading rhetorically is efferent reading, focusing not on the experience of reading but on the information the text conveys and upon the way an argument is established and supported in a text. Some arguments are written in an engaging style that is a pleasure to read, while others are written in a highly emotional tone that arouses a visceral response in the reader. A text that inspires aesthetic reading must sometimes be read several times in order for the reader to focus on the structure of the argument beneath the creative language.

Some theorists say that critical thinking is "thinking about thinking" or "reasoning about reasoning," and that is exactly what reading rhetorically involves—reasoning about whether or not a text presents a reasoned argument. A good way to begin reading rhetorically is to be aware of the essential elements of an argument and identify these elements in the text you are evaluating. See the Checklist of Essential Elements in an Argument presented below.

Checklist of Essential Elements in an Argument

☑ *A debatable issue.* By definition, for a text to be an argument, there must be at least two sides that can be asserted and supported.

☑ *A clearly stated position, claim statement, or thesis.* Arguments assert different kinds of claims, such as taking a position on an issue of fact, asserting a cause and effect relationship, declaring the value of some entity, or advocating a solution to a problem; but, in each case, after you read the argument, you should be able to restate or summarize the position, claim, or thesis in one or two sentences.

☑ *An audience.* To evaluate an argument, you need to know the original intended audience or place of publication, so that you can decide if the argument takes into account the audience's attitudes, background, and other factors. Ask yourself, for example, if the writer is assuming too much or too little background knowledge on the part of the audience or if the writer is using language that assumes the reader's agreement on the issue when that assumption is not warranted.

☑ *Evidence from reliable sources.* Quotes, statistics, and other evidence should be credited to reputable sources, even if your text is not a document that offers academic-style citations. The evidence should be sufficient to support the author's position or thesis.

☑ *Acknowledgment of the opposing argument.* A good rhetorician does not ignore any potential weaknesses in the argument. It is better to acknowledge points in favor of the opposing argument and then, if possible, refute the opposition's strong points than it is to allow an audience to poke holes in an argument.

☑ *A conclusion and/or call to action.* An argument can be concluded in a variety of effective ways, but it is important to note that it does, indeed, conclude. The conclusion can be a call to action on the part of the audience, but it should not be the beginning of an additional argument that is not supported by the evidence presented.

Reading 2.4

The Web Means the End of Forgetting

by Jeffrey Rosen

Several years ago, Stacy Snyder was a fairly typical 25-year-old college student training to be a teacher. That all changed forever when she did something that she probably thought was harmless fun—she posted a photo of herself on a social network site. In this article published in *The New York Times*, Jeffrey Rosen uses Snyder's case to illustrate how notions of privacy are changing because of the ever-growing presence and popularity of social networking sites. What is even more alarming, according to Rosen, is that photos and information, once posted on the web, are there forever. The web does not forget, and this lack of forgetting is changing society's ability to forgive and forget.

You may enjoy posting status updates about your life on a MySpace, Facebook, or Twitter account; however, with employers increasingly conducting background checks on such sites, it's very important to be careful about what you choose to post. This includes status updates, photographs, and videos. If you read the following article carefully, you may never look at social networking sites quite the same again.

Four years ago, Stacy Snyder, then a 25-year-old teacher in training at Conestoga Valley High School in Lancaster, Pa., posted a photo on her MySpace page that showed her at a party wearing a pirate hat and drinking from a plastic cup, with the caption "Drunken Pirate." After discovering the page, her supervisor at the high school told her the photo was "unprofessional," and the dean of Millersville University School of Education, where Snyder was enrolled, said she was promoting drinking in virtual view of her underage students. As a result, days before Snyder's scheduled graduation, the university denied her a teaching degree. Snyder sued, arguing that the university had violated her First Amendment rights by penalizing her for her (perfectly legal) after-hours behavior. But in 2008, a federal district judge rejected the claim, saying that because Snyder was a public employee whose photo didn't relate to matters of public concern, her "Drunken Pirate" post was not protected speech.

When historians of the future look back on the perils of the early digital age, Stacy Snyder may well be an icon. The problem she faced is only one example of a challenge that, in big and small ways, is confronting millions of people around the globe: how best to live our lives in a world where the Internet records everything and forgets nothing—where every online photo, status update, Twitter post and blog entry by and about us can be stored forever. With websites like LOL Facebook Moments, which collects and shares embarrassing personal revelations from Facebook users, ill-advised photos and online chatter are coming back to haunt people months or years after the fact.

Examples are proliferating daily: there was the 16-year-old British girl who was fired from her office job for complaining on Facebook, "I'm so totally bored!!"; there was the 66-year-old Canadian psychotherapist who tried to enter the United States but was turned away at the border—and barred permanently from visiting the country—after a border guard's Internet search found that the therapist had written an article in a philosophy journal describing his experiments 30 years ago with LSD. According to a recent survey by Microsoft, 75 percent of U.S. recruiters and human-resource professionals report that their companies require them to do online research about candidates, and many use a range of sites when scrutinizing applicants—including search engines, social networking sites, photo- and video-sharing sites, personal websites and blogs, Twitter and online gaming sites. Seventy percent of U.S. recruiters report that they have rejected candidates because of information found online, like photos and discussion-board conversations and membership in controversial groups.

Technological advances, of course, have often presented new threats to privacy. In 1890, in perhaps the most famous article on privacy ever written, Samuel Warren and Louis Brandeis complained that because of new technology—like the Kodak camera and the tabloid press—"gossip is no longer the resource of the idle and of the vicious but has become a trade." But the mild society gossip of the Gilded Age pales before the volume of revelations contained in the photos, video and chatter on social media sites and elsewhere across the Internet. Facebook, which surpassed MySpace in 2008 as the largest social-networking site, now has nearly 500 million members, or 22 percent of all Internet users, who spend more than 500 billion minutes a month on the site. Facebook users share more than 25 billion pieces of content each month (including news stories, blog posts and photos), and the average user creates 70 pieces of content a month. There are more than 100 million registered Twitter users, and the Library of Congress recently announced that it will be acquiring—and permanently storing—the entire archive of public Twitter posts since 2006.

In Brandeis's day—and until recently, in ours—you had to be a celebrity to be gossiped about in public: today all of us are learning to expect the scrutiny that used to be reserved for the famous and the infamous. A 26-year-old Manhattan woman told *The New York Times* that she was afraid of being tagged in online photos because it might reveal that she wears only two outfits when out on the town—a Lynyrd Skynyrd T-shirt or a basic black dress. "You have movie-star issues," she said, "and you're just a person."

We've known for years that the web allows for unprecedented voyeurism, exhibitionism and inadvertent indiscretion, but we are only beginning to understand the costs of an age in which so much of what we say, and of what others say about us, goes into our permanent—and public—digital files.

The fact that the Internet never seems to forget is threatening, at an almost existential level, our ability to control our identities; to preserve the option of reinventing ourselves and starting anew; to overcome our checkered pasts.

In a recent book, "Delete: The Virtue of Forgetting in the Digital Age," the cyberscholar Viktor Mayer-Schönberger cites Stacy Snyder's case as a reminder of the importance of "societal forgetting." By "erasing external memories," he says in the book, "our society accepts that human beings evolve over time, that we have the capacity to learn from past experiences and adjust our behavior." In traditional societies, where missteps are observed but not necessarily recorded, the limits of human memory ensure that people's sins are eventually forgotten. By contrast, Mayer-Schönberger notes, a society in which everything is recorded "will forever tether us to all our past actions, making it impossible, in practice, to escape them." He concludes that "without some form of forgetting, forgiving becomes a difficult undertaking."

It's often said that we live in a permissive era, one with infinite second chances. But the truth is that for a great many people, the permanent memory bank of the web increasingly means there are no second chances—no opportunities to escape a scarlet letter in your digital past. Now the worst thing you've done is often the first thing everyone knows about you.

THE CRISIS—AND THE SOLUTION?

Concern about these developments has intensified this year, as Facebook took steps to make the digital profiles of its users generally more public than private. Last December, the company announced that parts of user profiles that had previously been private—including every user's friends, relationship status and family relations—would become public and accessible to other users. Then in April, Facebook introduced an interactive system called Open Graph that can share your profile information and friends with the Facebook partner sites you visit.

What followed was an avalanche of criticism from users, privacy regulators and advocates around the world. Four Democratic senators—Charles Schumer of New York, Michael Bennet of Colorado, Mark Begich of Alaska and Al Franken of Minnesota—wrote to the chief executive of Facebook, Mark Zuckerberg, expressing concern about the "instant personalization" feature and the new privacy settings. In May, Facebook responded to all the criticism by introducing a new set of privacy controls that the company said would make it easier for users to understand what kind of information they were sharing in various contexts.

Facebook's partial retreat has not quieted the desire to do something about an urgent problem. All around the world, political leaders, scholars and citizens are searching for responses to the challenge of preserving control of our identities in a digital world that never forgets. Are the most promising solutions going to be technological? Legislative? Judicial? Ethical? A result of shifting social norms and cultural expectations? Or some mix of the above? Alex Türk, the French data protection commissioner, has called for a "constitutional right to oblivion" that would allow citizens to maintain a greater degree of anonymity online and in public places. In Argentina, the writers Alejandro Tortolini and Enrique Quagliano have started a campaign to "reinvent forgetting on the Internet," exploring a range of political and technological ways of making data disappear. In February, the European Union helped finance a campaign called "Think B4 U post!" that urges young people to consider the "potential consequences" of publishing photos of themselves or their friends without "thinking carefully" and asking permission. And in the United States, a group of technologists, legal scholars and cyberthinkers are exploring ways of recreating the possibility of digital forgetting. These approaches share the common goal of reconstructing a form of control over our identities: the ability to reinvent ourselves, to escape our pasts and to improve the selves that we present to the world. [. . .]

[. . .] In the near future, Internet searches for images are likely to be combined with social-network aggregator search engines, like today's Spokeo and Pipl, which combine data from online sources—including political contributions, blog posts, YouTube videos, web comments, real estate listings and photo albums. Increasingly these aggregator sites will rank people's public and private reputations, like the new website Unvarnished, a reputation marketplace where people can write anonymous reviews about anyone. In the Web 3.0 world, Michael Fertik, a Harvard Law School graduate, predicts people will be rated, assessed and scored based not on their creditworthiness but on their trustworthiness as good parents, good dates, good employees, good baby sitters or good insurance risks.

One legal option for responding to online setbacks to your reputation is to sue under current law. There's already a sharp rise in lawsuits known as Twittergation—that is, suits to force websites to remove slanderous or false posts. Last year, Courtney Love was sued for libel by the fashion designer Boudoir Queen for supposedly slanderous comments posted on Twitter, on Love's MySpace page and on the designer's online marketplace-feedback page. But even if you win a U.S. libel lawsuit, the website doesn't have to take the offending material down any more than a newspaper that has lost a libel suit has to remove the offending content from its archive.

Some scholars, therefore, have proposed creating new legal rights to force websites to remove false or slanderous statements. Cass Sunstein, the Obama administration's regulatory czar, suggests in his new book, "On Rumors," that there might be "a general right to demand retraction after a clear demonstration that a statement is both false and damaging." (If a newspaper or blogger refuses to post a retraction, they might be liable for damages.) Sunstein adds that websites might be required to take down false postings after receiving notice that they are false—an approach modeled on the Digital Millennium Copyright Act, which requires websites to remove content that supposedly infringes intellectual property rights after receiving a complaint.

As Stacy Snyder's "Drunken Pirate" photo suggests, however, many people aren't worried about false information posted by others—they're worried about true information they've posted about themselves when it is taken out of context or given undue weight. And defamation law doesn't apply to true information or statements of opinion. Some legal scholars want to expand the ability to sue over true but embarrassing violations of privacy—although it appears to be a quixotic goal.

Daniel Solove, a George Washington University law professor and author of the book, *The Future of Reputation*, says that laws forbidding people to breach confidences could be expanded to allow you to sue your Facebook friends if they share your embarrassing photos or posts in violation of your privacy settings. Expanding legal rights in this way, however, would run up against the First Amendment rights of others. Invoking the right to free speech, the U.S. Supreme Court has already held that the media can't be prohibited from publishing the name of a rape victim that they obtained from public records. Generally, American judges hold that if you disclose something to a few people, you can't stop them from sharing the information with the rest of the world.

That's one reason that the most promising solutions to the problem of embarrassing but true information online may be not legal but technological ones. Instead of suing after the damage is done (or hiring a firm to clean up our messes), we need to explore ways of preemptively making the offending words or pictures disappear.

Zuckerberg said in January to the founder of the publication TechCrunch that Facebook had an obligation to reflect "current social norms" that favored exposure over privacy. "People have really gotten comfortable not only sharing more information and different kinds but more openly and with more people, and that social norm is just something that has evolved over time," he said.

However, norms are already developing to recreate off-the-record spaces in public, with no photos, Twitter posts or blogging allowed. Milk and Honey, an exclusive bar on Manhattan's Lower East Side, requires potential members to sign an agreement promising not to blog about the bar's goings on or to post photos on social-networking sites, and other bars and nightclubs are adopting similar policies. I've been at dinners recently where someone has requested, in all seriousness, "Please don't tweet this"—a custom that is likely to spread.

But what happens when people transgress those norms, using Twitter or tagging photos in ways that cause us serious embarrassment? Can we imagine a world in which new norms develop that make it easier for people to forgive and forget one another's digital sins? [. . .]

[. . .] Perhaps society will become more forgiving of drunken Facebook pictures in the way Samuel Gosling, the University of Texas, Austin, psychology professor says he expects it might. And some may welcome the end of the segmented self, on the grounds that it will discourage bad behavior and hypocrisy: it's harder to have clandestine affairs when you're broadcasting your every move on Facebook, Twitter and Foursquare. But a humane society values privacy, because it allows people to cultivate different aspects of their personalities in different contexts; and at the moment, the enforced merging of identities that used to be separate is leaving many casualties in its wake. Stacy Snyder couldn't reconcile her "aspiring-teacher self" with her "having-a-few-drinks self": even the impression, correct or not, that she had a drink in a pirate hat at an off-campus party was enough to derail her teaching career.

That doesn't mean, however, that it had to derail her life. After taking down her MySpace profile, Snyder is understandably trying to maintain her privacy: her lawyer told me in a recent interview that she is now working in human resources; she did not respond to a request for comment. But her success as a human being who can change and evolve, learning from her mistakes and growing in wisdom, has nothing to do with the digital file she can never entirely escape. Our character, ultimately, can't be judged by strangers on the basis of our Facebook or Google profiles; it can be judged by only those who know us and have time to evaluate our strengths and weaknesses, face to face and in context, with insight and understanding. In the meantime, as all of us stumble over the challenges of living in a world without forgetting, we need to learn new forms of empathy, new ways of defining ourselves without reference to what others say about us and new ways of forgiving one another for the digital trails that will follow us forever.

Activity 2.6 Discuss "The Web Means the End of Forgetting"

1. What is the significance of the title, "The Web Means the End of Forgetting"?

2. What does Jeffrey Rosen mean when he suggests that in the future Stacy Snyder may be an icon?

3. What is the main point in Jeffrey Rosen's main essay? What is he arguing?

4. Does Rosen offer sufficient evidence to make you take his argument seriously? Why or why not?

5. Are you a member of any social networking sites? What can you do in order to protect your reputation?

6. A woman interviewed in the article said, in regard to being tagged in online photos, "you have movie-star issues—and you're just a person." If you are a member of any social networking sites, do you tag friends in photos? Is it important to be careful about this? Why or why not?

Activity 2.7 What Is the Current State of Identity Protection in Social Networking Sites?

In your group, explore news, watchdog, and government sites to see if any new laws or other protections have been implemented to safeguard individuals posting personal information on the web. Report what you learn to the class.

Close Reading of a Text

Rhetorical reading involves careful and patient attention to the text, even reading the text several times. Following are several strategies for reading critically. You do not need to use all of the reading strategies suggested for each essay you read, but as you begin to read critically, you should try all of the strategies at least once to see which ones supplement your natural reading and learning style.

1. **Learn about the author.** Knowing whether an author is a biologist, a professional writer, or a politician can guide your expectations of the essay. If you are reading in a magazine or journal, you can often discover information in the contributor's notes at the beginning or end of the essay or at the beginning or end of the magazine. Many books have a dust jacket or a page giving a short biography of the author. As you learn about the author, jot down any impressions you may have about the author's purpose in writing the essay. Does the author have an obvious agenda in promoting a certain viewpoint on the topic?

2. **Skim the text.** Once you've gotten to know the author a little, it is helpful to read the essay quickly and superficially by reading the introduction, the first sentence in every paragraph, and the conclusion. Read quickly. When you skim a text, you are not trying to understand it. You are preparing for the more careful read that will follow. If the essay tells a story, skimming will give you a good sense of the chronology of the story. When is the story taking place? How much time seems to pass? If the essay is argumentative, skimming will provide knowledge of the basic structure of the argument and will introduce you to the main points of support. If the essay is primarily informative, you will learn some of the important distinctions and classifications the author uses to organize the information.

It may be interesting to note whether you can get the gist of the reading by skimming. Has the writer provided topic sentences for paragraphs or sections? If so, the writer is trying to make his or her message easily accessible.

3. **Explore your own knowledge and beliefs on the subject.** Make a list of what you already know about the topic of the text. Then make a list of what you believe about this topic. Finally, make a note beside each entry that marks where that information or belief came from.

4. **Reflect on the topic.** The final step before reading is reflecting on what you expect from the essay before you begin a careful reading. What does the title lead you to expect from the essay? Does your quick glance at the essay seem to support the title? How do you feel about the essay so far? Does it anger you, interest you, bore you? Do you think you have any experience that relates to the essay? Will your experience and the author's experience lead you to the same conclusions? One effective way to reflect is to freewrite on the topic of the essay. Exploring what you know before you embark on a careful reading of the essay can deepen your responses.

5. Annotate. Read the essay slowly, thinking about what meaning the author is trying to convey. It is a good idea to annotate as you read, particularly points that seem important and/or raise questions in your mind. If you don't want to write in your text, try photocopying assigned essays so you can annotate them. You'll probably develop your own system of annotation as you begin to use this technique more often, but here are some basic guidelines to help you begin your annotations:

- Underline sentences, phrases, and words that seem important to the essay.

- Circle words you don't know but think you understand from the context. Then you can look them up later to see if the dictionary definition matches the definition you assumed from the context.

- Write questions in the margins. If the margins aren't large enough to write a complete question, a couple of words to remind you of what you were thinking and a question mark will do. You can also write brief comments in the margins, again just a few words to remind you of your thoughts.

- Number or put check marks in the margin by major points. Careful annotation of each point in the margin will help you later if you choose to outline.

- Use arrows, lines, and symbols in the margins to connect ideas in the essay that seem related or depend on each other.

- Note transitions, sentence structures, examples, topic sentences, and other rhetorical moves that seem particularly effective in the essay by writing a brief comment or an exclamation mark in the margin next to the underlined text.

See page 60 for an example of an annotated article.

6. Outline. An excellent way to distill the meaning of a text is to create an informal outline of the argument. If, as part of annotating the essay, you jot down the main subject of each paragraph in the margin, this will allow you to see the organization of the essay and outline it easily. An outline should list the focus of the essay and track how that focus unfolds paragraph by paragraph. If you are outlining a narrative essay, the outline will probably follow the chronology of the events. Outlining an informative essay, you might find that the outline tracks the steps of a process or reveals divisions and classifications. Outlining an argumentative essay, you'll probably find your outline works to prove a thesis by making statements which support that thesis, raising objections and refuting them, or, perhaps, proposing solutions to solve a problem.

7. Freewrite about the text. Another way to distill the meaning of a text after you have read it carefully is to lay the essay aside and freewrite for a few minutes about the content and purpose of the essay. If you have not tried freewriting before, it is easy. You simply put your pen to the paper, focus the topic in your mind, and write whatever comes to mind about the topic for a set period of time, perhaps five minutes. If you cannot think of anything to write, you write, "I can't think of anything to write," and then you continue writing what is in your mind. You may find it helpful to begin your freewriting by writing, "This essay is about . . ." and continue writing, explaining to yourself what you think the essay is about.

8. Summarize the text. Write a summary of what you consider to be the primary meaning of the text. Your summary should answer these questions about claims, support, purpose, and audience:

- What is the author of the essay trying to show or prove (claim)?

- What does the writer use to convince me that he or she is well informed or right (support)?

- Why did the writer choose to write this essay (purpose)?

- Who is the author addressing or writing for (audience)?

To write a clear summary, you have to understand the essay. You might test your understanding by reading the essay again and deciding whether your summary is accurate. Writing summaries helps you understand your assignments and prepares you for the numerous summaries you will complete.

Responding to Oral and Visual Media

Increasingly, young "politically minded viewers" are plugging into YouTube, Facebook, and comedy shows like "The Daily Show" and other alternative media instead of traditional news outlets. According to a *New York Times*

Reading 2.2

President Barack Obama on the Death of Osama bin Laden

One man affected so many

Good evening. Tonight, I can report to the American people and to the world that the United States has conducted an operation that killed Osama bin Laden, the leader of al Qaeda, and a terrorist who's responsible for the murder of thousands of innocent men, women, and children.

Where was I when it happened?

visual image— good technique

strong verbs

It was nearly 10 years ago that a bright September day was darkened by the worst attack on the American people in our history. The images of 9/11 are seared into our national memory— hijacked planes cutting through a cloudless September sky; the Twin Towers collapsing to the ground; black smoke billowing up from the Pentagon; the wreckage of Flight 93 in Shanksville, Pennsylvania, where the actions of heroic citizens saved even more heartbreak and destruction.

President Barack Obama announced the death of Osama bin Laden.

Presidential seal— ethos

refers to children— pathos

And yet we know that the worst images are those that were unseen to the world. The empty seat at the dinner table. Children who were forced to grow up without their mother or their father. Parents who would never know the

article, surveys and interviews during the 2008 presidential election indicate that "younger voters tend to be not just consumers of news and current events but conduits as well—sending out e-mailed links and videos to friends and their social networks. And in turn, they rely on friends and online connections for news to come to them." **Word of mouth** (via e-mail) is replacing traditional media as the major news filter, at least for young viewers. In this new process, moreover, "viewers" or "writers of e-mail" move seamlessly back and forth between e-mail, text-messaging, television viewing, and Internet surfing, appreciating and sharing the choicest rhetorical pieces with others. "We're talking about a generation that doesn't just like seeing the video in addition to the story—they expect it," said Danny Shea, 23, the associate media editor for *The Huffington Post* (huffingtonpost.com). "And they'll find it elsewhere if you don't give it to them, and then that's the link that's going to be passed around over e-mail and instant message." This multistream, cross-platform method of communication among younger viewers/readers is a fertile forum for rhetorical analysis.

Actually, the lines between oral, written, and visual "texts" have always been somewhat blurred. Speeches delivered orally in person or on television have a visual component, as the audience sees the speaker present the text. A written text is also, in a sense, visual because the audience's mind must process the little squiggles of ink on paper or on the computer screen into words. A visual text such as an advertisement or cartoon often includes written text, and, even if it does not, the image will inspire thoughts that are often distilled into language for expression. Reasonably, many of the same techniques used to analyze written and oral texts also can be applied to visual media (cartoons, advertisements, television, etc.).

Reading 2.5

I know I said I love you,

I know you know it's true,
I've got to put the phone down,
and do what we got to do.

One's standing in the aisleway,
Two more at the door,
We've got to get inside there,
Before they kill some more.

Time is runnin' out,
Let's roll.
Time is runnin' out,
Let's roll.

No time for indecision,
We've got to make a move,
I hope that we're forgiven,
For what we got to do

Let's Roll

by Neil Young

Music lyrics are performance texts, just as are speeches. They are written to be heard, not written to be read. However, you can analyze the argument in song lyrics, such as "Let's Roll," reprinted here, which was written by Neil Young. The song was inspired by the last words of a passenger named Todd Beamer, who died in the hijacking of Flight 93 on September 11, 2001. To analyze the song's lyrics rhetorically, you can consider whether the lyrics have a debatable issue, a clear thesis or claim, evidence to support that claim, a particular audience, and a conclusion. With a song, moreover, you can also consider the impact of the lyrics as they are presented by a vocalist accompanied by musical instruments. How does the musical presentation of the lyrics affect their impact as an argument?

How this all got started,
I'll never understand,
I hope someone can fly this thing,
And get us back to land.

Time is runnin' out,
Let's roll.
Time is runnin' out,
Let's roll.

No one has the answer,
But one thing is true,
You've got to turn on evil,
When it's coming after you,
You've gotta face it down,
And when it tries to hide,
You've gotta go in after it,
And never be denied,

Time is runnin' out,
Let's roll.

Let's roll for freedom,
Let's roll for love,
We're going after Satan,
On the wings of a dove,
Let's roll for justice,
Let's roll for truth,
Let's not let our children,
Grow up fearful in their youth.

Time is runnin' out,
Let's roll.
Time is runnin' out,
Let's roll.
Time is runnin' out,
Let's roll.

Activity 2.8 **Respond to Song Lyrics**

1. Reflect on what you know about the September 11 attacks. At the end of the first stanza, Young writes, "I've got to put the phone down, and do what we got to do." What is the call to action he is making here? What rhetorical significance does it have in this historical context?

2. Who is Young referring to when he says, "We're going after Satan"? What action is he advocating?

Activity 2.9 **Consider a Song as an Argument**

In your small group, explore the Internet for a song that seems to make an argument, and answer the following questions. Share your findings with the class.

1. What message is the artist/group trying to transmit with the song?

2. What are some lyrics that help to support this message?

3. How would you describe the musical style of the song? In what ways does the style of singing and instrumentation help the rhetorical message?

Responding to Visual Rhetoric

Methods of analyzing visual rhetoric draw upon several theoretical traditions. In art criticism, viewers may look for symbolism in an image or consider what meaning the artist was trying to convey. Semiotics views images as having intertextuality, as similar images come to have similar meanings, and those meanings may create similar emotions in the viewer. Rhetoricians, as you might expect, consider the argument that an image may present to a viewer. They think about how the subject of the image is presented in relation to other elements in the visual, how the image is cropped, and what types of lighting and colors are present. Rhetoricians also pay particular attention to the interplay between the visual image and any text that may appear with the image and how the two together construct an argument.

Courtesy BMW premium advertising.

In the BMW advertisement shown above, for example, a beautiful blonde-haired young woman is presented without clothes and lying down with her hair artfully arranged in waves. *Salon* magazine reprinted a copy of the BMW advertisement, pointing out that, "in small print scrawled across her bare shoulder, it reads: 'You know you're not the first.' As your eyes drift to the bottom of the advertisement—and the top of her chest—you learn that it's an advertisement for BMW's premium selection of used cars."

Of course, sexual appeal has been used for decades to sell a whole range of products. However, what do you think is BMW's argument here? *Salon* thinks the ad is implying, "Used cars, used women" and that the ad gives a "whole new meaning" to BMW's slogan, printed in the ad: "Sheer Driving Pleasure."

The image that appears below, surprisingly, isn't advertising a car. No, it is selling a community college, West Hills College, capitalizing on the idea that with all the money you would save by going to a community college, you could buy a nice car.

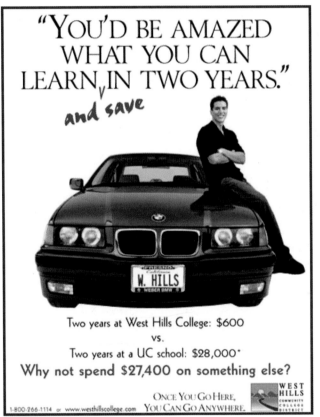

Courtesy West Hills College

Activity 2.10 **Interpret Advertisements**

1. What is the symbolism of the beautiful young woman (presumably naked) posed as she is in the BMW advertisement?

2. What meaning do you think the tag line, "You know you're not the first," adds to the image? Then, when you realize that the image is an ad for BMW used cars, does your interpretation of this tag line's meaning change?

3. What are the creators of the West Hills College advertisement trying to say by showing the image of the student sitting on the car?

4. The use of fonts is another important element in transmitting a message in an advertisement. In the West Hills College ad, why are the words "and save" written in a different font and inserted with the caret?

5. As a college student, would you be convinced by the West Hills advertisement? Why or why not? What elements exist in the ad that would or would not convince you to attend the college mentioned?

6. Do you find the BMW advertisement amusing, objectionable, or appealing? Does it make you want to buy a used BMW?

Activity 2.11 Find Advertisements with Effective Arguments

Bring to class an advertisement that you think makes an effective argument. It can be torn from a magazine or downloaded from the Internet. In your small group, evaluate each advertisement for its effectiveness in selling something, and choose the one with the most effective argument. Present your choice to the class along with an explanation of why you think it is effective.

Interaction between Texts and Images

Many of the texts we encounter in everyday life—in newspapers, magazines, and on the Internet—are not texts in isolation but texts combined with images. Indeed, when readers first glance at one of these media, likely their attention is caught first by photos, then by headlines. Only after being engaged by these attention-getting visual elements (for headlines are visual elements as well as written) are readers likely to focus on the written text. Student writers today, like professionals, have access to the use of visual elements in their compositions, and adding photos can not only catch the reader's attention but also emphasize particular points of an argument or create an overall mood.

All-Star Rockers Salute Buddy Holly

by Andy Greene

R&R

All-Star Rockers Salute Buddy Holly

McCartney, Cee Lo, the Black Keys, Kid Rock and more cut killer covers disc

When Buddy Holly died in a plane crash in 1959, he was just 22 years old and had been writing and recording songs for only about two years. But that music—including immortal hits like "Not Fade Away" and "Peggy Sue"—has had an incalculable impact on rock history. "He was a major influence on the Beatles," Paul McCartney told Rolling Stone recently. "John and I spent hours trying to work out how to play the opening riff to "That'll Be the Day," and we were truly blessed by the heavens the day we figured it out. It was the first song John, George and I ever recorded."

A half-century later, McCartney has returned to Holly's catalog, cutting a smoking rendition of "It's So Easy." It's one of 19 newly recorded Holly covers—by an all-star lineup including the Black Keys, My Morning Jacket, Kid Rock Fiona Apple, Patti Smith, and Lou Reed—for the tribute

NOT FADE AWAY
Holly in 1950. McCartney and Cee Lo recorded new songs commemorating Holly's 75th birthday.

disc *Rave on Buddy Holly*, spearheaded by Randall Poster, music supervisor of movies such as *The Royal Tenenbaums* and *I'm Not There*. "We wanted to commemorate Buddy's 75th birthday," Poster says. "I've used a lot of his songs in movies, and they're so powerful and so ripe for interpretation."

Florence and the Machine cut a New Orleans-flavored version of "Not Fade Away" while on tour in the Big Easy last year. "My grandmother took me to the musical *Buddy: The Buddy Holly Story* when I was a kid, and it changed my life," says singer Florence Welch. "When we were in New Orleans, we decided

it would be good to use the environment around us, so we brought in local Cajun musicians." Cee Lo Green tackled the relatively obscure "You're So Square (Baby, I Don't Care)." "We wanted to keep the rockabilly intact," he says. "But we broadened it and gave it a bit of something unique to me. There's something Americana about it, something country and something African."

Smith selected "Words of Love." "During the song she talks in Spanish and is sort of channeling [Holly's widow] Maria Elena Holly," says Poster. "It's so romantic and so novel. More times than not, we were just overwhelmed by the power of the renditions that we received." Despite Holly's extremely brief career, Poster thinks the set could have been even longer: "There's probably a half-dozen more songs we could have done. If I had more time and more of a budget, I would have kept on going." ANDY GREENE

Activity 2.12 **Analyze Interaction between Texts and Images**

Read the article, "All-Star Rockers Salute Buddy Holly," by Andy Greene, published in *Rolling Stone* magazine. Look at how the images and layout work together and answer the questions:

1. What rhetorical purpose do the photos of these musicians achieve in relation to the article? Hint: think about the ethos (credibility, reputation, power) of these particular musicians, especially when they appear together on the page.

2. Consider the way the text is wrapped around the pictures. In particular, notice how this layout suggests a close relationship between Buddy Holly, Paul McCartney, and Cee Lo Green. What does this layout signify?

Activity 2.13 **Write a Summary**

Summarizing is an excellent technique to use when preparing for an exam or researching for an essay. It allows you to discern the main points of a text to see what is beneficial for you to know for the exam or paper. With a classmate, search for an article from a newspaper or magazine that presents a strong argument. Read the article, and list the main points individually. After you've listed the main points, put them into paragraph form. Caution: Beware of the temptation to add your own analysis of what the text is saying. For example, if you are summarizing a scientist's article on global warming, you need to be careful not to reveal your personal opinion about whether or not global warming is occurring or whether or not human actions are to blame. In this assignment, you summarize only. You do not argue or analyze.

When you're finished, compare your summary with that of your partner.

Kindle users love reading. But let's face it—a book is in your hands.

Sure, Amazon's Kindle makes it possible to read more books, clears up a lot of shelf space, fits snugly in anyone's baggage and can actually be cheaper in the long run. But each reading feels the same. The only difference is the words you read and your reaction to them. You begin to miss that sometimes rough feel of a hardback book, along with the slick, almost slippery design

How to Make a Kindle Cover from a Hollowed Out Hardback Book

by Justin Meyers

The author of the following article explains why you would want to make a Kindle cover out of an old book instead of buying a new Kindle cover. What does the article say are the drawbacks of the Kindle? Think about it. These instructions are an argument, saying in text and photos that as wonderful as the Kindle is, it does not satisfy the needs of a reader to touch and smell a book. The author attempts to rectify the Kindle's shortcomings through these instructions for making a cover out of a book.

Notice also how the author uses photos to illustrate his text. If you had just the text and no photos, following the instructions would be much more difficult.

of a paperback. Each book seems to have a smell of its own, something unique. And getting your hands dirty with ink from the finely written words was half the journey.

The Kindle erases that part of your reading experience. It feels the same, smells the same and even looks the same. Instead of turning pages, which is different sizes, thicknesses and colors from book to book, you're pressing the same button over and over again. In some ways, reading a classic on your Kindle actually devalues its adventure. But the eBook reader is convenient, practically weightless and serves up immediate literature consumption.

So where's the compromise?

Well, you can have the best of both worlds—sort of . . .

ebonical has crafted the perfect Kindle case—out of a hardcover book. Kindle cases can be expensive, so making a homemade Kindle cover is the perfect weekend project. And chances are you already have the perfect book for your Kindle collecting dust on your bookshelf. If not, you'll need to shop the local bookstores.

"I decided to carve out the pages of a printed book and thus complete the poetic circle of digital book readers destroying the printed word.

"Getting the right book turned out to be harder than I thought as most hardcover books are designed to be a particular size and variance is slight. Too small and the edges would be brittle. Too large and it would just become a hassle and ruin the point of having the small digital reader in the first place. With some time spent scouring thrift shops and second hand book stalls I managed, with some luck, to find what seemed to be the right book."

So, then how do you actually make the Kindle book cover?

STEP 1 Gather the Materials

- Your perfectly-sized hardcover book
- Hobby PVA glue (polyvinyl acetate) or Elmer's white glue
- Paintbrush
- Scalpel, box cutter or other sharp utility knife
- Ruler
- Pencil
- More books (for use as weights)

STEP 2 Crafting Your Kindle Case

Getting your book ready for your Kindle is an easy process, though a lengthy one.

You begin by choosing where you want your hole to start. Once you have your spot picked, you use the paintbrush to spread the glue onto the edges of the pages where the hole will be cut. Use your extra books to weigh it down during the drying process.

When dry, open the book back up to your chosen starting point. Use the ruler and pencil to mark your hole the size of the Kindle. Once all marked, use your utility knife to start cutting on the outline. It's probably best to use your ruler as a straight edge to help guide the blade along, for a better, straighter cut. This is the longest step, because you have a lot to cut through. The time will vary depending on 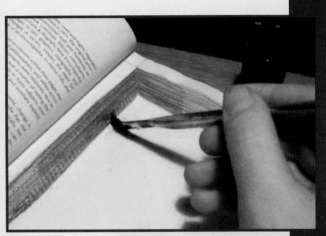 how deep your book is. I wouldn't recommend *War and Peace*.

Once you've gotten all the way to the back cover, the rest is easy. Just clean up the edges of your cuts as best you can, then use your paintbrush again to spread some glue along the cut edges.

TIP: When choosing your first page to cut, it's good to actually save it for later. Don't cut with the rest of them. When you have your hole fully cut open and have applied the glue, apply another thin line on the top border of your actual first page cut (essentially, the second page). Then close the book and add the weights to the top and let dry. Saving the first page helps reduce the chance of you accidentally gluing unwanted pages to cut ones, causing you to have to cut the pages you didn't want to cut to open the hole back up. Saving your first page makes it premeditated.

After fully dried, open it up and cut the final page (first page) to open the hole up. Then, you'll need to let it dry again, with the book open. After dried, that's it. You're done!

Activity 2.14 **Write and Illustrate Instructions**

Write and illustrate your own set of instructions for an activity that includes an argument. For example, during a lawn party at the White House, First Lady Michelle Obama served Carrot Lemonade to children who gave the drink rave reviews. Such a recipe could include an introduction explaining that creating healthy adaptations of popular foods and drinks for children only works if they taste good. Or, you might write instructions for how to remove geotags from photos before posting them on Facebook or other social networking sites. In your instructions you could explain that this process prevents people that you don't know from learning where you took the picture—and possibly learning where you live if you took it at home. Your argument would be that it is important to protect your privacy when you post photos on the Internet.

Try out your instructions on a friend, so you are sure you have included all the necessary steps and illustrated them adequately. Don't forget to include a brief statement of your argument, as does the writer of the Kindle cover article.

Activity 2.15 **Create Your Own Blog**

Read an article on the Internet related to a topic in which you're interested. Make sure the article has a substantial amount of text, as well as related images. In your blog, discuss how the text and the images both contribute to the article's rhetorical message. Include the title of the article, the author, the name of the publication or web page, and a link to the article.

Activity 2.16 **Write in Your Commonplace Book**

What do you read for fun? Magazines, blogs, books? Do you engage in what Louise Rosenblatt calls "aesthetic reading"? (See the section titled, "Ways of Reading Rhetorically") Write down a quote in your commonplace book from something that you have read for fun. First, reflect about what the quote means to you. Then, comment about why it is important to read things for fun and how that experience is different than reading to learn.

3
ANALYZING RHETORICALLY

Praxis in Action

Analyzing Arguments Improves My Writing by Eurydice Saucedo

Reading enables my creative mind to soar to undreamed-of worlds, to visit the deepest of memories, and to laugh as words describe a child's joy. Yes, reading enables me to be a bigger dreamer, but it also opens my eyes to better understand this world we live in.

Reading essays teaches me definitions and meanings, and, with practice, allows me to discern the validity and reliability of arguments. I can distinguish between fair representation of an issue, embellishment of truth, and bitter sarcasm. Every sentence has more than just simple grammar and punctuation. Every text, just like everything else in life, needs to be taken with a grain of salt, slowly simmered, and thought about before the final evaluation can be made. If I know rhetorical concepts, I can recognize when a text is trying to persuade me of something, and I can decide if the writer presents a good argument and sufficient evidence to merit serious consideration.

Reading and analyzing texts helps me learn how to structure my own argument. I may find a flaw in an argument, for example, a lack of acknowledgement of a counterargument that causes me to distrust a text. This causes me to be more careful to include the counterargument in my own text. And when I read and reread a classic argument such as Martin Luther King's "I Have a Dream" speech, I may make note of a strategy that I can use later. For example, Dr. King's adapting of President Lincoln's memorable language, saying, "five score years ago" instead of Lincoln's "four score and seven years ago" is highly effective. Perhaps I will try adapting a highly memorable quote when it fits in my argument.

One of the best ways to become a better writer is to read good writing.

Eurydice Saucedo writes, "Every text, just like everything else in life, needs to be taken with a grain of salt, slowly simmered, and thought about before the final evaluation can be made."

73

Discover the Kairos—The Opening for Argument

Ancient Greek archer

Kairos is a Greek word often translated as the right or opportune moment to do something, though it has no exact English translation. The first recorded use of the word kairos is in Homer's *Iliad*, where it appears as an adjective referring to an arrow striking the "deadliest spot" on the human body. When the word appears again later in Greek writing as a noun—a kairos—it retains this essential meaning as an opening or aperture. Twelve bronze axes with ring openings for wooden shanks are positioned in a line, so archers can practice by aiming at the kairos or ring opening, with the arrow passing down the line, through each ax. Clearly, launching an arrow through the kairos of twelve axes placed a yard apart required strength, training, practice, and a precise visual and muscle awareness of place. When people today say, "I saw my opening, and I took it, " they are conveying this meaning of kairos as an opening, combined with the idea of kairos as an opportunity.[1]

Ancient bronze ax with a ring hole for a wooden shank

Each time a rhetor (a speaker or writer) constructs an argument, he or she is working within a context of a certain moment, a particular time and place, that come together in a unique opportunity or opening for action—a kairos. A kairos both constrains and enables what a rhetor can say or write effectively in a particular situation. So, to compose the most effective text, a rhetor must do more than develop a thesis or statement of the main idea that takes a position about the subject—he or she must discover the kairos of the argument and its ramifications. What opportunities does the kairos present for making a persuasive argument, and what restrictions may be wise in consideration of the audience or occasion?

Use Kairos to Make Your Own Argument

Consider the following suggestions for determining the kairotic moment for your argument—the opening of sensitivity where you can shoot your metaphoric arrow:

- *Consider timeliness.* What is going on right now with the issue and how can you emphasize that in an argument? For example, if you are writing

---

[1] Thomas Rickert, "Invention in the Wild: On Locating Kairos in Space-Time," in *The Locations of Composition.* eds. Christopher J. Keller and Christian R. Weisser (Albany: SUNY Press, 2007) pp. 72–73.

about the death penalty, choose to write about the current cases on death row or the most recent person to be executed. Or, if your topic is about the unemployed exhausting their government benefits and you have, yourself, recently become unemployed, you can use your own experience as an illustration of the problem.

■ *Know your audience.* What are the characteristics of the audience? Do they agree with your position on the issue or not? What is their educational level and the extent of their knowledge about the subject? For example, if you are writing about immigration policy reform, does your audience believe there is a need for reform? Do they have personal experience with illegal or legal immigrants? You can judge the amount of background information you need to provide based upon the characteristics of your audience. Also, the most important members of the audience, so far as an argument is concerned, are not those who already agree with you but those who are neutral or even slightly opposed to your position but willing to listen. Be careful not to phrase your argument in ways that are insulting to people who do not agree with you, for if you do so, they will stop listening to you.

■ *Find a place to stand.* In the reading that follows, Martin Luther King, Jr., stood in front of the Lincoln Memorial as he gave his famous speech, "I Have a Dream." This location greatly impacts the speech and increases King's ethos, which we discuss in more detail below. You can make a similar rhetorical move, for example, if you live in a border community because you stand, metaphorically and physically, at an important juncture for issues such as immigration, free trade, and national security.

When Martin Luther King, Jr., gave his "I Have a Dream" speech, his words were carefully crafted to take into consideration the setting in front of the Lincoln Memorial. He said, "Five score years ago, a great American, in whose symbolic shadow we stand today, signed the Emancipation Proclamation." The words "five score" recall the "four score and seven years ago" of Lincoln's words in the Gettysburg Address. And King also pointed out that he and his audience that day stood in the "symbolic shadow" of the president who signed the Emancipation Proclamation. In these ways, he made use of Lincoln's shadow to legitimize what he was saying about civil rights.

In other ways, however, the kairos of the moment limited what he could say. His audience included both the thousands of people in front of him who were dedicated to the cause of racial equality and also the audience of those millions watching on television who may or may not have agreed with his message. Thus, the tone of his message needed to be subtly measured not to antagonize those among his audience, particularly the television audience, who may have opposed aspects of the civil rights movement such as school integration. However, he spoke to let both his supporters and his opponents know, "The whirlwinds of revolt will continue to shake the foundations of our nation until the bright day of justice emerges." Yes, King advocated nonviolent demonstrations, but they were demonstrations nonetheless; he was putting opponents on notice that the disruptions caused by demonstrations would continue "until justice emerges." King consistently took the high road, while maintaining the power of the kairotic moment when he spoke. This is one reason why his words continue to be studied decades after his death.

Reading 3.1

I Have a Dream
by Martin Luther King, Jr.

Martin Luther King, Jr., delivered this speech on August 28, 1963, at the Lincoln Memorial in Washington, D.C., as part of the March on Washington for Jobs and Freedom. A Baptist minister, King received the Nobel Peace Prize in 1964 for his efforts to end racial discrimination through nonviolent means. He was assassinated in 1968.

I am happy to join with you today in what will go down in history as the greatest demonstration for freedom in the history of our nation.

Five score years ago, a great American, in whose symbolic shadow we stand today, signed the Emancipation Proclamation. This momentous decree came as a great beacon light of hope to millions of Negro slaves who had been seared in the flames of withering injustice. It came as a joyous daybreak to end the long night of their captivity.

But one hundred years later, the Negro still is not free. One hundred years later, the life of the Negro is still sadly crippled by the manacles of segregation and the chains of discrimination. One hundred years later, the Negro lives on a lonely island of poverty in the midst of a vast ocean of material prosperity. One hundred years later, the Negro is still languished in the corners of American society and finds himself an exile in his own land. And so we've come here today to dramatize a shameful condition.

In a sense we've come to our nation's capital to cash a check. When the architects of our republic wrote the magnificent words of the Constitution and the Declaration of Independence, they were signing a promissory note to which every American was to fall heir. This note was a promise that all men, yes, black men as well as white men, would be guaranteed the "unalienable Rights" of "Life, Liberty and the pursuit of Happiness." It is obvious today that America has defaulted on this promissory note, insofar as her citizens of color are concerned. Instead of honoring this sacred obligation, America has given the Negro people a bad check, a check which has come back marked "insufficient funds."

But we refuse to believe that the bank of justice is bankrupt. We refuse to believe that there are insufficient funds in the great vaults of opportunity of this nation. And so, we've come to cash this check, a check that will give us upon demand the riches of freedom and the security of justice.

We have also come to this hallowed spot to remind America of the fierce urgency of Now. This is no time to engage in the luxury of cooling off or to take the tranquilizing drug of gradualism. Now is the time to make real the promises of democracy. Now is the time to rise from the dark and desolate valley of segregation to the sunlit path of racial justice. Now is the time to lift our nation from the quicksands of racial injustice to the solid rock of brotherhood. Now is the time to make justice a reality for all of God's children.

It would be fatal for the nation to overlook the urgency of the moment. This sweltering summer of the Negro's legitimate discontent will not pass until there is an invigorating autumn of freedom and equality. Nineteen sixty-three is not an end, but a beginning. And those who hope that the Negro needed to blow off steam and will now be content will have a rude awakening if the nation returns to business as usual. And there will be neither rest nor tranquility in America until the Negro is granted his citizenship rights. The whirlwinds of revolt will continue to shake the foundations of our nation until the bright day of justice emerges.

But there is something that I must say to my people, who stand on the warm threshold which leads into the palace of justice: In the process of gaining our rightful place, we must not be guilty of wrongful deeds. Let us not seek to satisfy our thirst for freedom by drinking from the cup of bitterness and hatred. We must forever conduct our struggle on the high plane of dignity and discipline. We must not allow our creative protest to degenerate into physical violence. Again and again, we must rise to the majestic heights of meeting physical force with soul force.

The marvelous new militancy which has engulfed the Negro community must not lead us to a distrust of all white people, for many of our white brothers, as evidenced by their presence here today, have come to realize that their destiny is tied up with our destiny. And they have come to realize that their freedom is inextricably bound to our freedom.

We cannot walk alone.

And as we walk, we must make the pledge that we shall always march ahead.

We cannot turn back.

There are those who are asking the devotees of civil rights, "When will you be satisfied?" We can never be satisfied as long as the Negro is the victim of the unspeakable horrors of police brutality. We can never be satisfied as long as our bodies, heavy with the fatigue of travel, cannot gain lodging in the motels of the highways and the hotels of the cities. We cannot be satisfied as long as the negro's basic mobility is from a smaller ghetto to a larger one. We can never be satisfied as long as our children are stripped of their selfhood and robbed of their dignity by a sign stating: "For Whites Only." We cannot be satisfied as long as a Negro in Mississippi cannot vote and a Negro in New York believes he has nothing for which to vote. No, no, we are not satisfied, and we will not be satisfied until "justice rolls down like waters, and righteousness like a mighty stream."[2]

I am not unmindful that some of you have come here out of great trials and tribulations. Some of you have come fresh from narrow jail cells. And some of you have come from areas where your quest—quest for freedom left you battered by the storms of persecution and staggered by the winds of police brutality. You have been the veterans of creative suffering. Continue to work with the faith that unearned suffering is redemptive. Go back to Mississippi, go back to Alabama, go back to South Carolina, go back to Georgia, go back to Louisiana, go back to the slums and ghettos of our northern cities, knowing that somehow this situation can and will be changed.

Let us not wallow in the valley of despair, I say to you today, my friends.

And so even though we face the difficulties of today and tomorrow, I still have a dream. It is a dream deeply rooted in the American dream.

I have a dream that one day this nation will rise up and live out the true meaning of its creed: "We hold these truths to be self-evident, that all men are created equal."

I have a dream that one day on the red hills of Georgia, the sons of former slaves and the sons of former slave owners will be able to sit down together at the table of brotherhood.

I have a dream that one day even the state of Mississippi, a state sweltering with the heat of injustice, sweltering with the heat of oppression, will be transformed into an oasis of freedom and justice.

I have a dream that my four little children will one day live in a nation where they will not be judged by the color of their skin but by the content of their character.

I have a dream today!

I have a dream that one day, down in Alabama, with its vicious racists, with its governor having his lips dripping with the words of "interposition" and "nullification"—one day right there in Alabama little black boys and black girls will be able to join hands with little white boys and white girls as sisters and brothers.

I have a dream today!

I have a dream that one day every valley shall be exalted, and every hill and mountain shall be made low, the rough places will be made plain, and the crooked places will be made straight; "and the glory of the Lord shall be revealed and all flesh shall see it together."[3]

This is our hope, and this is the faith that I go back to the South with.

With this faith, we will be able to hew out of the mountain of despair a stone of hope. With this faith, we will be able to transform the jangling discords of our nation into a beautiful symphony of brotherhood. With this faith, we will be able to work together, to pray together, to struggle together, to go to jail together, to stand up for freedom together, knowing that we will be free one day.

And this will be the day—this will be the day when all of God's children will be able to sing with new meaning:

> My country 'tis of thee, sweet land of liberty, of thee I sing.
> Land where my fathers died, land of the Pilgrim's pride,
> From every mountainside, let freedom <u>ring</u>!

> And if America is to be a great nation, this must become true.

> And so let freedom ring from the prodigious hilltops of New Hampshire.
> Let freedom ring from the mighty mountains of New York.
> Let freedom ring from the heightening Alleghenies of Pennsylvania.
> Let freedom ring from the snow-capped Rockies of Colorado.
> Let freedom ring from the curvaceous slopes of California.

But not only that:
Let freedom ring from Stone Mountain of Georgia.
Let freedom ring from Lookout Mountain of Tennessee.
Let freedom ring from every hill and molehill of Mississippi.
From every mountainside, let freedom ring.

And when this happens, when we allow freedom to ring, when we let it ring from every village and every hamlet, from every state and every city, we will be able to speed up that day when all of God's children, black men and white men, Jews and Gentiles, Protestants and Catholics, will be able to join hands and sing in the words of the old Negro spiritual:

Free at last! Free at last!

Thank God Almighty, we are free at last![4]

[2] Amos 5:24 (rendered precisely in The American Standard Version of the Holy Bible)

[3] Isaiah 40:4–5 (King James Version of the Holy Bible). Quotation marks are excluded from part of this moment in the text because King's rendering of Isaiah 40:4 does not precisely follow the KJV version from which he quotes (e.g., "hill" and "mountain" are reversed in the KJV). King's rendering of Isaiah 40:5, however, is precisely quoted from the KJV.

[4] "Free at Last" from American Negro Songs by J. W. Work.

Activity 3.1 Use Microsoft's Comment Feature to Annotate a Text

If you download Dr. Martin Luther King's speech from AmericanRhetoric.com, you can make use of Microsoft's Comment feature to annotate the speech with your comments, as is done in the example below. In Microsoft Word, highlight the text you want to annotate, go to the "Insert" pull-down menu, and select "Comment." A box will appear where you can enter your comment.

I am happy to join with you today in what will go down in history as the greatest demonstration for freedom in the history of our nation.

Five score years ago, a great American, in whose symbolic shadow we stand today, signed the Emancipation Proclamation. This momentous decree came as a great beacon light of hope to millions of Negro slaves who had been seared in the flames of withering injustice. It came as a joyous daybreak to end the long night of their captivity.

> 2/7/09 12:38 AM
> **Comment:** Reference to Lincoln's Gettysburg Address

But one hundred years later, the Negro still is not free. One hundred years later, the life of the Negro is still sadly crippled by the manacles of segregation and the chains of discrimination. One hundred years later, the Negro lives on a lonely island of poverty in the midst of a vast ocean of material prosperity. One hundred years later, the Negro is

Activity 3.2 **Discuss "I Have a Dream"**

Read the "I Have a Dream" speech by Rev. Martin Luther King, Jr., and, if possible, watch the speech. It is archived at http://www .americanrhetoric.com, where it is listed as the most requested speech and #1 in its list of the top 100 American speeches.

1. Discuss the kairos of Dr. King's speech. What was the occasion? Who was his audience, both present and absent? What were the issues he spoke about?

2. How did Dr. King take advantage of the kairos of the situation in the wording of his speech?

3. Why do you think the speech continues to be so popular and influential?

Activity 3.3 **Identify the Kairos**

Identifying the kairos in Martin Luther King's speech in front of the Lincoln Memorial is easy. In some speeches, however, identifying the kairos is more difficult. Every speech and every text has a kairos, but some rhetors are better at identifying it and utilizing it than others. Identify the kairos in the following readings that have appeared thus far in the text. Then discuss in your group how the writer or speaker does or does not utilize kairos to maximum effect.

1. "Violent Rhetoric and Arizona Politics" (Chapter 1, p. 14)

2. "The Sleepover Question" (Chapter 1, p. 18)

3. "San Ysidro Shooting Survivor Lives His Dream of Being a Cop" (Chapter 1, p. 22)

4. "President Barack Obama on the Death of Osama bin Laden" (Chapter 2, p. 41)

5. "The Web Means the End of Forgetting" (Chapter 2, p. 50)

Activity 3.4 **Analyze an Audience**

Select a group that you do not belong to and analyze it as a potential audience. As one method, you might locate a blog on the Internet that advocates a point of view different from your own. For example, if you believe in global warming, read a blog frequented by those who do not share that belief. If you are a Democrat, look for a Tea Party or Republican blog. Find a yoga blog if you are a football fan. Read blog entries for a week and write a one-page analysis. Answer these questions:

1. What are the two or three issues of primary interest to the group? What is the general position on each issue?

2. Who are these people? Where do they live? What is their educational level?

3. What is the extent of their knowledge about the issues of primary interest? Are they familiar with the evidence, or do they just repeat opinions?

4. What types of appeals would make a difference to the readers of this blog: ethos, pathos, or logos? How so?

Aristotle's Persuasive Appeals

Some theorists associate the rhetorical triangle directly with Aristotle's **appeals** (or proofs): ethos, pathos, and logos. **Ethos** refers to the writer's (or speaker's) credibility; **pathos** refers to emotion used to sway the audience; and, finally, **logos** refers to the writer's purpose (or subject), for an effective argument will include evidence and other supporting details to back up the author's claims.

Aristotle wrote:

> Of those proofs that are furnished through the speech there are three kinds. Some reside in the character [*ethos*] of the speaker, some in a certain disposition [*pathos*] of the audience and some in the speech itself, through its demonstrating or seeming to demonstrate [*logos*].

Contemporary theorist Wayne C. Booth said something similar:

> The common ingredient that I find in all writing that I admire—excluding for now novels, plays, and poems—is something that I shall reluctantly call the rhetorical stance, a stance which depends upon discovering and maintaining in any writing situation a

proper balance among the three elements that are at work in any communicative effort: the available arguments about the subject itself [*logos*], the interests and peculiarities of the audience [*pathos*], and the voice, the implied character of the speaker [*ethos*].

Arguments from Logos

Logos or reason was Aristotle's favorite of the three persuasive appeals, and he bemoaned the fact that humans could not be persuaded through reason alone, indeed that they sometimes chose emotion over reason. Aristotle also used the term *logos* to mean rational discourse. To appeal to logos means to organize an argument with a clear claim or thesis, supported by logical reasons that are presented in a well-organized manner that is internally consistent. It can also mean the use of facts and statistics as evidence. However, logos without elements of pathos and ethos can be dry, hard to understand, and boring.

Consider the following logical argument that advocates the televising of executions.

Reading 3.2

Executions Should Be Televised
by Zachary B. Shemtob and David Lat

Mr. Shemtob is an assistant professor of criminal justice at Central Connecticut State University. Mr. Lat, a former federal prosecutor, is the founder of *Above the Law*, a legal blog.

Earlier this month, Georgia conducted its third execution this year. This would have passed relatively unnoticed if not for a controversy surrounding its videotaping. Lawyers for the condemned inmate, Andrew Grant DeYoung, had persuaded a judge to allow the recording of his last moments as part of an effort to obtain evidence on whether lethal injection caused unnecessary suffering.

Though he argued for videotaping, one of Mr. DeYoung's defense lawyers, Brian Kammer, spoke out against releasing the footage to the public. "It's a horrible thing

In this opinion piece published in *The New York Times*, Zachary B. Shemtob and David Lat argue what they know is going to be an unpopular position in the United States—that executions should be televised. Shemtob is an assistant professor of criminal justice at Connecticut State University and Lat is a former federal prosecutor who also founded a legal blog, *Above the Law*. They reason, "democracy demands maximum accountability and transparency." Knowing that their position contradicts present policy, they carefully address possible objections to their position, such as the idea that executions are too gruesome to put on television.

that Andrew DeYoung had to go through," Mr. Kammer said, "and it's not for the public to see that."

We respectfully disagree. Executions in the United States ought to be made public.

Right now, executions are generally open only to the press and a few select witnesses. For the rest of us, the vague contours are provided in the morning paper. Yet a functioning democracy demands maximum accountability and transparency. As long as executions remain behind closed doors, those are impossible. The people should have the right to see what is being done in their name and with their tax dollars.

This is particularly relevant given the current debate on whether specific methods of lethal injection constitute cruel and unusual punishment and therefore violate the Constitution.

There is a dramatic difference between reading or hearing of such an event and observing it through image and sound. (This is obvious to those who saw the footage of Saddam Hussein's hanging in 2006 or the death of Neda Agha-Soltan during the protests in Iran in 2009.) We are not calling for opening executions completely to the public—conducting them before a live crowd—but rather for broadcasting them live or recording them for future release, on the Web or TV.

When another Georgia inmate, Roy Blankenship, was executed in June, the prisoner jerked his head, grimaced, gasped and lurched, according to a medical expert's affidavit. The *Atlanta Journal-Constitution* reported that Mr. DeYoung, executed in the same manner, "showed no violent signs in death." Voters should not have to rely on media accounts to understand what takes place when a man is put to death.

Cameras record legislative sessions and presidential debates, and courtrooms are allowing greater television access. When he was an Illinois state senator, President Obama successfully pressed for the videotaping of homicide interrogations and confessions. The most serious penalty of all surely demands equal if not greater scrutiny.

Opponents of our proposal offer many objections. State lawyers argued that making Mr. DeYoung's execution public raised safety concerns. While rioting and pickpocketing occasionally marred executions in the public square in the 18th and 19th centuries, modern security and technology obviate this concern. Little would change in the death chamber; the faces of witnesses and executioners could be edited out, for privacy reasons, before a video was released.

Of greater concern is the possibility that broadcasting executions could have a numbing effect. Douglas A. Berman, a law professor, fears that people might come to equate human executions with putting pets to sleep. Yet this seems overstated. While public indifference might result over time, the initial broadcasts would undoubtedly get attention and stir debate.

Still others say that broadcasting an execution would offer an unbalanced picture—making the condemned seem helpless and sympathetic, while keeping the victims of the crime out of the picture. But this is beside the point: the defendant is being executed precisely because a jury found that his crimes were so heinous that he deserved to die.

Ultimately the main opposition to our idea seems to flow from an unthinking disgust—a sense that public executions are archaic, noxious, even barbarous. Albert Camus related in his essay "Reflections on the Guillotine" that viewing executions turned him against capital punishment. The legal scholar John D. Bessler suggests that public executions might have the same effect on the public today; Sister Helen Prejean, the death penalty abolitionist, has urged just such a strategy.

That is not our view. We leave open the possibility that making executions public could strengthen support for them; undecided viewers might find them less disturbing than anticipated.

Like many of our fellow citizens, we are deeply conflicted about the death penalty and how it has been administered. Our focus is on accountability and openness. As Justice John Paul Stevens wrote in *Baze v. Rees*, a 2008 case involving a challenge to lethal injection, capital punishment is too often "the product of habit and inattention rather than an acceptable deliberative process that weighs the costs and risks of administering that penalty against its identifiable benefits."

A democracy demands a citizenry as informed as possible about the costs and benefits of society's ultimate punishment.

Collaborate Activity 3.5 **Analyze an Argument from Logos**

1. In your small group, go over the Checklist of Essential Elements in an Argument (Chapter 2), and decide if the authors of this article fulfill each one. Be prepared to defend your decisions to the class.

2. Shemtob and Lat present a logical argument about why executions should be televised. Ignoring your own reaction to their editorial, outline the main points.

3. How do the authors handle their audience's possible emotional objections to their argument? Give an example.

4. What is your reaction to the argument that executions should be televised? Did reading and evaluating the article cause you to see the issue differently? If so, in what way?

Deductive Reasoning

Aristotle was the first person in Western culture to write systematically about logic, and he is credited with developing and promoting syllogistic or **deductive reasoning** in which statements are combined to draw a **conclusion**. He wrote that "a statement is persuasive and credible either because it is directly self-evident or because it appears to be proved from other statements that are so." This logical structure is called a **syllogism**, in which premises lead to a conclusion. The following is perhaps the most famous syllogism:

Major premise: All humans are mortal.

Minor premise: Socrates is human.

Conclusion: Socrates is mortal.

The **major premise** is a general statement accepted by everyone that makes an observation about all people. The second statement of the syllogism is the **minor premise**, which makes a statement about a particular case within the class of all people. Comparison of the two premises, the general class of "all humans" and the particular case of "Socrates" within the class of "all humans" leads to the conclusion that Socrates also fits in the class "mortal," and thus his death is unavoidable. Thus, the logic moves from the general to the particular.

Similarly, if you try the pumpkin bread at one Starbucks and like it, you may infer that you will like the pumpkin bread at another Starbucks. The argument would look like this:

Major premise: Food products at Starbucks are standardized from one Starbucks to another.

Minor premise: You like the pumpkin bread at one Starbucks.

Conclusion: You will like the pumpkin bread at another Starbucks.

However, if your major premise is wrong, and the owner of one Starbucks substitutes an inferior stock of pumpkin bread, then your conclusion is wrong. Deductive reasoning is dependent upon the validity of each premise; otherwise the syllogism does not hold true. If the major premise that food products are standardized at all Starbucks franchises does not hold true, then the argument is not valid. A good deductive argument is known as a valid argument and is such that if all its premises are true, then its conclusion must be true. Indeed, for a deductive argument to be valid, it must be absolutely impossible for both its premises to be true and its conclusion to be false.

Inductive Reasoning

Aristotle identified another way to move logically between premises, which he called "the progress from particulars to universals." Later logicians labeled this type of logic as **inductive reasoning**. Inductive arguments are based on probability. Even if an inductive argument's premises are true, that doesn't establish with 100 percent certainty that its conclusions are true. Even the best inductive argument falls short of deductive validity.

Consider the following examples of inductive reasoning:

Particular statement: Milk does not spoil as quickly if kept cold.

General statement: All perishable foods do not spoil as quickly if kept cold.

Particular statement: Microwaves cook popcorn more quickly than conventional heat.

General statement: All foods cook more quickly in a microwave.

In the first example, inductive reasoning works well because cold tends to prolong the useable life of most perishable foods. The second example is more problematic. While it is true that popcorn cooks more quickly in a microwave oven, the peculiarities of microwave interaction with food molecules does not produce a uniform effect on all food stuffs. Rice, for example, does not cook much, if any, faster in a microwave than it does on a stovetop. Also, whole eggs may explode if cooked in their shells.

A good inductive argument is known as a strong (or "cogent") inductive argument. It is such that if the premises are true, the conclusion is likely to be true.

Activity 3.6 **Identify Deductive and Inductive Reasoning**

In your small group, identify an example of a deductive argument and list the premises and conclusion. Then identify an inductive argument and identify the particular statement and the general statement. Report to the class.

Logical Fallacies

Generally speaking, a **logical fallacy** is an error in reasoning, as opposed to a factual error, which is simply being wrong about the facts. A **deductive fallacy** (sometimes called a *formal fallacy*) is a deductive argument that has premises that are all true, but they lead to a false conclusion, making it an invalid argument. An **inductive fallacy** (sometimes called an *informal fallacy*) appears to be an inductive argument, but the premises do not provide enough support for the conclusion to be probable. Some logical fallacies are more common than others and, thus, have been labeled and defined. Following are a few of the most well-known types:

Ad hominem (to the man) are arguments that attempt to discredit a point of view through personal attacks upon the person who has that point of view. These arguments are not relevant to the actual issue because the character of the person that holds a view says nothing about the truth of that viewpoint.

> *Example*: Noam Chomsky is a liberal activist who opposes American intervention in other countries. Noam Chomsky's theory of transformational grammar, which suggests that humans have an innate ability to learn language, is ridiculous.

Non sequitur (Latin for "it does not follow") arguments have conclusions that do not follow from the premises. Usually, the author has left out a step in the logic, expecting the reader to make the leap over the gap.

> *Example*: "Well, look at the size of this administration building; it is obvious this university does not need more funding."

Either/or or **false dichotomy** arguments force an either/or choice when, in reality, more options are available. Issues are presented as being either black or white.

> *Example*: With all the budget cuts, "we either raise tuition or massively increase class size."

Red herring arguments avoid the issue and attempt to distract with a side issue.

> *Example*: "Why do you question my private life issues, when we have social problems with which to deal?"

Ad populum (Latin for "appeal to the people") arguments appeal to popularity. If a lot of people believe it, it must be true.

> *Example*: "Why shouldn't I cheat on this exam? Everyone else cheats."

Ad verecundium (Latin for "argument from that which is improper") arguments appeal to an irrelevant authority.

> *Example*: "If the President of Harvard says it is a good idea, then we should follow suit." Or, "That is how we have always done it."

Begging the question arguments simply assume that a point of view is true because the truth of the premise is assumed. Simply assuming a premise is true does not amount to evidence that it *is* true.

> *Example*: A woman's place is in the home; therefore, women should not work.

Confusing cause and effect is a common problem with scientific studies in which the fact that two events are correlated implies that one causes the other.

> *Example*: Obese people drink a lot of diet soda; therefore, diet soda causes obesity.

Post hoc (from the Latin phrase "Post hoc, ergo proper hoc," or after this, therefore because of this) is a fallacy that concludes that one event caused another just because one occurred before the other.

Example: The Great Depression caused World War II.

In a **straw man** fallacy, a position of an opponent is exaggerated or weakened, so that it is easier for the opponent to argue against it.

Example: Pro-choice advocates believe in murdering unborn children.

A **slippery slope** argument asserts that one event will inevitably lead to another event.

Example: the Dilbert cartoon below:

DILBERT: © Scott Adams/Dist. by United Feature Syndicate, Inc.

These logical fallacies are summarized in the chart that follows.

Chart of Fallacies and Examples		
Fallacy	**The Error in Reasoning**	**Example**
Ad hominem	When speakers attack the person making the argument and not the argument itself.	"We can't believe anything he says; he is a convicted felon."

Fallacy	The Error in Reasoning	Example
Ad populum	When we attempt to persuade people by arguing our position is reasonable because so many other people are doing it or agree with it.	"Why shouldn't I cheat on this exam? Everyone else cheats."
Ad verecundium	An appeal to persuasion based on higher authority or tradition.	"If the president of Harvard says it is a good idea, then we should follow suit." Or, "That is how we have always done it."
Begging the question	When a speaker presumes certain things are facts when they have not yet been proven to be truthful.	"Oh, everyone knows that we are all Christians."
Confusing cause and effect	A common problem with scientific studies in which the fact that two events are correlated implies that one causes the other.	"Obese people drink a lot of diet soda; therefore, diet soda causes obesity."
Either/or	Presents two options and declares that one of them must be correct while the other must be incorrect.	"We either raise tuition or massively increase class size."
Non sequitur	When you make an unwarranted move from one idea to the next.	"Well, look at the size of this administration building; it is obvious this university does not need more funding."
Post hoc	Assumes that because one event happened after another, then the preceding event caused the event that followed.	"Every time Sheila goes to a game with us, our team loses. She is bad luck."
Red herring	When a speaker introduces an irrelevant issue or piece of evidence to divert attention from the subject of the speech.	"Why do you question my private life issues, when we have social problems with which to deal?"
Slippery slope	Assumes that once an action begins it will follow, undeterred, to an eventual and inevitable conclusion.	"If we let the government dictate where we can pray, soon the government will tell us we cannot pray."

Fallacy	The Error in Reasoning	Example
Straw man	When a speaker ignores the actual position of an opponent and substitutes a distorted and exaggerated position.	"Oh, you think we should agree to a cut in our salaries. Why do you want to bleed us dry?"

Activity 3.7 **Identify Logical Fallacies**

Match the following types of logical fallacies with the examples below:

Types:

Ad hominem   Post hoc

Begging the question   Straw man

Confusing cause and effect   Slippery slope

Examples:

1. Legalization of medical marijuana will lead to increased marijuana use by the general population.

2. Twenty-one is the best age limit for drinking because people do not mature until they are 21.

3. If you teach birth control methods, more teenage girls will get pregnant.

4. The culture wars of the 1960s were a result of parents being unable to control their children after the post–World War II baby boom.

5. Al Gore claims that global warming is a dangerous trend. Al Gore is a liberal. Therefore, there is no global warming.

6. Immigration reform advocates want to separate families and children.

Activity 3.8 **Create Examples of Logical Fallacies**

In your small group, work through the chart of logical fallacies above and create a new example for each type of fallacy. Then report to the class, one fallacy at a time, with the instructor making a list of each group's examples on the chalk board. Discuss any examples that are not clear cases of a particular fallacy.

Arguments from Pathos

Pathos makes use of emotion to persuade an audience.

Aristotle wrote:

> Proofs from the disposition of the audience are produced whenever they are induced by the speech into an emotional state. We do not give judgment in the same way when aggrieved and when pleased, in sympathy and in revulsion.

Effective rhetors know their audiences, particularly what emotions they hold that are relevant to the issue under consideration. What motivates them? What are their fears, their hopes, their desires, and their doubts? If the audience has the same emotions as you do, fine. However, if they do not already hold those emotions, you need to bring them to share the hurt, the anger, or the joy that will persuade them to share your viewpoint—through the stories you tell, the statistics you cite, and the reasoning you offer.

For example, when Martin Luther King, Jr., in his "I Have a Dream" speech (reprinted earlier in this chapter) referred to the "hallowed spot" of the Lincoln Memorial, he was appealing to his audience's feelings of patriotism and reverence for the accomplishments of President Lincoln. Subtly, he was also garnering this emotion toward Lincoln in contemporary support of civil rights. Lincoln had issued the Emancipation Proclamation that declared all slaves to be free, yet, according to King, America had not lived up to Lincoln's promise.

Reading 3.3

People for Sale
by E. Benjamin Skinner

Most people imagine that slavery died in the 19th century. Since 1810, more than a dozen international conventions banning the slave trade have been signed. Yet today there are more slaves than at any time in human history.

And if you're going to buy one in five hours, you'd better get a move on. First, hail a taxi to JFK International Airport and hop on a direct flight to Port-au-Prince, Haiti. The flight takes three hours. After landing, take a tap-tap, a flatbed pickup retrofitted with benches and a canopy, three-quarters of the way up Route de Delmas, the capital's main street. There, on

E. Benjamin Skinner has written on a wide range of topics. His articles have appeared in *Newsweek International, Travel and Leisure*, and other magazines. This essay was adapted from *A Crime So Monstrous: Face-to-Face with Modern-Day Slavery* and appeared in *Foreign Policy*.

a side street, you will find a group of men standing in front of Le Réseau (the Network) barbershop. As you approach, a man steps forward: "Are you looking to get a person?"

Meet Benavil Lebhom. He smiles easily. He has a trim mustache and wears a multicolored striped golf shirt, a gold chain, and Doc Martens knockoffs. Benavil is a courtier, or broker. He holds an official real estate license and calls himself an employment agent. Two-thirds of the employees he places are child slaves. The total number of Haitian children in bondage in their own country stands at 300,000. They are restavèks, the "stay-withs," as they are euphemistically known in Creole. Forced, unpaid, they work in captivity from before dawn until night. Benavil and thousands of other formal and informal traffickers lure these children from desperately impoverished rural parents with promises of free schooling and a better life.

The negotiation to buy a child slave might sound a bit like this:

"How quickly do you think it would be possible to bring a child in? Somebody who could clean and cook?" you ask. "I don't have a very big place; I have a small apartment. But I'm wondering how much that would cost? And how quickly?"

"Three days," Benavil responds.

"And you could bring the child here?" you inquire. "Or are there children here already?"

"I don't have any here in Port-au-Prince right now," says Benavil, his eyes widening at the thought of a foreign client. "I would go out to the countryside."

You ask about additional expenses. "Would I have to pay for transportation?"

"Bon," says Benavil. "A hundred U.S."

Smelling a rip-off, you press him, "And that's just for transportation?"

"Transportation would be about 100 Haitian," says Benavil, "because you'd have to get out there. Plus, [hotel and] food on the trip. Five hundred gourdes"—around $13.

"OK, 500 Haitian," you say.

Now you ask the big question: "And what would your fee be?" Benavil's eyes narrow as he determines how much he can take you for.

"A hundred. American."

"That seems like a lot," you say, with a smile so as not to kill the deal. "Could you bring down your fee to 50 U.S.?"

Benavil pauses. But only for effect. He knows he's still got you for much more than a Haitian would pay. "Oui," he says with a smile.

But the deal isn't done. Benavil leans in close. "This is a rather delicate question. Is this someone you want as just a worker? Or also someone who will be a 'partner'? You understand what I mean?"

You don't blink at being asked if you want the child for sex. "Is it possible to have someone who could be both?"

"Oui!" Benavil responds enthusiastically.

If you're interested in taking your purchase back to the United States, Benavil tells you that he can "arrange" the proper papers to make it look as though you've adopted the child.

He offers you a 13-year-old girl.

"That's a little bit old," you say.

"I know of another girl who's 12. Then ones that are 10, 11," he responds.

The negotiation is finished, and you tell Benavil not to make any moves without further word from you. You have successfully arranged to buy a human being for 50 bucks.

It would be nice if that conversation were fictional. It is not. I recorded it in October 2005 as part of four years of research into slavery on five continents. In the popular consciousness, "slavery" has come to be little more than just a metaphor for undue hardship. Investment bankers routinely refer to themselves as "high-paid wage slaves." Human rights activists may call $1-an-hour sweatshop laborers slaves, regardless of the fact that they are paid and can often walk away from the job.

The reality of slavery is far different. Slavery exists today on an unprecedented scale. In Africa, tens of thousands are chattel slaves, seized in war or tucked away for generations. Across Europe, Asia, and the Americas, traffickers have forced as many as 2 million into prostitution or labor. In South Asia, which has the highest concentration of slaves on the planet, nearly 10 million languish in bondage, unable to leave their captors until they pay off "debts," legal fictions that in many cases are generations old.

Few in the developed world have a grasp of the enormity of modern-day slavery. Fewer still are doing anything to combat it. . . . Between 2000 and 2006, the U.S. Justice Department increased human trafficking prosecutions from 3 to 32, and convictions from 10 to 98. By the end of 2006, 27 states had passed anti-trafficking laws. Yet, during the same period, the United States liberated only about 2 percent of its own modern-day slaves. As many as 17,500 new slaves continue to enter bondage in the United States every year . . . Many feel that sex slavery is particularly revolting—and it is. I saw it firsthand. In a Bucharest brothel, I was offered a mentally handicapped suicidal girl in exchange for a used car. But for every woman or child enslaved in commercial sex, there are some 15 men, women, and children enslaved in other fields, such as domestic work or agricultural labor.

Save for the fact that he is male, Gonoo Lal Kol typifies the average slave of our modern age. (At his request, I have changed his name.) Like a majority of the world's slaves, Gonoo is in debt bondage in South Asia. In his case, in an Indian quarry. Like most slaves, Gonoo is illiterate and unaware of the Indian laws that ban his bondage and provide for sanctions against his master. His story, told to me near his four-foot-high stone and grass hutch, represents the other side of the "Indian Miracle."

Gonoo lives in Lohagara Dhal, a forgotten corner of Uttar Pradesh, a north Indian state that contains 8 percent of the world's poor. I met him one evening in December 2005 as he walked with two dozen other laborers in tattered and filthy clothes. Behind them was the quarry. In that pit, Gonoo, a member of the historically outcast Kol tribe, worked with his family 14 hours a day. His tools were a hammer and a pike. His hands were covered in calluses, his fingertips worn away.

Gonoo's master is a tall, stout, surly contractor named Ramesh Garg. He makes his money by enslaving entire families forced to work for no pay beyond alcohol, grain, and subsistence expenses. Slavery scholar Kevin Bales estimates that a slave in the 19th-century American South had to work 20 years to recoup his or her purchase price. Gonoo and the other slaves earn a profit for Garg in two years.

Every single man, woman, and child in Lohagara Dhal is a slave. But, in theory at least, Garg neither bought nor owns them. The seed of Gonoo's slavery, for instance, was a loan of 62 cents. In 1958 his grandfather borrowed that amount from the owner of a farm where he worked. Three generations and three slave masters later, Gonoo's family remains in bondage.

Recently, many bold, underfunded groups have taken up the challenge of tearing out the roots of slavery. Some gained fame through dramatic slave rescues. Most learned that freeing slaves is impossible unless the slaves themselves choose to be free. Among the Kol of Uttar Pradesh, for instance, an organization called Pragati Gramodyog Sansthan (PGS)—the Progressive Institute for Village Enterprises—has helped hundreds of families break the grip of the quarry contractors.

The psychological, social, and economic bonds of slavery run deep, and for governments to be truly effective in eradicating slavery, they must partner with groups that can offer slaves a way to pull themselves up from bondage. One way to do that is to replicate the work of grassroots organizations such as the India-based MSEMVS (Society for Human Development and Women's Empowerment). In 1996 the group launched free transitional schools where children who had been enslaved learned skills and acquired enough literacy to move on to formal schooling. The group also targeted mothers, providing them with training and start-up materials for microenterprises. . . . In recent years, the United States has shown an increasing willingness to help fund these kinds of organizations, one encouraging sign that the message may be getting through.

For four years, I encountered dozens of enslaved people, several of whom traffickers like Benavil actually offered to sell to me. I did not pay for a human life anywhere. And, with one exception, I always withheld action to save any one person, in the hope that my research would later help to save many more. At times, that still feels like an excuse for cowardice. But the hard work of real emancipation can't be the burden of a select few. For thousands of slaves, grassroots groups like PGS and MSEMVS can help bring freedom. Until governments define slavery in appropriately concise terms, prosecute the crime aggressively in all its forms, and encourage groups that empower slaves to free themselves, however, millions more will remain in bondage. And our collective promise of abolition will continue to mean nothing at all.

Activity 3.9 **Analyze an Argument from Pathos**

After reading Skinner's essay on slavery, reread the passage in which he negotiated to buy a child slave. Then freewrite for five minutes about how that negotiation made you feel.

Most people feel emotional when they read about a child in distress, and Skinner further highlights that emotional effect by putting this particular episode in dialogue, always a point of emphasis in an essay. Do you think Skinner deliberately appealed to pathos in this part of his essay? Discuss in your group.

List other areas where the essay evokes an emotional response. Consider why, and freewrite on the feelings and beliefs that are brought into play. How did the author know that you would probably react this way?

Although much of Skinner's argument relies on pathos, he also provides statistics and references to authorities to bolster his argument. Identify the paragraphs which provide statistics or other evidence that would qualify as logos.

Arguments from Ethos

No exact translation exists in English for the word *ethos*, but it can be loosely translated as the credibility of the speaker. This credibility generates good will which colors all the arguments, examples, and quotes the rhetor utilizes in his text. Rhetors can enhance their credibility by evidence of intelligence, virtue, and goodwill and diminish it by seeming petty, dishonest, and mean-spirited. In addition, a speaker or writer can enhance his or her own credibility by references to quotes or the actions of authorities or leaders.

Aristotle wrote:

> Proofs from character [ethos] are produced, whenever the speech is given in such a way as to render the speaker worthy of credence—we more readily and sooner believe reasonable men on all matters in general and absolutely on questions where precision is impossible and two views can be maintained.

For example, Martin Luther King, Jr., pointed out in his "I Have a Dream" speech, that, according to the framers of the Constitution and the Declaration of Independence, "unalienable Rights" of "Life, Liberty and the pursuit of Happiness" apply equally to black men and white men. He was, in effect, borrowing the ethos of Thomas Jefferson and the framers of the Constitution in support of the unalienable rights of blacks.

Consider the following article and how the author's credibility or ethos enhances the appeal of his arguments.

Reading 3.4

I remember the first time the concept of another world entered my mind. It was during a walk with my father in our garden in Sri Lanka. He pointed to the Moon and told me that people had walked on it. I was astonished: Suddenly that bright light became a place that one could visit.

Schoolchildren may feel a similar sense of wonder when they see pictures of a Martian landscape or Saturn's rings. And soon their views of alien worlds may not be confined to the planets in our own solar system.

Alien Life Coming Slowly into View
by Ray Jayawardhana

Ray Jayawardhana, the author of "Alien Life Coming Slowly into View," which was originally published in *The New York Times*, is a professor of astronomy and astrophysics at the University of Toronto. He is also the author of *Strange New Worlds: The Search for Alien Planets and Life Beyond Our Solar System*.

After millenniums of musings and a century of failed attempts, astronomers first detected an exoplanet, a planet orbiting a normal star other than the Sun, in 1995. Now they are finding hundreds of such worlds each year. Last month, NASA announced that 1,235 new possible planets had been observed by Kepler, a telescope on a space satellite. Six of the planets that Kepler found circle one star, and the orbits of five of them would fit within that of Mercury, the closest planet to our Sun.

By timing the passages of these five planets across their sun's visage—which provides confirmation of their planetary nature—we can witness their graceful dance with one another, choreographed by gravity. These discoveries remind us that nature is often richer and more wondrous than our imagination. The diversity of alien worlds has surprised us and challenged our preconceptions many times over.

It is quite a change from merely 20 years ago, when we knew for sure of just one planetary system: ours. The pace of discovery, supported by new instruments and missions and innovative strategies by planet seekers, has been astounding.

What's more, from measurements of their masses and sizes, we can infer what some of these worlds are made of: gases, ice or rocks. Astronomers have been able to take the temperature of planets around other stars, first with telescopes in space but more recently with ground-based instruments, as my collaborators and I have done.

Two and a half years ago, we even managed to capture the first direct pictures of alien worlds. There is something about a photo of an alien planet—even if it only appears as a faint dot next to a bright, overexposed star—that makes it "real." Given that stars shine like floodlights next to the planetary embers huddled around them, success required painstaking efforts and clever innovations. One essential tool is adaptive optics technology, which, in effect, takes the twinkle out of the stars, thus providing sharper images from telescopes on the ground than would otherwise be possible.

At the crux of this grand pursuit is one basic question: Is our warm, wet, rocky world, teeming with life, the exception or the norm? It is an important question for every one of us, not just for scientists. It seems absurd, if not arrogant, to think that ours is the only life-bearing world in the galaxy, given hundreds of billions of other suns, the apparent ubiquity of planets, and the cosmic abundance of life's ingredients. It may be that life is fairly common, but that "intelligent" life is rare.

Of course, the vast majority of the extra-solar worlds discovered to date are quite unlike our own: many are gas giants, and some are boiling hot while others endure everlasting chills. Just a handful are close in size to our planet, and only a few of those may be rocky like the Earth, rather than gaseous like Jupiter or icy like Neptune.

But within the next few years, astronomers expect to find dozens of alien earths that are roughly the size of our planet. Some of them will likely be in the so-called habitable zone, where the temperatures are just right for liquid water. The discovery of "Earth twins," with conditions similar to what we find here, will inevitably bring questions about alien life to the forefront.

Detecting signs of life elsewhere will not be easy, but it may well occur in my lifetime, if not during the next decade. Given the daunting distances between the stars, the real-life version will almost certainly be a lot less sensational than the movies depicting alien invasions or crash-landing spaceships.

The evidence may be circumstantial at first—say, spectral bar codes of interesting molecules like oxygen, ozone, methane and water—and leave room for alternative interpretations. It may take years of additional data-gathering, and perhaps the construction of new telescopes, to satisfy our doubts. Besides, we won't know whether such "biosignatures" are an indication of slime or civilization. Most people will likely move on to other, more immediate concerns of life here on Earth while scientists get down to work.

If, on the other hand, an alien radio signal were to be detected, that would constitute a more clear-cut and exciting moment. Even if the contents of the message remained elusive for decades, we would know that there was someone "intelligent" at the other end. The search for extraterrestrial intelligence with radio telescopes has come of age recently, 50 years after the first feeble attempt. The construction of the Allen Telescope Array on an arid plateau in northern California greatly expands the number of star systems from which astronomers could detect signals.

However it arrives, the first definitive evidence of life elsewhere will mark a turning point in our intellectual history, perhaps only rivaled by Copernicus's heliocentric theory or Darwin's theory of evolution. If life can spring up on two planets independently, why not on a thousand or even a billion others? The ramifications of finding out for sure that ours isn't the only inhabited world are likely to be felt, over time, in many areas of human thought and endeavor—from biology and philosophy to religion and art.

Some people worry that discovering life elsewhere, especially if it turns out to be in possession of incredible technology, will make us feel small and insignificant. They seem concerned that it will constitute a horrific blow to our collective ego.

I happen to be an optimist. It may take decades after the initial indications of alien life for scientists to gather enough evidence to be certain or to decipher a signal of artificial origin. The full ramifications of the discovery may not be felt for generations, giving us plenty of time to get used to the presence of our galactic neighbors. Besides, knowing that we are not alone just might be the kick in the pants we need to grow up as a species.

Explore

Activity 3.10 **Analyzing an Argument from Ethos**

1. In the above article, Ray Jayawardhana draws upon the ethos of his position as a professor of astronomy and astrophysics to formulate a convincing argument for the strong possibility of the existence of alien life. In your group, discuss how Jayawardhana's profession increases the credibility of his argument.

2. How do you think this essay would compare to essays by people of more credentials who argue that no alien life exists? What kinds of other evidence could Jayawardhana have offered that would strengthen his argument?

3. Is Jayawardhana appealing to pathos with his opening narrative? What effect does he want to have on his audience by describing this childhood memory?

Combining Ethos, Pathos, and Logos

The ethos, pathos, and logos appeals are equally important and merit equal attention in the writing process. No text is purely based on one of the three appeals, though more of the argument in a particular text may be based on one appeal rather than another. In each writing situation, however, an effective rhetor will think about how each plays into the structure of the argument.

In today's world, for example, a public speaker's effectiveness is affected by the ability to use a teleprompter, or, if one is not available, to memorize a speech well enough so he or she can speak without frequently referring to notes. If a speaker's eyes flit from left to right across the text of a teleprompter, it shows on television. This reduces the credibility, or ethos, of the speaker, no matter how well the other appeals are executed in the speech. The equivalent of presentation for a written text would be to produce a document that is essentially free from grammatical errors, spell-checked, and printed on good paper stock with the correct margins and type size. If the document does not look professional, it will lose credibility or ethos no matter what it says.

To give another example, E. Benjamin Skinner's essay, "People for Sale," relies on the highly emotional image of a child being sold into slavery for its major appeal. However, if you read back through the essay, you will see that it has a clear thesis, which could be stated as the following: Slavery exists in the present time, even in the United States, and it is not even that difficult to buy a slave. The essay is well organized and offers a variety of evidence, including statistics and first-person observation. Logos may not stand out as the primary appeal in Skinner's essay, but it is nevertheless strong in its appeal to logos.

If you want to develop your writing skills, it is essential that you pay attention to each of Aristotle's appeals—ethos, pathos, and logos.

Activity 3.11 **Writing about Ethos, Pathos, and Logos**

Choose one of the texts in Chapters 1, 2, or 3 and write an essay that identifies the ethos, pathos, and logos of the particular text. Then discuss how the three appeals together are used by the author to produce an effective essay. Alternatively, discuss which of the appeals is weak in the particular essay and how that affects the effectiveness of the essay.

Photos Heighten Ethos or Pathos

When Steve Jobs was in the process of turning over the reins of Apple to Tim Cook, the two appeared in a series of photos in a variety of publications. For example, see the photo below (from wired.com). Notice the "twinning effect," as both Jobs and Cook wear blue jeans and black pullover sweaters. In a not-so-subtle way, Apple was using ethos to visually state that since Jobs and Cook look alike, they must be alike. Thus, Cook would be successful in running Apple.

Photos can be equally effective in presenting pathos, though logos is more problematic.

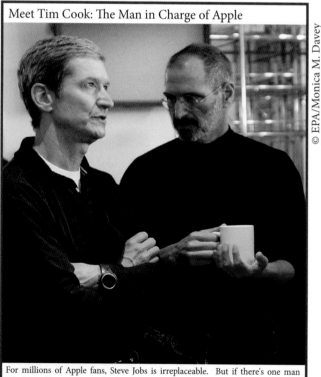

Meet Tim Cook: The Man in Charge of Apple

© EPA/Monica M. Davey

For millions of Apple fans, Steve Jobs is irreplaceable. But if there's one man Jobs himself trusts to stand in his shoes it is his second in command Apple Chief Operating Officer Tim Cook.

Activity 3.12 Logos Activity: Write a Letter to the Editor

In the following letter, originally published on the blog, *The Frisky* (www.thefrisky.com), the author uses both humor and logic to argue that *The New Yorker* reviews shouldn't give away the ending of movies.

An Open Letter To The New Yorker
via The Frisky on 4/25/11

Dear *New Yorker*,

Obviously, you are an awesome magazine. However, I have one small, teensy weensy beef. Could you please—possibly—stop ruining the ending of movies for me? Last night, on a 10-hour flight from Buenos Aires to New York, I sat down determined to catch up on your last three issues. In one, I read a review of Jake Gyllenhaal's newish movie, "Source Code." I had been planning to see it. Emphasis on the *had*. While you didn't go into details, you told me how it unfolds in the end. Which sort of takes the wind out of a movie's sail, doesn't it? But even worse, in a fantastic article about Anna Faris and her specific brand of girl humor, you let me know the surprise twist ending of her upcoming click, "What's Your Number?" Which. Doesn't. Even. Come. Out. Until. SEPTEMBER. Reading this reminded me of the collective sigh of 100 students in my Intro to Film Studies class in college when our professor told us the secret to "Chinatown" before we watched.

Choose one of your favorite magazines and write a letter to the editor. You can protest something the magazine has done recently that bothered you, or you can praise something that it has done well. Your letter does not need to be long, but you need to make your argument clear and support it with specific examples. If appropriate for your target publication, use humor as does the author of the letter to the editor of *The New Yorker*.

After you have written your letter to the editor, write a paragraph describing your target publication, what you have written in your letter, and why your letter is an illustration of logos.

Activity 3.13 **Pathos Activity: Portray an Emotion in a Collage**

Think of an emotion that you've been feeling lately and that you are willing to explore. Create a collage to express that emotion. Use these criteria.

- You can create your collage with cut and paste paper or you can create it through a computer program.

- Have little white space. Use colors with emotional connotations (blue for calm, for example).

- Have at least three images. You can find these on the Internet or in magazines, or take your own photos.

- Before you begin your collage, write down the emotion you are trying to explore and describe how you plan to represent it. In other words, make a plan, even though you will likely deviate from it.

- When you finish, write a paragraph describing the experience of creating the collage. Turn your paragraph in with your collage.

Activity 3.14 Ethos Activity: Create a Professional Facebook Page

Facebook is not just used to tell your friends about what you did over the weekend. Corporations use it as a networking tool. As you learned in the reading in Chapter 2, "The Web Means the End of Forgetting," it is a good idea to be cautious about what you post about yourself on Facebook because information and photos may be seen by unintended audiences, including future employers. Some individuals choose to have two Facebook pages, one for their personal friends and one for networking.

For this assignment, create a professional Facebook page similar to the one shown here. Consider in your small group what information and photos you want to post on a page you will use for networking. In effect, you are creating an ethos for yourself by these choices.

After you have completed your Facebook page, write a paragraph that explains the ethos you wanted to project in your page and how your content choices project that ethos.

Activity 3.15 Write a Rhetorical Analysis

In this essay you will make use of rhetorical vocabulary to analyze a text or combined text and images. The sample student essay in Chapter 7 (see page 190) analyzes a speech archived on the American Rhetoric website (http://www.americanrhetoric.com), which features many presidential and other prominent speeches. Alternatively, you can write a rhetorical analysis of a Facebook page, a newspaper or magazine article, or website.

In your analysis, apply several of the rhetorical concepts you have studied this semester:

- Speaker or writer—Does the speaker's identity affect the text?

- Purpose—What was the speaker or writer trying to achieve?

- Audience—Who was the speech/text directed to? Are there multiple audiences?

- Rhetorical appeals—How does the speaker or writer use ethos, pathos, and logos?

- Kairos—What is special about the rhetorical moment of the text/speech in terms of place and time?

Activity 3.16 **Write on Your Blog**

In your blog, do a freewrite exercise in which you argue for some type of policy change related to a topic you are interested in writing about. What is the kairos of your topic? Where can you use the three rhetorical appeals (pathos, ethos, and logos)?

Activity 3.17 **Write in Your Commonplace Book**

Do a search on the Internet for kairos, ethos, pathos, and logos. Print out and paste a short section about each from the Internet. Then comment briefly about each section.

4
INVENTING RHETORICALLY

Praxis in Action

How I Do Invention by Adam Webb

Before I start a research and writing project, I like to explore as many perspectives, arguments, or interpretations of a topic as possible. After I have chosen my topic, I write down everything I know about it. Next, I read broadly about my topic. I call this early stage of the research process "reading around," similar to information gathering.

Then, I usually ask myself a series of questions, such as: (1) Why is this topic important to me? (2) What has been said or written on this topic? (3) Who has already written on this topic? (4) How do these perspectives or arguments relate to my own perspective on this topic? and (5) How has media, such as television or the Internet, portrayed this topic? If I don't know the answers, either from my personal knowledge or my "reading around," I ask individuals who are knowledgeable about my topic. By answering these questions, I usually develop a larger contextual framework in which I can better understand and situate myself within the various perspectives on my topic. This is all before I start to integrate specific material from research sources.

Next, I start locating any recurring terms, themes, symbols, connections, or references as well as listing other ideas, beliefs, or values that might be relevant to my topic. In order to keep track of my ideas and information, I like to use Dragon Dictation, a note-taking and voice recording program application on my smartphone. I sometimes use this application to start writing an outline of my ideas.

By this time, I know what I want to argue and the general framework of my project. Then I can begin adding in specific paraphrases and quotes from my research.

Adam Webb has developed his own process for doing research that he applies to different projects.

Aristotle's Classification of Rhetoric

Aristotle, in *The Art of Rhetoric* (or *On Rhetoric*), laid the groundwork for today's persuasive writing by being the first to write systemically about how to teach rhetoric. His teacher Plato, in contrast, had distrusted rhetoric. Plato deplored the way rhetoricians (or politicians) of his era skillfully manipulated the people of Athens, particularly the masses of up to 10,000 voters in the Assembly or 500 in the juries of the law courts. Aristotle, on the other hand, perceived great potential in rhetoric, when taught properly. Rhetoric, as he envisioned it, could be both persuasive and ethical, and in *The Art of Rhetoric* he laid out an organization and classification of rhetoric as he believed it should be taught.

Aristotle divided the process of writing and delivering a composition into five parts. The first of these was **invention**, during which the writer or speaker expanded a topic into ideas that were later arranged into a text or speech. According to the ancient Greeks, the rhetor *invented* these ideas, though they may have mirrored or adapted thoughts presented by previous rhetors. Today, we call this the **prewriting stage** of the writing process, an adaptation of Aristotle's invention stage.

In the previous chapter, we discussed the three appeals or means that a rhetor can use to persuade an audience: ethos, pathos, and logos. In *The Art of Rhetoric*, Aristotle divides these appeals or means of persuasion into two types of proofs: artistic and inartistic. Today, these proofs are still part of the writing process though we call them by different names.

Artistic Proofs

Artistic proofs are logical arguments constructed by rhetors from ideas plucked from their minds. An individual then develops these thoughts into a line of reasoning and, in the process, explores and narrows the topic, creates a thesis, and determines the ideas that need to be conveyed to the audience. These proofs are the ones that Aristotle and other ancient rhetoricians believed were critically important, for they are the ones developed from the *rhetor's own mind* and, thus, *invented*. These ideas can be shaped into two types of arguments—deductive and inductive—which we will discuss in the next few pages.

Inartistic Proofs

Inartistic proofs are direct evidence that the speaker might use to support the argument, such as testimony, documents, and anything else that rhetors do not invent through their own thinking. Today, we would call these proofs research. They, also, are essential to writing, but they should *support* the writer's ideas, rather than lead them.

For Aristotle's students, the use of artistic and inartistic proofs might not have been a two-step process—first one and then the other, though the proofs are arranged that way in *The Art of Rhetoric*, as they are in this book. Rather, similar to the process used by Adam Webb (see the *Praxis in Action* at the beginning of this chapter), they might have developed both proofs in an alternating or recursive process. After developing basic ideas for a composition through invention, these students would then collect information from authorities (testimony), what Webb refers to as "reading around." Then they would return to inventing artistic proofs about the project, followed by more references to inartistic proofs. Today, we have more resources for research than did the ancient Greeks, but this does not make artistic proofs any less important. The differences between artistic and inartistic proofs are summarized in the table below.

Aristotle's Artistic and Inartistic Proofs	
Artistic Ideas from the rhetor's own mind, thus *invented*	**Inartistic** Information gained from external sources
Personal knowledge	Authorities
Observation	Testimony
Patterns of reasoning	Documents

The Five Canons of Rhetoric

Greek and Roman teachers of rhetoric divided rhetoric into five parts or canons. These canons corresponded to the order of activities in creating a speech, as they perceived the process: Invention, arrangement, style, memory, and delivery. These five parts are described in many handbooks of rhetorical instruction, including the *Rhetorica ad Herennium*, which was composed by an unknown author between 86 and 82 CE:

> The speaker . . . should possess the faculties of Invention, Arrangement, Style, Memory, and Delivery. Invention is the

devising of matter, true or plausible, that would make the case convincing. Arrangement is the ordering and distribution of the matter, making clear the place to which each thing is to be assigned. Style is the adaptation of suitable words and sentences to the matter devised. Memory is the firm retention in the mind of the matter, words, and arrangement. Delivery is the graceful regulation of voice, countenance, and gesture.

Today, classes in composition or writing studies still emphasize the necessity of **invention**, now interpreted as prewriting activities that enable writers to develop the logic and words needed for effective arguments. **Arrangement** involves organizing an argument into a logical format that leads the reader easily from the thesis to the conclusion. **Style** has to do with the author's voice and tone and the structure of sentences and paragraphs. **Memory** is used somewhat differently today, as students are no longer required to memorize compositions for oral presentation. Instead, memory is utilized in ways such as remembering how and where to retrieve information from the Internet, books, and other reference materials. Finally, **delivery**, which once involved gestures and tone of voice in an oral presentation, today has to do with document design, so that the final product is presented in a professional manner according to Modern Language Association (MLA) or American Psychological Association (APA) style. Delivery also involves grammatical accuracy because surface errors detract from the effective impact of a document. See the table below for a summary of the five parts of rhetoric.

The Five Parts (or Canons) of Rhetoric		
English	**Greek**	**Latin**
invention	*heuresis*	*inventio*
arrangement	*taxis*	*dispositio*
style	*lesis*	*elocutio*
memory	*mneme*	*memoria*
delivery	*hypocrisis*	*actin*

The Modern Writing Process Overview

Prewriting (Inventing)

Writing is not only about putting the pen to paper. As did rhetors in ancient Greece and Rome, you have to think deeply and critically about a subject before you begin a composition. The "invention" step of the writer's process is designed to help you find a worthwhile topic and develop your ideas about that topic before you start to write a draft. It includes writing, discussion, and research, as well as informal writing to help you explore your thoughts and feelings about a subject. Whatever method you choose, keep a record of your thoughts and discoveries as you spend this time in close examination of your subject.

Drafting

It may seem odd that writing a draft should come in the middle of the writer's process. However, research has shown that students and professionals alike write more effective essays when they don't reach for the pen too quickly. If you have spent enough time in the invention stage, the actual drafting stage may go more quickly. After writing the first draft, in succeeding drafts you can add details, observations, illustrations, examples, expert testimony, and other support to help your essay entertain, illuminate, or convince your audience.

Revising

Today, we talk more about the revision stage of writing than did ancient rhetoricians. If you are a student who tends to write assigned essays at the last minute, you may have missed this step entirely, yet many writers claim this is the longest and most rewarding step in the writing process. To revise, you must, in a sense, learn to let go of your writing. Some students think their first drafts should stay exactly the way they are written because they are true to their feelings and experience. Many writers find, however, that first drafts assume too much about the reader's knowledge and reactions. Sometimes readers, reading a first draft essay, are left scratching their heads and wondering what it is the writer is trying to convey. Writers who revise try to read their writing as readers would, taking note of gaps in logic, the absence of clear examples, the need for reordering information, and so on. Then they can revise their content with the reader in mind.

Editing and Polishing

Once writers have clarified their messages and the methods by which they will present those messages, one more step must be taken. Particularly because their compositions are written, rather than presented orally, they must go over their work again to check for correct spelling, grammar, and punctuation, as well as the use of Standard Written English. Some students finish with an essay, print it, and turn it in without ever examining the final copy. This is a critical mistake, because misspelled words and typographical and formatting errors can make an otherwise well-written essay lose its credibility. The five canons of rhetoric and the modern writing process are summarized in the table below.

The Five Canons of Rhetoric and the Modern Writing Process	
Five Canons of Rhetoric	**Modern Writing Process**
Invention—Devising the arguments that will make the case convincing, often basing them on models of famous speeches.	Prewriting—Determining the thesis, points of argument, counterargument, and rebuttal. Researching evidence to support the argument.
Arrangement—Ordering the argument into a logical format. Style—Finding suitable words and figures of speech. [Note: This may have been a recursive process, but the ancients did not consider that aspect important.]	Drafting, revising, and editing— Putting ideas and prewriting into a useable form through a recursive process of drafting, revising, and editing.
Memory—Retaining the argument in the mind, including its content and arrangement.	Remembering how and where to retrieve information from the Internet, books, and other reference materials.
Delivery—Effective use of voice and gestures to present argument.	Publication—Putting text, images, and other elements in a suitable format and releasing the document to an audience.

Activity 4.1 Compare the Five Canons of Rhetoric and the Modern Writing Process

In your group, reread the discussions in this chapter on the five canons of rhetoric and the modern writing process and review the table above. What parts of the five canons correspond to the modern writing process?

What step in the five canons is not included in the contemporary writing process? If the similarities and differences are not clear to you, consult the Internet. If you search for either "Five Canons of Rhetoric" or "Writing Process" you will find resources. What explanations can you offer for the differences? The similarities?

Stasis Theory Identifies Critical Point in Controversy

Stasis theory presents a series of four questions that were developed by Greek and Roman rhetoricians, primarily Aristotle, Quintilian, and Hermagoras. Answering these questions for an issue enabled rhetors to determine the critical (or stasis) point in a disagreement. This was a technique the ancients developed for the law courts to enable advocates to focus their arguments on the crux of the case. Quintilian, the great Roman teacher of rhetoric, explained in regard to a defendant:

> By far the strongest mode of defense is if the charge which is made can be denied; the next, if an act of the kind charged against the accused can be said not to have been done; the third, and most honorable, if what is done is proved to have been justly done. If we cannot command these methods, the last and only mode of defense is that of eluding an accusation, which can neither be denied nor combated, by the aid of some point of law, so as to make it appear that the action has not been brought in due legal form.

In other words, Quintilian is saying that in law cases, advocates have four choices in developing a focus for their arguments. You have probably watched a courtroom drama on television or film and can recall various defenses made on behalf of defendants. The strongest and most obvious defense is that the defendant is not guilty, that is, he or she did not do the deed in question. The same was true in Quintilian's day. However, sometimes an argument of innocence is not possible, perhaps because it seems obvious that the defendant did perform the deed in question. Thus, the advocate must develop a different strategy. For example, in defense of one accused of murder, the attorney may argue self-defense or mitigating circumstances (such as that the killing was an act of war). In rare cases, other defenses are offered; for example, if the supposed victim's body has not been found, the advocate can argue that the victim

Marcus Fabius Quintilianus (Quintilian) was a Roman orator from Spain who taught stasis theory.

may still be alive. An attorney can discover these possible defenses by using stasis theory to analyze the situation.

Another great advantage of stasis theory is that, if pursued diligently, it prevents the rhetor from making the mistake of organizing an argument by simply forwarding reasons why he or she is correct and the opposition is wrong. That approach may please people who agree with the rhetor, but it will not likely gain any support from the opposition. Answering the stasis questions carefully forces the writer to consider aspects of the issue that may have been overlooked but are crucial to an effective argument.

The wording of the four questions has varied somewhat over time, but essentially they are questions of fact, definition, quality, and policy. The same questions can be applied to any issue, not only issues of law. The four stasis questions are as follows:

1. What are the facts? (conjecture)

2. What is the meaning or nature of the issue? (definition)

3. What is the seriousness of the issue? (quality)

4. What is the best plan of action or procedure? (policy)

Many writers prefer stasis theory to other prewriting techniques because answering the questions determines whether or not the different sides of an argument are at stasis. Being at **stasis** means that the opponents are in agreement about their disagreement—the stasis point—which can be identified by one of the four stasis questions. If the sides are at stasis, they have common ground to build upon, for they are arguing the same issue. There is, thus, a greater chance the sides can reach a workable consensus or compromise. If opponents are not at stasis, there is much more work to be done to reach consensus.

The point where the opposing sides agree upon their disagreement is the stasis point.

For example, in the argument about the teaching of evolution and/or intelligent design in schools, the two sides are not in agreement about how to discuss the issue. Those in favor of teaching evolution claim intelligent design should not be called science, which is an issue of definition. Those who propose teaching intelligent design along with (or instead of) evolution tend to focus on "proving" evidence, an issue of fact. Until the two sides can agree upon what is the stasis point, or crux of the issue, they cannot debate effectively. They are not presenting arguments about the same question.

The four stasis questions can be broken into the subquestions listed in the following table. If you want to find the stasis point, work through the list for your issue, answering all of the subquestions. However, for each question, you must identify not only how *you* would answer the question but also how the opposing side or sides would answer. For example, if you are considering the issue of global warming, people with different positions will not agree on the facts. Thus, you must identify the basic facts of global warming represented by your side, and then identify the facts that might be presented by the opposing side.

Stasis Questions

Fact

- Did something happen?
- What are the facts?
- Is there a problem/issue?
- How did it begin and what are its causes?
- What changed to create the problem/issue?
- Can it be changed?

It also may be useful to ask the following critical questions of your own research and conclusions:

- Where did I obtain my data and are these sources reliable?
- How do I know they're reliable?

Definition

- What is the nature of the problem/issue?
- What exactly is the problem/issue?
- What kind of a problem/issue is it?
- To what larger class of things or events does it belong?
- What are its parts, and how are they related?

It also may be useful to ask the following critical questions of your own research and conclusions:

- Who/what is influencing my definition of this problem/issue?
- How/why are these sources/beliefs influencing my definition of the issue?

Quality

- Is it a good thing or a bad thing?
- How serious is the problem/issue?
- Who might be affected by this problem/issue (stakeholders)?
- What happens if we don't do anything?
- What are the costs of solving the problem/issue?

It also may be useful to ask the following critical questions of your own research and conclusions:

- Who/what is influencing my determination of the seriousness of this problem/issue?
- How/why are these sources/beliefs influencing my determination of the issue's seriousness?

Policy

- Should action be taken?
- Who should be involved in helping to solve the problem/address the issue?
- What should be done about this problem?
- What needs to happen to solve this problem/address this issue?

It also may be useful to ask the following critical questions of your own research and conclusions:

- Who/what is influencing my determination of what to do about this problem/issue?
- How/why are these sources/beliefs influencing my determination of what to do about this issue?

Source: Adapted from Purdue Owl Resource on Stasis Theory, http://owl.english.purdue.edu/owl/resource/736/1.

Using Stasis Questions

To illustrate the use of stasis questions, a team of writers working together to compose a report on racism in America might use the stasis questions to talk through information they will later use in their report. In the following sample dialogue, team members disagree about what actions are racist.

"Flying the Confederate battle flag is racist."

"Flying the Confederate battle flag is *not* racist."

"Yes, it is, because it represents the Confederate states that supported slavery, and it's generally accepted that slavery in America was racist."

"Flying the Confederate battle flag is not racist, because it's a part of American history and Southern heritage."

These two team members disagree about whether or not flying the Confederate battle flag is a racist act. This sort of disagreement might lead to a complete breakdown of group work if common ground cannot be found.

In this example, the team members go on to agree that some people still exhibit the Confederate battle flag (*fact*) on their vehicles and on their clothes, but that the flag is also displayed in museums (*fact*). They go on to agree that the issue is still very important to some people since a number of American states have recently debated the flag in legislatures and assemblies (*quality*). Moreover, group members note that a number of legal suits have been filed for and against the display of the flag in public places, so it's clear the issue still matters to a lot of people (*quality*).

In this sense, the team members have achieved stasis on two of the four stases—*fact* (people still display the flag, though in different places) and *quality* (it's a very important issue). Where the team members disagree, however, is in the stases of *definition* (is the display of the flag "racist"?) and *policy* (what should we do about this?).

Thinking about this disagreement using stasis theory allows people to build common ground so that parties who disagree can move toward resolution and action even if they can't agree on all levels. For example, team members who disagree about whether or not flying the Confederate battle flag is racist might still be able to agree on what to do about it.

"Ok, we disagree about whether flying the flag is racist, but we can agree that flying the flag is probably protected under the First Amendment to the United States Constitution—that flying the flag is protected by our freedom of speech."

"Yeah."

"So, people are free to display the flag on their vehicles, on their clothes, and on their property, as well as in museums. But, state legislatures and assemblies will have to debate and vote on whether or not the flag can be displayed on publicly funded property or in public symbols, such as state flags and seals."

"That sounds pretty democratic. Sure."

Not every team situation is going to end this amicably; however, by using the stasis questions to help keep the dialogue going—on a reasonable course—team members can find common ground and work toward action that is acceptable to most, if not all, of the group members.*

Stasis Theory and Kairos

As you will remember from Chapter 3, the *kairos* of an argument is the context, opportune moment, or point in time in which the rhetor, the audience, the issue, and the current situation provide opportunities and constraints for an argument. If you keep kairos in mind as you analyze an issue, you take advantage of timeliness. For example, if you want to write an argument about the death penalty, you might consider that United States courts are increasingly questioning the validity of eyewitness testimony, evidence which has been the deciding factor in many death penalty cases.

As part of your use of stasis theory, consider the four questions in relation to kairos:

1. How do recent developments (new facts) or the local situation affect the issue? Will it change your audience's perception of the facts?

2. Does the current situation affect your audience's definition of the issue? Is it defined differently by an audience in this location than elsewhere?

3. Have recent events made the issue more or less important to your audience? Is it more or less important in your location than elsewhere?

4. Do recent events, locally or widely, affect the need or lack of need for action, in your audience's perception?

As a rhetorician, it is important for you to be aware of the history of a controversy. But it is equally important to have an awareness of the kairos of the argument. Such an awareness enables you to adopt a "ready stance" and adjust your argument, so that it reflects an awareness of your audience's position and interests, as well as contemporary developments in the issue.

---

* Allen Brizee, "Stasis Theory for Teamwork," *Purdue Owl*, April 17, 2010, http://owl.english.purdue.edu/owl/ (Accessed October 3, 2011).

Such a flexible stance may afford you an opportunity to be persuasive that you might otherwise miss.

Activity 4.2 **Identify the Defense in a Television or Film Courtroom Drama**

As your instructor directs, watch a courtroom drama on television or film and decide what defense the defendant's attorney is offering. Report your conclusion to your small group or the class. Then, after you have discussed the stasis questions, identify which of the four questions the attorney in the drama is focusing upon as the crux of the defense. Discuss with your group or the class.

Activity 4.3 **Use Stasis Theory to Explore Your Topic**

Choose an issue that interests you and answer all the stasis questions in the table on pages 117-118, both for your position and for the opposing argument. Elaborate with three or four sentences for each subquestion that is particularly relevant to your topic. Is your issue at stasis for any of the questions? Report to your group or to the class.

Activity 4.4 **Evaluate a Public Debate**

Locate a public debate that has been reported recently in newspaper editorials, television programs, or other media that can be analyzed by using stasis theory. In a paper of 350 to 500 words, do the following:

- Describe the context (kairos).
- Identify the sides of the argument and their principal points.
- Decide which stasis question each side is primarily addressing.
- Determine whether or not the issue is at stasis and explain your answer.
- Include a citation in MLA or APA format for your source or sources.

Activity 4.5: Use Stasis Theory to Analyze a Case

Professors Vijay Govindarajan and Christian Sarkar launched a competition on the *Harvard Business Network* blog for designs to build $300 houses for the poor. Word of the competition spread quickly, and a wide variety of people began to write about the competition—in editorials in *The New York Times*, the *Economist,* and in a companion blog, http://www.300house.com/blog.

Your Task: Read the four articles written about the $300 house competition that appear on the following pages. Discuss them in class and in small groups. In particular, note that Matias Echanove and Rahul Srivastava write in their *New York Times* op-ed essay, "Hands Off Our Houses," that the idea of a $300 house is impractical and will fail in places such as Mumbai, India. In contrast, "A $300 Idea that Is Priceless," the editorial from the *Economist,* praises the design competition for initiating an "explosion of creativity." Work through the stasis questions, with one side of the controversy being those who support this design initiative.   The other side would be those who foresee problems in applying this idealistic initiative in the real world, a viewpoint that is expressed in "Hands Off Our Houses."

Write a paper of approximately 750 words in which you do the following:

- Briefly present the idea of the design competition.

- Summarize the arguments of those in favor of the initiative.

- Explain the reservations expressed in "Hands Off Our Houses."

- Identify a stasis point, if one exists, and explain why you think the sides have common ground on that particular stasis question.

- Discuss whether the discovery of common ground might allow individuals involved in this debate to talk to one another and work toward solutions for the problem of substandard housing in slums worldwide.

- As your instructor directs, cite your sources in APA or MLA style.

David A. Smith, the founder of the Affordable Housing Institute (AHI) tells us that "markets alone will never satisfactorily house a nation's poorest citizens ... whether people buy or rent, housing is typically affordable to only half of the population."

The $300 House: A Hands-On Lab for Reverse Innovation?

by Vijay Govindarajan

Published in the *HBR Blog Network.*

The result? Smith points to a "spontaneous community of self-built or informally built homes—the shanty towns, settlements, and ever-expanding slums that sprout like mushrooms on the outskirts of cities in the developing world."

We started discussing the issue, examining the subject through the lens of reverse innovation.

Here are five questions Christian and I asked ourselves:

1. How can organic, self-built slums be turned into livable housing?

2. What might a house-for-the-poor look like?

3. How can world-class engineering and design capabilities be utilized to solve the problem?

4. What reverse-innovation lessons might be learned by the participants in such a project?

5. How could the poor afford to buy this house?

Livable Housing. Our first thought was that self-built houses are usually built from materials that are available—cardboard, plastic, mud or clay, metal scraps and whatever else is nearby. Built on dirt floors, these structures are prone to collapse and catching fire. Solution: replace these unsafe structures with a mass-produced, standard, affordable, and sustainable solution. We want to create the $300-House-for-the-Poor.

Look and Feel. To designers, our sketch of this house might be a bit of a joke, but it's useful nonetheless to illustrate the concept, to get started. We wanted the house to be an ecosystem of products and solutions designed around the real needs of the inhabitants. Of course it would have to be made out of sustainable, green materials, but more crucially, it would have to be durable enough to withstand torrential rains, earthquakes, and the stress of children playing. The house might be a single room structure with drop-down partitions for privacy. Furniture—sleeping hammocks and fold-down chairs would be built in. The roof would boast an inexpensive solar panel and battery to light the house and charge the mobile phone and tablet computer. An inexpensive water filter would be built in as well.

In effect, the house is really a one-room shed designed around the family ecosystem, a lego-like aggregation of useful products that "bring good things to life" for the poor.

World-Class Design. Our next question was: "Who will do this?" We decided that it would have to be a collaboration between global design and engineering companies and non-profits with experience solving problems for the poor. The usual suspects ran through our minds—IDEO, GE, TATA, Siemens, Habitat-for-Humanity, Partners In Health, the Solar Electric Light Fund, the Clinton Global Initiative, the Gates Foundation, Grameen. Governments may play an important part in setting the stage for these types of cross-country innovation projects.

The Reverse Innovation Payoff. Participating companies will reap two rewards. First, they will be able to serve the unserved, the 2.5 billion who make up the bottom of the pyramid. Second, they create new competencies which can help transform lives in rich countries by creating breakthrough innovations to solve several problems (scaled housing for hurricane victims, refugees, and even the armed forces).

A House of One's Own: Affordability. To move beyond charity, the poor must become owners of their homes, responsible for their care and upkeep. The model of social business introduced by Muhammad Yunus resonates strongly with us. Micro-finance must surely play a role in making the $300 House-for-the-Poor a viable and self-sustaining solution.

Of course, the idea we present here is an experiment. Nevertheless, we feel it deserves to be explored. From the one-room shacks in Haiti's Central Plateau to the jhuggi clusters in and around Delhi, to the favelas in São Paulo, the problem of housing-for-the-poor is truly global.

We ask CEOs, governments, NGOs, foundations: Are there any takers?

Reading 4.2

Mumbai, India

Hands Off Our Houses

by Matias Echanove and Rahul Srivastava

Published in *The New York Times.*

Last summer, a business professor and a marketing consultant wrote on The Harvard Business Review's website about their idea for a $300 house. According to the writers, and the many people who have enthusiastically responded since, such a house could improve the lives of millions of urban poor around the world. And with a $424 billion market for cheap homes that is largely untapped, it could also make significant profits.

The writers created a competition, asking students, architects and businesses to compete to design the best prototype for a $300 house (their original sketch was of a one-room prefabricated shed, equipped with solar panels, water filters and a tablet computer). The winner will be announced this month. But one expert has been left out of the competition, even though her input would have saved much time and effort for those involved in conceiving the house: the person who is supposed to live in it.

We work in Dharavi, a neighborhood in Mumbai that has become a one-stop shop for anyone interested in "slums" (that catchall term for areas lived in by the urban poor). We recently showed around a group of Dartmouth students involved in the project who are hoping to get a better grasp of their market. They had imagined a ready-made constituency of slum-dwellers eager to buy a cheap house that would necessarily be better than the shacks they'd built themselves. But the students found that the reality here is far more complex than their business plan suggested.

To start with, space is scarce. There is almost no room for new construction or ready-made houses. Most residents are renters, paying $20 to $100 a month for small apartments.

Those who own houses have far more equity in them than $300—a typical home is worth at least $3,000. Many families have owned their houses for two or three generations, upgrading them as their incomes increase. With additions, these homes become what we call "tool houses," acting as workshops, manufacturing units, warehouses and shops. They facilitate trade and production, and allow homeowners to improve their living standards over time.

None of this would be possible with a $300 house, which would have to be as standardized as possible to keep costs low. No number of add-ons would be able to match the flexibility of need-based construction.

In addition, construction is an important industry in neighborhoods like Dharavi. Much of the economy consists of hardware shops, carpenters, plumbers, concrete makers, masons, even real-estate agents. Importing pre-fabricated homes would put many people out of business, undercutting the very population the $300 house is intended to help.

Worst of all, companies involved in producing the house may end up supporting the clearance and demolition of well-established neighborhoods to make room for it. The resulting resettlement colonies, which are multiplying at the edges of cities like Delhi and Bangalore, may at first glance look like ideal markets for the new houses, but the dislocation destroys businesses and communities.

The $300 house could potentially be a success story, if it was understood as a straightforward business proposal instead of a social solution. Places like refugee camps, where many people need shelter for short periods, could use such cheap, well-built units. A market for them could perhaps be created in rural-urban fringes that are less built up.

The $300 house responds to our misconceptions more than to real needs. Of course problems do exist in urban India. Many people live without toilets or running water. Hot and unhealthy asbestos-cement sheets cover millions of roofs. Makeshift homes often flood during monsoons. But replacing individual, incrementally built houses with a ready-made solution would do more harm than good.

A better approach would be to help residents build better, safer homes for themselves. The New Delhi–based Micro Homes Solutions, for example, provides architectural and engineering assistance to homeowners in low-income neighborhoods.

The $300 house will fail as a social initiative because the dynamic needs, interests and aspirations of the millions of people who live in places like Dharavi have been overlooked. This kind of mistake is all too common in the trendy field of social entrepreneurship. While businessmen and professors applaud the $300 house, the urban poor are silent, busy building a future for themselves.

Reading 4.3

When *The New York Times* printed "Hands Off Our Houses," an op-ed about our idea for a $300 House for the poor, we were both delighted and dismayed—delighted because the $300 House was being discussed, and dismayed because authors Matias Echanove and Rahul Srivastava, co-founders of the Institute of Urbanology, didn't seem to have read the series of blog posts about our idea.

The $300 House: A Hands-On Approach to a Wicked Problem
by Vijay Govindarajan with Christian Sarkar

Published in the *HBR Blog Network*

Nearly every criticism the authors levy in their op-ed is answered in 12 blog posts, a magazine article from January/February 2011, a video interview, and a slideshow that integrated community and commentary, which were published between last October and this May.

In critiquing our vision, the authors cite Micro Homes Solutions as "a better approach." In fact, the leaders of that venture were invited several months ago to contribute a blog post to our series as a way of joining the discussion and helping us understand what they've seen on the ground there. They declined to be part of the conversation.

The authors also write that students who tried to write a business plan to serve the poor and who visited poor urban areas of India found "the reality here is far more complex than their business plan suggested."

Yet a fundamental tenet of our project and the blog series about it is that slums present complex challenges that can't be fixed with a clever shack alone. Rather than creating an echo chamber of rah-rah rhetoric, we told blog authors to focus on one of the many knotty issues that Echanove and Srivastava cite in their critique. From the start we asked: What are the complexities of financing these homes? How do you get energy and infrastructure into such dwellings? How do you get corporations to invest in a significant way? We acknowledged that we didn't have the answers. "Just because it is going to take longer than it should doesn't mean we should walk away," wrote Seth Godin in one of the posts. "It's going to take some time, but it's worth it."

The op-ed suggests that the $300 House doesn't acknowledge that "space is scarce" in urban poor areas. Yet, Sunil Suri wrote in a post on the urban challenge that "slums by their nature are located where land and space are limited." Suri proposed potential solutions, including innovative materials, new ways of thinking of the construction process, and building up.

The authors also say that "one expert has been left out of the challenge . . . the person who is supposed to live in it." But a post in the series on the co-creation challenge from Gaurav Bhalla addressed this squarely. "It will be unfortunate if the house were to be designed by those who will never live in it," wrote Bhalla. "Investments need to be made understanding the daily habits and practices of people for whom the house is being designed." Bhalla used the case study of the chulha stove, co-created by businesses, NGOs, and slum dwellers, to make his point. We are also bringing students to India and Haiti to do ethnographic research that will inform development of a $300 House, and when prototypes are developed, they will be deployed and tested with those who will live in them.

Echanove and Srivastava also state that a $300 House "would have to be as standardized as possible to keep costs low. No number of add-ons would be able to match the flexibility of need-based construction." While we agree that a one-size-fits-all approach will not work, we disagree that a $300 House would be inflexible. Core tenets from a blog post about the overall design challenge of creating a $300 House by Bill Gross include "give your customers options" and "make it aspirational." And David Smith's entry on the financial challenge shows that flexibility can be born out of financing options as well. A need-based approach alone also ignores the scale of the problem we are facing. "Triple the U.S. population by three. That's how many people around the world live on about a dollar a day," Godin writes. "Triple it again and now you have the number that lives on $2. About 40% of the world lives on $2 or less a day." In any situation where scale is required, so is some level of standardization.

The most puzzling critique in the op-ed was that "construction is an important industry in neighborhoods like Dharavi. Much of the economy consists of hardware shops, carpenters, plumbers, concrete makers, masons, even real-estate agents. Importing prefabricated homes would put many people out of business, undercutting the very population the $300 house is intended to help."

In fact, our contest's design briefing said these dwellings should be "self built and/or self-improvable." It also stated that the design should rely as much as possible on local materials, which of course would be harvested and crafted by local workers. Our goal is to increase demand for local trades, not drive them away. And the idea that jobs would disappear belies the fact that with progress comes new jobs; teachers for the kids who can now go to school; health care professionals for the families that can now afford check-ups; technology professionals who could service solar panels or internet access devices; farmers who could manage shared crop spaces in the neighborhoods. The $300 House project is a housing ecosystem project.

Finally, Echanove and Srivastava state that "The $300 house could potentially be a success story, if it was understood as a straightforward business proposal instead of a social solution."

We disagree completely. We do support other applications for low-cost housing—bringing these dwellings back to the industrialized world for hurricane relief, for example, would be a reverse innovation success story. However, trying to pigeonhole ideas as either "for good" or "for profit" is an outmoded way of thinking.

The authors have an implicit negative view on business. For them, profit seems to be a dirty word. For us, good business and social innovation are one and the same. The rising tide of New Capitalism, what Michael Porter calls "shared value" and what Umair Haque calls "thick value," is perhaps the most important reaction to the corruption and greed that spurred the most recent global economic crisis. The *Economist* was right when it suggested that this is a "can do" moment in history.

Our goal is neither to start yet another charity—one of our advisers, Paul Polak, tells us that "you can't donate your way out of poverty"—nor to start just another business. Rather we must encourage existing businesses to find ways to create new, scalable markets; to get NGOs to share their on-the-ground expertise; and to force governments to make it as simple as possible to work across the hybrid value chain in order to make such a project a reality and begin the process of instilling dignity in and creating options for individuals who now don't have either.

We are happy that Echanove and Srivastava share our passion for the problem of affordable housing, which is a wicked problem. We simply disagree with the idea that if it's a market, it can't also be a socially progressive solution. Trying to categorize the regeneration of slums as either a business problem or social problem is like trying to categorize a flame as either heat or light. It is both, always.

Reading 4.4

A $300 Idea that Is Priceless

from Schumpeter, a column in the *Economist*

Applying the world's business brains to housing the poor.

Friedrich Engels said in "The Condition of the Working Class in England," in 1844, that the onward march of Manchester's slums meant that the city's Angel Meadow district might better be described as "Hell upon Earth." Today, similar earthly infernos can be found all over the emerging world: from Brazil's favelas to Africa's shanties. In 2010 the United Nations calculated that there were about 827m people living in slums—almost as many people as were living on the planet in Engels's time—and predicted that the number might double by 2030.

Last year Vijay Govindarajan, of Dartmouth College's Tuck School of Business, along with Christian Sarkar, a marketing expert, issued a challenge in a *Harvard Business Review* blog: why not apply the world's best business thinking to housing the poor? Why not replace the shacks that blight the lives of so many poor people, thrown together out of cardboard and mud, and prone to collapsing or catching fire, with more durable structures? They laid down a few simple guidelines. The houses should be built of mass-produced materials tough enough to protect their inhabitants from a hostile world. They should be equipped with the basics of civilized life, including water filters and solar panels. They should be "improvable," so that families can adapt them to their needs. And they should cost no more than $300.

Mr. Govindarajan admits that the $300 figure was partly an attention-grabbing device. But he also argues that it has a certain logic. Muhammad Yunus, the founder of Grameen Bank, has calculated that the average value of the houses of people who have just escaped from poverty is $370. Tata Motors has also demonstrated the value of having a fixed figure to aim at: the company would have found it more difficult to produce the Tata Nano if it had simply been trying to produce a "cheap" car rather than a "one lakh" car (about $2,200).

The attention-grabbing certainly worked. The blog was so inundated with positive responses that a dedicated website, 300house.com, was set up, which has attracted more than 900 enthusiasts and advisers from all over the world. On April 20th Mr. Govindarajan launched a competition inviting people to submit designs for a prototype of the house.

Why has a simple blog post led to such an explosion of creativity? The obvious reason is that "frugal innovation"—the art of radically reducing the cost of products while also delivering first-class value—is all the rage at the moment. General Electric has reduced the cost of an electrocardiogram machine from $2,000 to $400. Tata Chemicals has produced a $24 purifier that can provide a family with pure water for a year. Girish Bharadwaj, an engineer, has perfected a technique for producing cheap footbridges that are transforming life in rural India.

Another reason is that houses can be such effective anti-poverty tools. Poorly constructed ones contribute to a nexus of problems: the spread of disease (because they have no proper sanitation or ventilation), the perpetuation of poverty (because children have no proper lights to study by) and the general sense of insecurity (because they are so flimsy and flammable). Mr. Govindarajan's idea is so powerful because he treats houses as ecosystems that provide light, ventilation and sanitation.

Numerous innovators are also worrying away at this nexus of problems. Habitat for Humanity, an NGO, is building durable houses of bamboo in Nepal. Idealab, a consultancy, is on the verge of unveiling a $2,500 house that will be mass-produced in factories, sold in kits and feature breakthroughs in ventilation, lighting and sanitation. Philips has produced a cheap cooking stove, the Chulha, that cuts out the soot that kills 1.6m people a year worldwide. The Solar Electric Light Fund is demonstrating that you can provide poor families with solar power for roughly the same cost as old standbys such as kerosene and candles.

Profits and other problems

These thinkers, like the advocates of the $300 house, must solve three huge problems to succeed. They must persuade big companies that they can make money out of cheap homes, because only they can achieve the economies of scale needed to hit the target price. They need to ensure sufficient access to microloans: $300 is a huge investment for a family of squatters living on a couple of dollars a day. And they need to overcome the obstacle that most slum-dwellers have weak or non-existent property rights. There is no point in offering people the chance to buy a cleverly designed house if they have no title to the land they occupy. Solving these problems will in turn demand a high degree of co-operation between people who do not always get on: companies and NGOs, designers and emerging-world governments.

However, the exciting thing about the emerging world at the moment is a prevailing belief that even the toughest problems can be solved. And a similar can-do moment, in the late 1940s, offers a striking historical precedent for the application of mass-production techniques to housing: as American servicemen flooded home after the second world war to start families, Levitt & Sons built Levittowns at the rate of 30 houses a day by mass-producing the components in factories, delivering them on lorries and using teams of specialists to assemble them.

Some emerging-world governments are beginning to realize that providing security of tenure is the only way to deal with the problem of ever-proliferating slums. And big companies that face stagnant markets in the West are increasingly fascinated by the "fortune at the bottom of the pyramid." Bill Gross of Idealab reckons the market for cheap houses could be worth at least $424 billion. But in reality it is worth far more than that: preventing the Earth from becoming what Mike Davis, a particularly gloomy follower of Marx and Engels, has termed a "planet of slums."

Other Invention Strategies

Great myths have grown up around writers who can supposedly sit down, put pen to paper, and write a masterpiece. If these myths had developed about any other type of artist—a musician or a painter—we would scoff about them and ask about the years of study and practice those artists had spent before they created their masterpieces. Since all of us can write to some degree, perhaps it seems more feasible that great authors simply appear magically amongst us. Alas, it is not so; like all talented artists, good writers must learn their craft through consistent and continuous practice. Similar to how the ancient Greeks used **topoi** (a strategy or heuristic made up of questions about a topic which allows a rhetor to construe an argument) to generate raw material for their compositions, many writers today use the following invention strategies as prewriting activities.

Freewriting

One practice method developed in the 1970s and often attributed to Peter Elbow, author of *Writing without Teachers*, is called freewriting. This method is just what it sounds like—writing that is free of any content restrictions. You simply write what is on your mind. This method is freeform, but there is some structure—you must set a time limit before you begin, and once you begin, you must not stop. The time period is usually 10 to 20 minutes, and you must keep your pen or pencil moving on the page—no hesitations, no corrections, no rereading. Don't worry about spelling, or punctuation, or grammar—just download onto the paper whatever comes to mind. It will seem awkward at best; some have said it is downright painful. But after a few weeks practice, you will realize it is effective and a wonderful individual method of getting at your thoughts on a subject.

Invisible Freewriting

If you just cannot stop paying attention to your spelling and grammar, or if you find yourself always stopping to read what you have written, you can freewrite invisibly. To do this, you will need carbon paper and a pen that is retracted or out of ink. You sandwich the carbon paper, carbon side down, between two sheets of paper and write on the top sheet with your empty pen. You cannot see what you are writing, but it will be recorded on the bottom sheet of paper. If you prefer to work on the computer, you can easily modify this technique by taping a blank sheet of paper over the monitor while you type.

Focused Freewriting

When freewriting, you are writing without sticking to any particular topic. You are exploring many ideas and your sentences may roam from your day at work, the letter you just got from your sister, or a story you read in the paper about a man who tracks the nighttime migrations of songbirds. With focused freewriting, you are trying to concentrate on one particular subject. You can write the name of that subject at the top of the page to remind you of your topic as you write. The rules are the same as the other types of freewriting, but you are focusing on one question or idea and exploring it in depth.

One drawback of focused freewriting is that students sometimes confuse it with a different step in the writing process, drafting. Remember that freewriting is "invention" work, intended only to help you explore ideas on paper. Drafting takes place only after you have explored, analyzed, and organized those ideas. Freewriting helps you think and write critically about a topic while drafting occurs once you have done the critical thinking necessary to come up with a unified, cohesive, and organized plan for an essay.

Listing/Brainstorming

This method of mapping is the least visual and the most straightforward. Unlike freewriting, where you write continuously, with listing you write down words and/or phrases that provide a shorthand for the ideas you might use in your essay, much as you would a grocery or "to-do" list. Brainstorming is a bit looser. Lists usually follow line after line on the page; brainstorming consists of words and phrases placed anywhere you want to write them on the page.

Clustering

When you think of a cluster, you think of several like things grouped together, often with something holding them together. Peanut clusters, a type of candy, are peanuts joined together with milk chocolate. Star clusters are groupings of stars, like the Pleiades or the Big Dipper, connected by their relative positions to each other in space. You can create clusters of like ideas by grouping your ideas around a central topic on a blank sheet of paper.

Organizing or Arranging

The "invention" process is intended to get our ideas out of our heads and onto a piece of paper, but rarely do these ideas arrive in the most logical or effective order. Take some time (an hour or so for a short essay) to analyze your inventions. Place all the ideas in a logical order, and join similar ideas. Next, look for your most significant point, the most important thing you want to say about your subject. This may become your tentative thesis. Then identify which of the other items on your list will help you communicate your point and delete items that are irrelevant to your thesis.

Reading 4.5

Take a Leap into Writing
by Craig Wynne

When I was working at Berkeley's College Academic Support Center, I often tutored second-language learners who struggled with sentences that had awkward constructions. Sometimes, I would say to a student, "What is it you're trying to say here?" The student inevitably could state the point orally with accuracy and clarity. I would then say to the student, "Write down what you just said." The student would write it down with pen and paper. Then I'd say, "Okay, pretend you're the professor. Which do you think is the easier sentence to understand: what you wrote or what you typed?" The student would say, "What I wrote. Whenever I type, I'm always afraid of what the professor will say."

Craig Wynne says, "When jumping out of an airplane, you don't have time to think about consequences. You just have to do it....The same principle applies to writing."

Around that time, I read an article in *Writer* magazine entitled "Forget the Rules and Take a Leap," by an author named Deanna Roy. In this article, Roy had been suffering from writer's block, and she found that skydiving was a way for her to release her thoughts without fear of saying the "wrong thing." So I decided to put this idea into practice myself for the purposes of teaching my students about overcoming their inhibitions when it came to writing.

When jumping out of an airplane, you don't have time to think about consequences. You just have to do it. You can see from the photo, jumping wasn't an easy thing for me to do, but afterwards I was glad I had gone through with taking that leap.

The same principle applies to writing. You need to find a way to write without thinking about whether your words are spelled correctly or whether the professor won't like the idea. Those thoughts get in the way with your writing process. Some students can write with that kind of freedom on a computer, but others find that with the computer comes an uninvited editor who looks over their shoulder and criticizes. Yet, they can escape that editor by talking out their thoughts and then writing with pen and paper. Whatever works. This doesn't mean that writing is ever going to be easy. It's just easier if you can get your thoughts down on a piece of paper before that internal editor starts looking for errors.

A professor named Peter Elbow developed a process called freewriting, which helps writers take that leap from thoughts into words. To freewrite, you put your pen to paper and just write. You don't want to think about whether something is spelled incorrectly or whether the professor will like an idea. Freewriting is the chance for you to get your ideas down on paper (or on the computer). When you freewrite, you don't stop. You just write. Even if you have an idea you think sounds completely stupid or off-the-wall, just write it down. You never know. Sometimes, those "silly" ideas could contain something you might be able to use for your assignment. When I start a project, I begin by letting all my ideas out in words in a row, even if they don't sound quite right. Professor Elbow remarked that freewriting results in a lot of words that are garbage. That's true. However, eventually, I come to words that express an idea I like. In order to get to the point of liking my words, I have to take that leap onto the page. Eventually, I have to worry about grammar, structure, and the end product, but not while I'm freewriting.

Activity 4.6 **Consider "Take a Leap into Writing"**

1. How do you write most easily? On a computer? With pen and paper? Share your experience getting words onto a page.

2. What do you think of Wynne's comparison of writing to skydiving? What do the two things have in common?

3. Do you have an internal editor that keeps you from writing freely? Can you describe your editor? What does it do?

Activity 4.7 **Focused Freewriting**

1. Write your topic at the top of a blank sheet of paper.

2. Write a list of at least 10 aspects or characteristics of your topic.

3. Choose two or three items from your list and do a focused freewriting on each item for five to eight minutes.

4. Add more items to your list if you have discovered new ideas during your freewriting.

Activity 4.8 **Begin with What You Know**

In your small group, make a list of controversial topics that you already have some knowledge about because of personal experience or course work. For example, one of you may be among the millions of Americans without health insurance or you may know someone else in this position. If so, you probably know about some of the failings of the American health care system. Alternatively, you may have lost a job during the 2009 recession or been unable to find a job when you needed one. If so, you probably have some thoughts about the efforts of the federal government to deal with the economic crisis. These personal connections with controversial issues give you a starting point for research on a topic. Share your group's list with the class.

Expand Your Personal Knowledge through Observation

Close observation for descriptive detail can enhance almost any topic. If you are writing a paper on the effectiveness of recycling in your community, you might take a trip to your community's processing area for recycled glass. There you could gather information through observing the glass recycling process. You also might be able to conduct short, informal interviews with the employees about the process.

You may need to call to get permission to visit certain places. You'll need to identify yourself and your topic. Usually you can get permission to visit and observe. However, if you cannot get permission to visit an area, you can ask your contact if there is a similar area nearby. Again, look at your research questions before you visit to decide which questions might be answered by your observations. For example, if you have read about recycling centers in other communities, during your visit to the local center, you could observe the similarities and differences in their procedures. Good writers always gather more detail than they actually use so they have choices about what to include.

The key to successful observation is tuning the senses. Can you remember what your room smelled like when you woke up this morning, the first thing you saw when you opened your eyes, the way your sheets or blanket felt against your skin, the sounds in the room after you turned off your alarm, or the taste of the orange juice or coffee you had with breakfast? Our minds are trained to ignore seemingly unimportant information, so if you can't remember any sensory details from your morning, you're not alone. When conducting an observation, however, those sensory responses are an important part of your research. Sitting in the place you're observing, freewrite for at least five minutes on each of the senses: touch, taste, smell, sight, and sound. You might even freewrite on each of the senses from several different vantage points, depending on the size of the place or the event you're observing. Take notes on the responses given by those you speak with.

Within fifteen minutes of leaving the place you have been observing, take a few minutes to read over your notes and write a few overall impressions or add details you missed in your description. Look again at your research questions and decide which ones have been answered by your visit.

Explore

Activity 4.9 **Observation Exercise**

In this exercise, describe your classroom. Alternatively, go to another setting such as a museum, restaurant, or library and describe that space and the people in it.

- How large is the space, approximately? Describe the shape of the room, and the color and texture of the walls, the ceiling, and the floor.

- How is the space furnished? Describe the color, shape, and style of the furnishings.

- What about representing the other senses? Is the room silent or noisy? Does it have a characteristic smell? Describe.

- How many people are in the room? What are they doing? Describe their ages, general style of dress, and possessions such as computers, backpacks, or purses.

- Pick two or three people that stand out in some way from the other occupants and write a sentence or two about each, describing what it is about each person that caught your attention.

Reading 4.6

BMW 1M: Miniature, Mighty and Miles of Fun
by Dan Neil

Dan Neil, auto columnist for *The Wall Street Journal*, reviewed the new BMW Coupe in his weekly column "Rumble Seat."

As you read the article that follows, pay attention to how the author uses details from both personal knowledge and close observation to enrich his writing.

Typically, car makers will choose a special color for the introduction of a special vehicle, known in the biz as the "launch color." In the case of the 1M Coupe—the Motorsports division variant of BMW's beastly looking 135i—the launch color is a sort of burnt tangerine, a phrase that also describes my own mental citrus after a weekend behind the wheel.

A bratty little barrel-racer of a car, with a spirit that seems to want to bite through the bit, the 1M Coupe is quick, playful, aggressive and laugh-out-loud fun to drive; indeed, it's as much fun as the law will allow. For BMW fanboys, I gather, that's just the problem.

A little history is in order: The M division began in the 1970s building highly tuned versions of the Werks' production cars, with more powerful engines, bigger brakes, more athletic legs and edgier electronics. Some of these cars have been, simply, epic. The M3 that I imprinted on was a '96 Euro-spec yellow coupe. That car is, to this day, the best handling five-seater I've ever driven.

Bratty Little Barrel Racer

(Note to Bavaria: Bring back the narrow-section steering wheel. And stop hogging all the good scenery.)

To describe the pleasures of that M3—known to the geek squad as the E36 model—is to define a kind of atavism that the Bimmerphiles pine for. Those cars were relatively simple (in-line six, manual transmission and spare amenities), with beautifully quick and sensitive steering and an easy progressiveness that meant you could let the rear end slide around without fear of losing it, catching the car with a dab of throttle and counter-steer. It wasn't the fastest car in the world but it was such a sheer limbic pleasure to drive, to wheel, to wield, to control. That's it: a sense of mastery. You got out of that car wearing a cape and a big S on your chest.

Most of all, that car was lightweight. That E36 coupe weighed about 3,200 pounds. By contrast, the current model-year M3 (E92) weighs fully 500 pounds more on a 2.4-inch-longer wheelbase. And while the current M3 has vastly more go-fast hardware—including a 414-horsepower V8, optional dual-clutch gearbox, cybernetic brakes and the M Variable Differential Lock (sounds like an outlawed wrestling hold, doesn't it?)—a certain something, call it a dynamic lucidity, has been lost.

And the fanboys feel betrayed. They whine, they fume, they wear black. You'd think Rudolph Valentino had just died or something. Why does the M3 have to be so heavy? What part of Ultimate Driving Machine does BMW itself not understand?

But everyone's favorite M3 of yore didn't have to have a monster stereo, navi, power seats, umpteen airbags or five-star crash structure. The M3 so fondly remembered has been essentially optioned up and regulated out of existence. Unless BMW discovers the formula for Flubber, that car isn't coming back.

And the bloat isn't confined to the weight scales. The current M3 is also punitively pricey, starting at $61,075 (with gas-guzzler tax) and luxed-out to nearly $70,000. More fanboy despair. Oh, Rudy!

To these disconsolate few, the news last year that the M division was going to hot up the 135i coupe (the E82 platform, in nerd-speak) must have sounded like salvation. The numbers were there. Not quite 3,400 pounds, with a twin-turbo 3.0-liter in-line six delivering 335 hp and 332 pound-feet of torque—with brief computer-summoned overboost of 369 pound-feet—and the sole choice of a six-speed manual transmission, the 1M Coupe sounded like more than just a cool car. It promised a return to form, an end to a kind of despised lavishness, a cure for what ails the BMW brand.

2012 BMW 1M Coupe

Base price: $47,010

Price as tested: $49,000 (est.)

Powertrain: Twin-turbo 3.0-liter in-line six cylinder with variable valve timing; six-speed manual transmission; rear wheel drive with variable differential lock

Horsepower/torque: 335 hp at 5,900 rpm/332 pound-feet at 1,500–4,500 rpm (369 pound-feet at overboost)

Length/weight: 172.4 inches/3,362 pounds

Wheelbase: 104.7 inches

EPA fuel economy: 19/26 mpg, city/highway

Cargo capacity: 8 cubic feet

Now that the car is here, is it? You know, it is, sort of.

To boil it down a bit, the 1M Coupe is the smaller car with the mighty M3's dirty bits, less 400 pounds. The same highly evolved suspension componentry, the same massive brakes behind the same stick-with-a-grip 35-series, 19-inch tires and wheels, the same electronically controlled rear differential, and the same M-tuned dynamics control, which allows drivers to color outside the lines safely at the track. And yes, you can turn the electronic interventions off. But once the nannies are dismissed, be advised, the car has a measure of the old-school, free-gimbaling character of the early M's. In other words, it can get away from you. Me? Oh, please. You'd like that, wouldn't you?

The 1M is certainly track-day ready, with a dry-sump engine-lubrication system with its own heat exchanger as well as a radiator for the heavy-duty six-speed transmission. The car I drove had a brake warning light come on—I think the 14-inch cross-drilled brakes got a little too warm after being lapped at Laguna Seca for a half-hour or so—but they never failed to haul the car down with a precise and determined yank rearward.

Here, at last, is a man's clutch—heavily weighted, with a smooth, precise uptake—and slick-shifting gearshift to go with it. Pedal position is just about perfect for heel-and-toe footwork.

Serene and smooth at low speeds, but with an increasingly impatient growl from the quad exhaust as the revs build, the 1M does several dynamic things particularly well. First, at corner exits, it pulls like hell, like it has deployed some magical torque spinnaker. BMW gives the 0–60 acceleration at 4.7 seconds, but the way this thing gets on the cam in second and third gear will bring a tear to your eye. Like my favorite M3 of olden days, the car is not unnervingly fast but it's hugely willing. This thing hits redline faster than one of the Real Housewives of Atlanta.

Second, it has splendid cornering grip, and the corner-to-corner transitions happen without a lot of heaving, rolling or rebound to unsettle the car or cause you to correct your line. The 1M Coupe has impeccable cornering manners, and the M Sport Seats lock you in driving position.

Third, it trail-brakes like a dream. Turn in to a corner with the brakes on and ease off the binders. The car's rear end slides gracefully to the outside, the world swivels and now you're looking at corner exit. Dig in the spurs, up come the revs. Hi-yo, Silbern, away!

So what could possibly be wrong? Well, for one thing, the 1M Coupe is a total buttaface, one of the ugliest, most disturbingly wrong car designs in modern history. The addition of all the massive wheel arches, lip spoilers, aero mods and the so-called Air Curtain front spoiler helps not at all. This car is the last revenge of former BMW styling head Chris Bangle. Jeez, put a flag over its head and drive for glory.

Second—at least to the fanboys—it's still too heavy, despite the fact it's actually 77 pounds lighter than the standard 135i. But I checked the trunk for lead bars and found none, and I found very little in the way of depleted uranium in the cabin.

I can only conclude that, for some old-schoolers, nothing BMW makes will ever be light enough again. That's too bad. This thing's a tangerine dream.

Activity 4.10 **Find Artistic and Inartistic Proofs in a Reading**

Much of Dan Neil's column, "BMW 1M: Miniature, Mighty and Miles of Fun," comes from his own personal experience and observation. For example, his description of the car as a, "bratty little barrel-racer of a car, with a spirit that seems to want to bite through the bit," is his own evaluation or thought and, thus, an artistic proof. So is the first sentence, "Typically, car makers will choose a special color for the introduction of a special vehicle, known in the biz as the 'launch color.'" That information comes from his long experience with reviewing cars. Also, his remark that the brake light came on in the car he drove is his observation.

However, the information that the car has "a dry-sump engine-lubrication system with its own heat exchanger as well as a radiator for the heavy-duty six-speed transmission" may have come from the manufacturer's promotional literature.

For this activity, go through the reading and highlight (or underline) the parts that you think come from Dan Neil's own knowledge or observation. These are the artistic proofs. Information he has obtained from other sources (such as the car company) would be inartistic proofs. If you aren't sure whether or not a sentence is his own knowledge or observation, make a note of that in the margin. Discuss this as a class.

Activity 4.11 Write a Product Review

Choose a new product in a category you know well, such as a computer or an MP3 player, and write a review as if you were a columnist for a newspaper, magazine, or blog. Using the techniques explained in this chapter, do prewriting to elicit what you know about the product and the product category. Then, observe the product and try it out, so that you can review its positives and negatives. If you need specific information that you do not know, consult the product advertising, packaging, or instruction manual.

Like Dan Neil's auto product review, you can use vivid language and insider slang in order to provide an enjoyable experience for your reader. Remember, however, that this is an argument. You need to evaluate whether the product is a good or bad selection for its target audience and why.

Activity 4.12 Write on Your Blog

Choose a controversial topic and speculate in your blog whether or not that topic is at a stasis point for any of the stasis questions.

Activity 4.13 Write in Your Commonplace Book

In your commonplace book, freewrite about how you do invention. What methods do you use to extract from your mind what you already know about a subject (what Aristotle would call artistic proofs)?

5
WRITING RHETORICALLY

Praxis in Action

How I Write by Matthew Harding

Writing can seem very daunting at times, especially when you have a major writing assignment that's worth as much as a test. It should be easy since you know about the assignment way ahead of time, but somehow the time ends up getting away from you because it's hard to get started. You end up both stressing about the paper and trying to write it at the last minute. One way that I reduce the pressure of a writing assignment is to start writing long before the paper is due, giving myself enough time to work on it.

If I tell myself that I am only going to write a certain amount at a time, say a page a day, it is less intimidating to write. While this method may seem drawn out, it works. Whenever I come back to the paper the next day, I always review what I have already written, so I can be sure I keep the topic in mind. This way, I avoid burning myself out, getting my ideas confused, or losing track of the topic and, ultimately, rushing to finish by the end. This allows me to come to my paper with a fresh perspective and new ideas with every installment I write. Once I finish that day's work I feel good because I am getting the paper done while also giving it my best effort, which also greatly reduces the stress of having to write it.

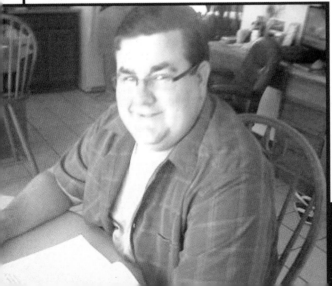

Matthew Harding points out that writing can be daunting even for experienced writers.

Through Writing, Enter the Conversation

Cicero's famous work, *On the Ideal Orator*, is not a treatise or handbook about how to be an effective rhetorician. Instead, it is a dialogue, a conversation. The setting is a villa outside Rome belonging to Lucius Licinius Crassus, and the time is 91 CE, an era of dangerous unrest in the Roman Empire. Prominent and respected citizens gather with Crassus to escape, for a while, the political crisis developing in the city. Crassus and his guests settle at leisure under a wide, spreading plane tree, not only to enjoy its shade but also to pay homage to Plato's *Phaedrus*, which similarly took place under a plane tree, though in Greece. They take time this day to dialogue about the attributes of an ideal orator. The purpose of the arguments they present to each other is not to win out over the others but, conversing together, to come to knowledge. It is not a trivial pursuit. Cicero reveals what his characters do not know—soon they will all die horribly as part of the civil unrest in Rome, violence traceable to the failure of leaders to resolve their differences in nonviolent dialogue.

Throughout ancient times, dialogue appears alongside rhetoric. It was through dialogue that rhetoricians such as Aristotle, Isocrates, and Cicero taught their students rhetorical skills. Today, in the writing classroom, group discussion or pairs dialogue is also part of the teaching process. A rhetorical text, too, is a conversation with previous texts, responding to ideas they have presented. In addition, arguments include paraphrases and quotes from others' compositions, making them part of the conversation. Moreover, writers composing texts must anticipate their audiences' reactions—questions they might ask or objections they might raise—so responses to these questions and objects can be included in the argument. This process of responding to audiences in advance continues the conversation.

Organize Your Essay

All texts are conversational, a characteristic reflected in the format or organization. In ancient times, orators began a speech by attracting the audience's attention in what was called the *exordium*, which we would call the opening or introduction. Next, they provided background information in a *narratio* (narration), followed by an *explication* in which they defined terms and enumerated the issues. During the *partition* they would express the thesis or main issue to be discussed, and in the *confirmation* they would provide evidence to support the thesis. Opposition arguments would be addressed in the *refutatio*, and the composition would be wrapped up with a *peroratio* or conclusion. The order of these different elements was not rigid in ancient times, nor is it today. Sometimes one or more sections were eliminated if they were not needed, but then, as now, an effective text included most of these elements. For example, if your audience is very familiar with a particular subject, you may not need to define terms, as you would with an audience who was unfamiliar with the material.

As did the ancient Greeks and Romans, when you write an argument, you begin with an introduction that gains your audience's attention and presents your thesis; likewise, you end with a conclusion that ties together what you have said or presents a call to action. However, you have a choice of several formats for what happens between that introduction and conclusion. Following are three prominent alternatives; your choice of which to use depends on your purpose and the type of evidence you have.

- Created by Stephen Toulmin, the **Toulmin model** for persuasion grew out of the 20th century emphasis upon empirical evidence and is *most effective for arguments that rely on evidence from scientific studies, surveys, or other data.* His model requires six elements. First, rhetors present a claim or statement that they want the audience to accept. Then, they back up the claim with data and facts, what Aristotle would have called inartistic proofs. A warrant links these data to the claim, explaining why the data make the claim valid. Backing provides additional support for the argument, while a counterclaim acknowledges any objections or weaknesses in the argument. And, finally, the rebuttal responds to any counterclaims, removing possible objections to the argument.

- The **Rogerian** (or common ground) **argument** is named for psychologist Carl Rogers. It is *most effective for arguments that attempt to establish common ground between opponents* on an issue. Rogerian argument begins with an introduction that states the problem to be considered. Second, in a much different move than the Toulmin pattern, the rhetor states the opposing argument in neutral language to demonstrate that he or she understands the other side's position, as well as instances when it may be valid. The assumption is that, since the rhetor has been willing to pay attention to the other side's position, they will, in fairness, listen as the rhetor states his or her own position, as well as discusses the instances when it is preferable. The Rogerian argument ends on a positive note, describing how the rhetor's position could, at least in some instances, benefit the opposition.

- The **general modern format** for argument is one that will probably be familiar to you from previous English classes. It is a *format that you can use when your argument does not fit neatly into either the Toulmin or Rogerian patterns.* Moreover, you can adapt it to serve the needs of your argument. It is the standard five-paragraph essay modified for presenting an argument, and, like that pattern, it can be expanded to accommodate longer essays. Similar to the five-paragraph essay, you begin with an introduction that attracts your audience's attention and states your thesis. Then two or three sections each present major points that support your thesis. The next section presents a counterargument, which anticipates audience questions or objections and is followed by a rebuttal of the counterargument. Finally, a conclusion ties the argument together, perhaps by reflecting back to the introduction or issuing a call for action.

Notice that all of these formats include an attempt to dialogue with the audience. In the Toulmin model, the warrant, in particular, is designed to help the audience make the logical link between the claim and the data offered as evidence. In a Rogerian argument, the rhetor carefully and in emotionally-neutral language demonstrates that he or she has been listening to the opposition and can even restate their argument fairly. The arguments produced via these models, even if they do not immediately convince, will not worsen the situation. The aim of well-intentioned rhetors is not to convince at any cost but to continue the conversation until reasonable solutions can be found. For a comparison of the different argument formats, see the table presented on pages 150–151.

Like the ancient Greeks, you will begin with an opening and end with a conclusion. However, in between the bookends of your essay, you have more flexibility to adapt the basic format than did the Romans.

Write a Thesis Statement

A **thesis** may be a sentence or a series of sentences, or in a few cases it may be implied rather than stated explicitly; but a thesis is at the heart of any piece of writing. If a reader cannot identify your thesis, the meaning of your text is not clear. How do you develop a thesis? First, you determine your occasion for writing—who is your audience, what is your purpose, and what special circumstances are there (if any)? Then you write a working thesis that makes an assertion or claim about your topic, something that will be affected by your audience and purpose. For example, if you are writing a research paper about the advantages and disadvantages of biodiesel fuel, your claim may be stated differently depending on whether your audience is an English class or a chemistry class. In the latter, you might need to use technical language that would be unfamiliar to your English professor.

Working theses are statements that develop and change as essays are written; they are basic frameworks that provide a connection for the ideas you have decided to convey to your reader. Later, after you have completed a draft of your text, examine your working thesis. If needed, rewrite your thesis so that it states the main idea of your essay in a clear and engaging fashion. Consider the following examples of thesis statements.

> The United States should implement a guest worker program as a way of reforming the illegal immigration problem.

> Nuclear power should be considered as part of a program to reduce the United States's dependence on foreign oil.

Compose an Introduction

Experienced writers have different methods of creating a good introduction. One writer who tends to discover his paper as he goes along swears the best way to write an introduction is to write the entire paper and then move the conclusion to the beginning of the essay and rewrite it as the introduction. Another writer lets the paper sit around for a few days before she writes her introduction. A third always writes two or three different introductions and tries them out on friends before deciding which to use. However you choose to write the introduction, make sure it is interesting enough to make your reader want to read on.

The introduction to your essay is an invitation to your reader. If you invite readers to come along with you on a boring journey, they won't want to follow. In magazine and

Essay Starters

If, after you have done extensive invention (prewriting and research), you still find it intimidating to face the blank computer screen, try one of the essay starters below. These are phrases to get the words flowing. Then, later, after you have written a rough draft, go back and revise the beginning. Delete the essay starter and, in its place, write a real introduction. As you probably know, you do not need to say, "In my opinion," because what you write in your essay, unless you attribute it to someone else, is your opinion. See the section in this chapter on writing introductions.

In my opinion . . .

I agree . . .

I disagree . . .

Studies show . . .

Experts say . . .

My paper is about . . .

I am writing this essay because . . .

In the beginning . . .

Argument Formats: A Comparison

Ancient Roman	General Modern Format
Standard pattern the ancients modified to suit the argument.	Good all-purpose format that can be adapted for the needs of the argument.
Introduction—Exordium Attracts the interest of the audience and identifies the argument.	**Introduction** Attracts the interest of the audience through its opening strategy and states the thesis.
Background or narration—Narratio Details the history or facts of the issue.	**First main point** Supports the thesis.
Definition—Explication Defines terms and outlines issues.	**Second main point** Supports the thesis.
Thesis—Partition States the particular issue that is to be argued.	**Third main point** Supports the thesis.
Proof—Confirmation Develops the thesis and provides supporting evidence.	**Counterargument** Acknowledges the opposing argument or arguments.
Refutation or opposition—Refutatio Addresses the arguments opposing the thesis.	**Rebuttal of counterargument** Refutes the opposing argument or arguments.
Conclusion—Peroratio Reiterates the thesis and may urge the audience to action.	**Conclusion** Ties together the elements of the composition and gives the reader closure. May summarize the essay and include a call to action.

Toulmin Model	Rogerian Argument
Good for an argument that relies on empirical evidence such as scientific studies or data collection.	**Good when the object is consensus or compromise, so that opponents can work together while retaining their positions.**
Claim Presents the overall thesis the writer will argue.	**Introduction** States the problem to be solved or the question to be answered. Often opponents will also agree there is a problem.
Data Supports the claim with evidence.	**Summary of opposing views** Describes the opposing side's arguments in a neutral and fair manner.
Warrant (also known as a bridge) Explains why or how the data support the claim. Connects the data to the claim.	**Statement of understanding** Concedes occasions when the opposing position might be valid.
Counterclaim Presents a claim that negates or disagrees with the thesis/claim.	**Statement of position** Avoids emotionally charged language, and identifies position.
Rebuttal Presents evidence that negates or disagrees with the counterclaim.	**Statement of contexts** Describes the specific contexts in which the rhetor's position applies/works well.
Conclusion Ties together the elements of the composition (if not included with the rebuttal).	**Statement of benefits** Presents benefits that may appeal to the self-interest of readers who may not yet agree with you; shows how your position benefits them. Ends on a positive note.
	Conclusion Ties together the elements of the composition (if not included in the statement of benefits).

newspaper writing, the introduction is sometimes called a *hook* because it hooks the reader into reading the text. If a magazine writer does not capture the reader's attention right away, the reader is not likely to continue. After all, there are other and possibly more interesting articles in the magazine. Why should readers suffer through a boring introduction? Depending on the topic and pattern of your essay, you might employ one of the following techniques to hook your readers and make them want to keep reading:

- An intriguing or provocative quotation
- A narrative or anecdote
- A question or series of questions
- A vivid sensory description
- A strongly stated opinion

Your introductory paragraph makes a commitment to your readers. This is where you identify the topic, state your thesis (implicitly or explicitly), and give your readers clues about the journey that will follow in the succeeding paragraphs. Be careful not to mislead the reader. Do not ask questions you will not answer in your paper (unless they are rhetorical questions). Do not introduce a topic in your introduction and then switch to another one in your paper.

Although the introduction is the first paragraph or so of the paper, it may not be the first paragraph the writer composes. If you have problems beginning your essay because you cannot immediately think of a good introduction, begin with the first point in your essay and come back to the introduction later.

If you have problems writing anything at all, consider the suggestions offered in the following essay.

Reading 5.1

The Truth about Writer's Block

by Judith Johnson

Judith Johnson suggests in this essay, first published in *Huffington Post Books*, that there is no such thing as writer's block. She suggests what writers experience is the ebb and flow of the writing process.

I don't choose to experience "writer's block" which I see as simply a matter of faulty perception. It is a mislabeling of a very natural part of the ebb and flow of the writing process. To say "I have writer's block" is to judge a temporary or permanent absence of writing momentum and productivity as wrong and therefore to see oneself as a failure in some way. The process of writing is an intricate interplay of conscious and unconscious dynamics and what actually lands on the page is a small part of it all. When we label and judge that process, we interfere with its natural flow and take a position of againstness with ourselves. It's all in how you look at it.

When a writer declares that he or she is experiencing writer's block, it is like grabbing hold of a fear (Fantasy Expectation Appearing Real) and fueling it with emotional distress. A way to reframe this is to simply trust that what appears to be a dry spell is a normal part of the process of being a writer and that either you need time to be away from the writing focus or that the process is largely unconscious at that time. Each writer has to make peace with this by finding their own particular rhythm and honoring that. For example, what works for me is not to have any rigid writing schedule, but rather to let the words come to me—and they always do—sooner or later. When working on a deadline, whether self-imposed or not, I never lose sight of the deadline, it is always there, but I don't beat myself up with it if time keeps passing and nothing is getting on paper. I'll notice that the topic is alive in me—turning this way and that finding its way to the paper. It takes a lot of trust to let this be. So far, it has never failed me.

I have lots of books and articles and projects on the back burner and no fear of running out of things to write about. I know that each piece of writing has a life of its own. For example, I have a poem that I started at the age of 16 that rumbles around in my head from time to time looking for its ending. I know it will end someday, but hasn't so far. That's not a problem to me—just a reality. I also keep what I call a "dump" file for each project and whether I am actively working on it or not, I capture ideas and information there.

In addition to building a strong bond of trust with yourself, here are some other keys to maintaining a good relationship with yourself as a writer:

Just Do It: There is a point at which every writer just has to sit down and write. Whether you write for five minutes or five hours straight doesn't matter, but if you are going to be a writer, you have to sit down and write.

Write with Freedom and Abandon, Then Edit Ruthlessly: It is important to give yourself permission to write whatever comes up without any judgment. Just focus on capturing your thoughts and ideas—forget about grammar, structure and eloquence. Just get a hold of whatever comes up. Then, just as Michelangelo described the sculpting process as discovering a statue inside every block of stone, each writer must ruthlessly revise and refine a piece of work until pleased with it.

Get Out of Your Own Way: If you get into a pattern of negativity and beating up on yourself when writing, find a way to be more loving with yourself and do not feed the negativity.

Patience: Writing takes enormous patience. As with any other art form, you are constantly revising and refining your work. For an artist the equation is never time is money, but rather "do I feel complete with this piece? Is it my best effort given the time I have available?"

Flexibility, Cooperation and Balance: There is always some level of agitation just under the surface that propels a writer forward giving momentum to the working process. But there are always other forces at work and writing is only one of many activities in an individual's life. Finding your own rhythm and being willing to cooperate with the other elements of life that often seem to intrude on the writer's solitary endeavor are like moving between shooting the rapids and gliding along on calm waters, never quite knowing which is going to present itself and when. Experience teaches us all to go with the flow and somehow that seems to yield maximum inner peace and outward productivity.

Keeping a Sense of Humor and Humility: I've learned never to take myself too seriously as a writer. I do my best and need to laugh at myself from time to time when I give too much importance to what I write. If people get value from what I write, that's great and positive feedback is extremely gratifying. However, while writing is ultimately about communication, I find it very funny that I don't write to communicate, but rather because I simply need to write—I am compelled to do so. If the end product of my endeavors is of value to others, that's great, but the solitary process of engaging in the art form itself is entirely for me and I think that is pretty funny.

Letting Go of the Illusion of Control: A really good writer is never in control of the writing process. You may find that having a rigid schedule works well for you or you might be someone who writes when the spirit moves you to do so. Either way, a good writer taps into the wellspring of human consciousness and like love, you can't make that happen on demand.

Is writing challenging? Absolutely! However, it is a great way to learn some profound lessons in life and to be of service to others.

Activity 5.1 Discuss "The Truth about Writer's Block"

1. How does Judith Johnson choose to reframe the concept of writer's block?

2. Johnson makes recommendations to deal with the "absence of writing momentum." Which of her suggestions makes the most sense to you? Which makes the least sense to you?

3. What do you think? Is there such a thing as "writer's block"?

Combine Your Ideas with Support from Source Materials

A research paper, by definition, makes use of source materials to make an argument. It is important to remember, however, that it is *your* paper, *not* what some professors may call a "research dump," meaning that it is constructed by stringing together research information with a few transitions. Rather, you, as the author of the paper, carry the argument in your own words and use quotes and paraphrases from source materials to support your argument. How do you do that? Here are some suggestions:

■ After you think you have completed enough research to construct a working thesis and begin writing your paper, collect all your materials in front of you (photocopies of articles, printouts of electronic sources, and books) and spend a few hours reading through the materials and making notes. Then, put all the notes and materials to the side and freewrite for a few minutes about what you can remember from your research that is important. Take this freewriting and make a rough outline of the main points you want to cover in your essay. Then you can go back to your notes and source materials to flesh out your outline.

■ Use quotes for the following three reasons:

1. You want to "borrow" the ethos or credibility of the source. For example, if you are writing about stem cell research, you may want to quote from an authority such as Dr. James A. Thomson, whose ground-breaking research led to the first use of stem cells for research. Alternatively, if your source materials include the *New England Journal of Medicine* or another prestigious publication, it may be worth crediting a quote to that source.

2. The material is so beautifully or succinctly written that it would lose its effectiveness if you reworded the material in your own words.

3. You want to create a point of emphasis by quoting rather than paraphrasing. Otherwise, you probably want to paraphrase material from your sources, as quotes should be used sparingly. Often, writers quote source material in a first draft and then rewrite some of the quotes into paraphrases during the revision process.

■ Introduce quotes. You should never have a sentence or sentences in quotation marks just sitting in the middle of a paragraph, as it would puzzle a reader. If you quote, you should always introduce the quote by saying something like this: According to Dr. James A. Thomson, "Stem cell research. . . . "

■ Avoid plagiarism by clearly indicating material that is quoted or paraphrased. See the appendix (at the end of the book) for more information about citing source material.

Support Your Thesis

After you have attracted the interest of your audience, established your thesis, and given any background information and definitions, you will next begin to give reasons for your position, which further develops your argument. These reasons are, in turn, supported by statistics, analogies, anecdotes, and quotes from authorities which you have discovered in your research or know from personal knowledge. Ideally, arrange your reasons so that the strongest ones come either at the beginning or at the end of this portion of the paper (points of emphasis) and the weaker ones fall in the middle.

Answer Opposing Arguments

If you are aware of a contradicting statistic or other possible objection to your argument, it may be tempting to ignore that complication, hoping your audience will not notice. However, that is exactly the worst thing you can do. It is much better to anticipate your audience's possible questions or objections and address them in your discussion. Doing so prevents you from losing credibility by either appearing to deceive your audience or being unaware of all the facts. Also, acknowledging possible refutations of your position actually strengthens your position by making you seem knowledgeable and fair-minded.

Vary Your Strategies or Patterns of Development

When composing your essay, you have many different strategies or **patterns of development** available to you. You may write entire essays whose sole strategy is argumentation or comparison and contrast, but more often, you will combine many of these different modes while writing a single essay. Consider the following strategies or patterns of development:

- *Analysis* entails a close examination of an issue, book, film, or other object, separating it into elements and examining each of the elements separately through other writing modes such as classification or comparison and contrast.

- *Argumentation* involves taking a strong stand on an issue supported by logical reasons and evidence intended to change a reader's mind on an issue or open a reader's eyes to a problem.

- *Cause and effect* is an explanation of the cause and subsequent effects or consequences of a specific action.

- *Classification* entails dividing and grouping things into logical categories.

- *Comparison and contrast* examines the similarities and differences between two or more things.

- *Definition* employs an explanation of the specific meaning of a word, phrase, or idea.

- *Description* uses vivid sensory details to present a picture or an image to the reader.

- *Exemplification* makes use of specific examples to explain, define, or analyze something.

- *Narration* uses a story or vignette to illustrate a specific point or examine an issue.

Write a Conclusion

After they have read the last paragraph of your essay, your readers should feel satisfied that you have covered everything you needed to and you have shared an insight. You may have heard the basic rules: A conclusion cannot address any new issues, and it should summarize the main points of the essay. Although these are valid and reliable rules, a summary is not always the best way to end an essay. The prohibition against new ideas in the final paragraph also might limit certain effective closures like a call to action or a question for the reader to ponder.

One effective technique for writing a conclusion is to refer back to your introduction. If you began with a narrative anecdote, a sensory description, or a question, you can tie a mention of it to your ending point. Or, if you are composing an argumentative essay, you might choose to summarize by using an expert quote to restate your thesis, giving the reader a final firm sense of ethos or credibility. You might also end with a single-sentence summary followed by a suggestion or a call to action for the reader. Another effective way to end an argument can be a paragraph that suggests further research.

A conclusion doesn't have to be long. As a matter of fact, it does not even need to be a separate paragraph, especially if your essay is short. If your closing comments are related to the final paragraph of the essay, one or two sentences can easily be added to the final body paragraph of the essay.

Consider Elements of Page Design

Professors now take it for granted that you word-process your paper using a professional looking typeface such as Times Roman. However, producing your text on a computer with Internet access gives you the option to do much more—including adding one or more images and other page design elements. Several of the assignments in this chapter offer you the opportunity to be creative with your project presentation. Even if you are required to submit your project in standard MLA or APA essay formats, however, you can still include one or more images, and it is important to consider where you place the images.

Some simple guidelines will help you design effective documents:

- Use space as a design element. Do not overcrowd your pages. Place material so that important parts are emphasized by the space around them.

- Rarely (if ever) use all capital letters. Words in all caps are hard to read, and on the Internet all caps is considered shouting.

- Use headings to group your information and make your pages easy to skim. Readers often like to skim pages before deciding what to read.

Indeed, many people will skim all the headlines, headings, and photo captions first, before reading the body text of any section.

■ Put important elements in the top left and lower right parts of the screen. English readers are trained to read from left to right, so our eyes naturally start at the upper left-hand corner of the screen. Our eyes, when skimming, don't flow line by line, but move in a Z pattern, as illustrated in the following diagram.

Eye movement when skimming a page

If you want to include a photo in your research paper, for example, you should put it either in the top left or the bottom right corner of the page, points of emphasis in the Z pattern. Today, with a sophisticated word processing program such as Microsoft Word, it is easy to import an image, size it, and move it to the desired place on a page. Once you have imported an image, you can click on it, hold your cursor at a corner, and enlarge or shrink the image by dragging the cursor. Also, by clicking on the image, you can activate the dialogue box that allows you to specify having the text run tightly around the image. Then you can easily move the image around on the page until you have placed it in a pleasing spot. Alternatively, Microsoft Word provides document templates that you can use for newsletters, brochures, and other types of projects.

If you look closely at the illustration on the next page, you may notice that the text surrounding the image does not seem to make any sense (though it is actually Latin). That's because the text is Lorem ipsum text, sometimes called placeholder or dummy text, which designers use to create page layouts before they have the real text from writers. If you want to try using Lorem ipsum yourself, just do a search on the Internet for that name, and you will find sites that provide paragraphs of the nonsense words that you can utilize as placeholder text.

The image in this article has been effectively placed in the lower right corner, which is a point of emphasis.

Including Images in Your Projects: Copyright Implications

United States copyright law includes a provision called "fair use" that allows copyrighted images to be used for educational projects. However, copyright laws are complicated, and the implications of using digital images is still being determined in the courts. Clearly, if you take the photo yourself, you own the copyright. Many photographers post photos on websites such as Flikr.com and give permission for "fair use" of the images on the Internet, so long as their work is credited. Others, however, post their work for viewers to enjoy but do not allow it to be copied. Scanning a photo from a published work and using it once for a class project falls more clearly under the spirit of the "fair use" law than does putting such an image up on the Internet. If you are doing a web page or blog project that includes images, be sure to contact the copyright owner to obtain permission.

Activity 5.2 Write a Research-Based Argument Paper

The Purpose of the Assignment

Writing a research paper gives you the opportunity to practice key academic writing skills, including locating and utilizing research materials, prewriting, drafting, and revision. It also requires you to take a position on a topic, create an argument, and support it with quotes and paraphrases from authoritative sources.

Purpose as a Writer

Your purpose as a writer is to convince readers to consider your argument carefully, and, if possible, to persuade them to agree with your point of view. To do this, include appropriate background material and definitions, as well as a consideration of opposing arguments.

Topic

Your topic should address a current issue about which you can take and support a position in the paper length your instructor specifies. Choose your topic carefully, as it should be one that engages your interest and enthusiasm.

Audience

Unless your instructor specifies otherwise, you can assume that your audience has general awareness of your issue but is unfamiliar with scholarly sources on the topic.

Sources

To do your research, you will need to utilize recent and credible sources that include a mix of recent books, scholarly articles, public speeches, and news articles. You may also use interviews, observation, and personal experience, if they are relevant to your topic. Sources will need to be cited in the text and in a works cited page or references page, according to MLA or APA style.

Information that you gather from your sources should support the argument you have created. A research paper is not an assignment in which you take information from sources and simply reorganize it into a paper. The expectation for this course is that you will use your sources to create an argument that is distinctly your own.

Thesis

Your essay should have a clear thesis that takes a position on an issue that can be supported within the word limitations of the assignment.

Rough Draft

As directed by your instructor, bring two copies of your rough draft essay to class for peer editing. The draft should have your sources credited in the text and should have a works cited page or references page.

Final Draft

Submit your final draft in MLA or APA format in a folder with your rough draft and copies of all of your source materials with the location of quotes or paraphrased material highlighted. If you are using material from a book or books, copy enough of the text before and after your quotes or paraphrases so that your instructor can determine the context of the material being quoted.

Reading 5.2

Film Review: *The Hangover* (2009)
by Owen Gleiberman

This film review by Owen Gleiberman appeared in EW.com. As you read the review, decide what you think is the author's position. How does he support his argument?

Going to Las Vegas for a "wild" bachelor party is now the ultimate middle-class hedonist cliché. It's not just that the jaunt has been done so often, in the movies as well as in life. It's that there's a contradiction embedded in the lure of the Vegas bacchanal. Men—and women too, of course—go there to be as reckless as humanly possible. But the naughtiness is so *organized* that there's not much recklessness left in it. Sure, you can craps-table your way to financial ruin, but the lap dances, the glorified college drinking binges, the ritualized ordering of hookers: It's all about as spontaneous as a shuffleboard tournament on a cruise ship.

The fun of *The Hangover*—what makes it more than just one what-happens-in-Vegas romp too many—is that the film completely understands all this. The four comrades who drive from Los Angeles to the Nevada desert to prepare for the wedding of Doug (Justin Bartha) aren't daring or cool; they aren't born swingers. They're an unglamorous Everyguy quartet, doing what they all think they're supposed to do. They're probably imitating Vegas movies as much as those films imitated reality.

Phil (Bradley Cooper), the one who's good-looking enough to strut into a casino like he owns it, is a junior-high teacher devoted to his wife and kid; Stu (Ed Helms), the group dweeb, is an anxious-eyed dentist who's like the 21st-century version of *American Graffiti*'s Terry the Toad, with a fascist girlfriend (Rachael Harris) who treats him like a slave; and Alan (Zach Galifianakis), so brick-stupid he qualifies as more nutzoid than dorkish, is a pudgy, bearded runt who stands up in the group's cruising convertible and shouts "Road trip!" That's an inside nod to the fact that Todd Phillips, the movie's director, made *Road Trip* as well, though it also indicates that these four think they're living inside a stupid teen comedy.

They arrive at their hotel, and the film then cuts to the next day, when they wake up in their trashed villa. There's a tiger in the bathroom, and a baby in the cabinet. Stu is missing his top right incisor; the groom is nowhere to be seen. And the thing is, none of them remembers . . . anything. *The Hangover* is structured, basically, as one long morning-after *OMG what have I done?*, and the kick of the film is that the discovery of what the characters have, in fact, done becomes the perfect comeuppance to their tidy fantasy of Vegas bliss. A light-buttered comic nightmare, like Martin Scorsese's *After Hours* (or Peter Berg's scandalous, overlooked *Very Bad Things* with things not nearly so bad), *The Hangover* is a riff on what the stuff you do when you're *really* out of control says about you.

The surprises in this movie are everything, so without giving much away, I'll just say that a Vegas chapel figures into the mix. So does a crowbar-wielding Asian gangster (Ken Jeong) who might be the epicene brother of Long Duk Dong in *Sixteen Candles*. There's also a juicy run-in with Mike Tyson. *The Hangover* has scattered laughs (many in the cathartically funny end-credit montage), but overall it's more amusing than hilarious. The most deftly acted character is Stu, played by Helms with a realistic alternating current of horror and liberation. As Alan, Zach Galifianakis makes blinkered idiocy a cartoon rush, though a little of him goes a long way. I wish Phillips, working from a script by the knockabout team of Jon Lucas and Scott Moore (*Ghosts of Girlfriends Past*), had nudged the characters closer to being a true shaggy-dog Apatow-style ensemble. You're always a little too aware that they're types. But it's fun seeing each of them have the "fun" they deserve.

Activity 5.3 **Discuss Review of *The Hangover***

1. Owen Gleiberman says that the "wild" bachelor party in Las Vegas has become a cliché. Is this true? What other films portray bachelor parties in Las Vegas?

2. What is different about the Vegas bachelor party in *The Hangover*, according to the review?

3. What is Gleiberman's thesis? What evidence does he offer to support his thesis?

4. Does the review make you want to see the movie, if you haven't? How so?

Activity 5.4 **Write a Film Review**

In this assignment, you are a film critic. Write a review that could appear in a newspaper, magazine, or blog. Your style and tone will be dictated by your audience, so identify the publication just under the title of your review by saying something like this: "Written for Undergroundfilms .com." Be sure to read several reviews published in your chosen media outlet.

1. Select a film you would like to review. Films that are social commentaries are particularly good for reviewing. It does not have to be a serious movie, but it should be one that makes you think about some social trend or historical event.

2. After you decide on a film, learn about its context. Who are the director, producer, and primary actors? What films have these individuals worked on before? Have they won awards? Are they known for a certain style? Read and annotate other reviews of the film, marking sections that you might paraphrase or quote to support your opinions.

3. What about the historical event or social context? Can you learn more about it to see if the film presents a reasonably accurate picture of that time and place (a kairos)? Is it based on a book? If so, what kind of a job does it do creating the world of the book?

4. Is the film persuasive? Does the film appeal to ethos, pathos, or logos? In what way?

5. Create a working thesis that makes an argument about the film. You can modify this thesis later, but it helps to identify early on what you want to argue.

6. Use some of the invention strategies in Chapter 4 to help you articulate what proofs you can use to support your argument.

7. Near the beginning of your draft, briefly summarize enough of the film that your review will be interesting to those who have not seen it. However, don't be a "spoiler." Don't ruin the film for potential viewers by giving away the ending.

8. Organize your essay into three main points that support your thesis and at least one counterargument that complicates or disagrees with your argument.

9. Write a compelling introduction that uses one of the approaches discussed in this chapter. You want your reader to be interested in what you have to say. For example, you might begin with a startling quote from the film or a vivid description of a pivotal scene.

10. Be sure to include specific examples and colorful details. These are essential to make your review interesting to the reader.

Activity 5.5: **Write an Op-Ed Argument**

The Op-Ed Project (www.theop-edproject.org) is an online initiative to "expand the range of voices" submitting op-ed essays to media outlets. According to its statistics, 80 to 90 percent of op-ed pieces are currently written by men, which is something it endeavors to change by helping women and members of other underrepresented groups develop the skills to get published in top media markets. Whether you are male or female, you may belong to an underrepresented group that is not having its voice heard as part of the national conversation about issues.

An op-ed is an opinion piece printed in a newspaper, magazine, blog, or other media outlet. The name derives from earlier times in print journalism when these opinion pieces would be printed on a page opposite the editorial page. Op-eds are written by individuals not affiliated with the publication, as opposed to editorials that are written by the publication's staff.

Tips for Op-Ed Writing from the Op-Ed Project

1. Own your expertise

Know what you are an expert in and why—but don't limit yourself. Consider the metaphors that your experience and knowledge suggest.

2. Stay current

Follow the news—both general and specific to your areas of specialty. If you write about Haiti, read the Haitian press. If you write about pop culture, read the media that cover it.

3. The perfect is the enemy of the good

In other words: write fast. You may have only a few hours to get your piece in before the moment is gone. But also . . .

4. Cultivate a flexible mind

Remember that a good idea may have more than one news hook; indeed, if the idea is important enough it can have many. So keep an eye out for surprising connections and new news hooks—the opportunity may come around again.

5. Use plain language

Jargon serves a purpose, but it is rarely useful in public debate, and can obfuscate—sorry, I mean cloud—your argument. Speak to your reader in straight talk.

6. Respect your reader

Never underestimate your reader's intelligence or overestimate her level of information. Recognize that your average reader is not an expert in your topic and that the onus is on you to capture her attention—and make the argument compel.

This assignment asks you to write an op-ed piece suitable for submission to a major newspaper or other media outlet. It does not require you to submit your text. That is up to you.

For this assignment, you need to do the following:

1. Read op-eds that appear in the major regional newspaper or other media outlet for your city, such as the *Chicago Tribune*, the *Washington Post*, or the *Arizona Republic*. The Op-Ed Project provides a list of the top 100 U.S. media outlets on its website. Read several op-eds to get a sense of the topics and style of the articles that the newspaper or other media outlet prints.

2. Notice that op-eds are not academic writing. They must be well-researched, but they also generally are written in a more casual and engaging style than traditional academic writing. You must first attract your audience's attention in order to present your case. Analyze how each op-ed you read captures the reader's interest.

3. Choose a topic that is timely and of interest to the readers of the publication that you choose. Research that topic using some of the tools in the research chapter of this textbook.

4. The length and structure of your op-ed should follow the pattern of pieces recently published in your publication.

5. Keep your audience in mind—the readers of the publication.

6. Follow the basic op-ed structure recommended by the Op-Ed Project, reprinted below.

7. Read the "Tips for Op-Ed Writing from the Op-Ed Project," in the sidebar.

(*Note*: A *lede* (or lead) is a journalism term that means the beginning of your article that catches your reader's attention and establishes your topic.)

Basic Op-Ed Structure from the Op-Ed Project
(*Note*: This is not a rule—just one way of approaching it.)

Lede (around a news hook)

Thesis (statement of argument—either explicit or implied)

Argument (based on evidence, such as stats, news, reports from credible organizations, expert quotes, scholarship, history, and first-hand experience)

- 1st Point
  - Evidence
  - Evidence
  - Conclusion
- 2nd Point
  - Evidence
  - Evidence
  - Conclusion
- 3rd Point
  - Evidence
  - Evidence
  - Conclusion

Note: In a simple, declarative op-ed ("policy X is bad; here's why"), this may be straightforward. In a more complex commentary, the 3rd point may expand on the bigger picture (historical context, global/geographic picture, mythological underpinnings, etc.) or may offer an explanation for a mystery that underpins the argument (e.g., why a bad policy continues, in spite of its failures).

"To Be Sure" paragraph (in which you preempt your potential critics by acknowledging any flaws in your argument and address any obvious counterarguments)

Conclusion (often circling back to your lede)

Activity 5.6 **Write on Your Blog**

Write an informal review of a film you have seen recently. What did you like and what did you dislike? Would you recommend the film to a friend?

Activity 5.7 **Write in Your Commonplace Book**

Find a piece from the Opinion/Editorial section of your local newspaper that interests you. If you were going to write a letter to the editor in response, what might you say?

The Casebook: In 2011, two professors launched a competition on the *Harvard Business Network* blog for designs to build $300 houses for the poor. Word of the competition spread quickly, and a wide variety of people began to write about the competition—in editorials in *The New York Times* and the *Economist* and in a companion blog, http://www.300house.com/blog.

Your Task: In Chapter 4 you read four articles about the $300 house competition. Read and discuss them in class and in small groups. Make a list of the different positions being argued in these texts and what evidence the writers offer to support their opinions. Then construct your own short research-based argument about the design competition or an op-ed essay (as your instructor specifies) agreeing with one of the positions or developing your own.

6
REVISING RHETORICALLY

Praxis in Action

How I Revise by Amber Lea Clark

Revising is an essential part of the writing process. One of the first things I do when I revise a paper is read with organization in mind. How is my introduction? Does my argument make sense? Did I transition well between points? Next, I look for words and phrases I have repeated too many times and look for other ways to say what I'm trying to say.

For me, a very necessary part of the revision process is reading the paper out loud to see how it flows. I look for any awkwardly worded sentences. It also helps me find typos and misused words. If I'm in a lab setting, I read very quietly, just mouthing the words. I might get a couple of funny looks but I don't care, it is a must when it comes to the revising process for me.

One of the best things to do in the revising process is set your paper aside and come back to it several hours or a day later. This requires some planning and an attempt not to procrastinate too much. Doing this allows me to look at my paper again with fresh eyes and see what I might have left out or want to say differently.

My mother always told me to have someone else give me feedback on my papers before I turn them in. This is valuable advice. I always have someone look over my papers and try to help others when they need someone to look at their papers. I ask the person who is proofing my paper to look for typos but also any sentences that do not make sense as they are worded. Is my argument coming through clearly?

Also, I always run my paper through the computer's spell check and grammar check. The computer will flag things as grammatically wrong that aren't, so I don't follow everything it says; but the computer also finds errors I haven't. Oh, be sure to spell the proper names right!

Amber Lea Clark says that one important part of her revision is setting her paper aside for a few hours or overnight and then looking at it with fresh eyes.

169

Revision Is Part of the Writing Process

In ancient times, the focus of the rhetor was upon the presentation of oral arguments in the form of speeches and students trained to perform in pressured situations before a law court or assembly. Though a speaker might spend time in preparation, most speeches were one-time opportunities. If the words were not well-chosen and well-spoken the first time, there was no second chance to influence an audience.

With modern written documents, a composition does not have to be perfect when the words first appear on the page. A document is not truly finished until it is transmitted to an audience, and, even then, important documents are often circulated in draft stages to colleagues for comments before they are presented to an audience.

Many writers claim that revising is the most rewarding step in writing, the time when they have words on a page to work with and can manipulate them to create a composition that communicates effectively. Yet, many students feel that their first drafts should stay exactly the way they've written them because these writings are truest to their feelings and experience. They are sure they have made their point clearly. In reality, a first draft often leaves the reader scratching his or her head and wondering what it was the writer meant to say. To communicate effectively, a writer must learn to interact with his reader to ensure he has communicated his message clearly.

Begin Revision by Rereading

The first step of revising is rereading. This step can be simple, if you are reading something written by someone else. When it is your own writing, it becomes infinitely more difficult. After all, you know what you meant to say—you know the research behind the writing and why you chose certain words or phrases. You even know how every sentence is supposed to read—even though you may have left out a word or two or three—and your mind can trick you into seeing the missing words right where they belong. Unfortunately, the reader does not have your understanding, and communication can break down. You need to learn to read your own work critically, as if it were written by a stranger. One of the first aids in this process is to read your work aloud. You can often hear stumbling blocks quicker than you can see them.

You can also learn to read your own work more objectively by reading and commenting on other writers' work. Look at the structure of essays, at the way the writers use transitions and topic sentences, and at the sentence structure and choice of words. As you learn to see how good writers put ideas and words together, you will begin to think about the readings in a more thorough manner—thinking of alternative, perhaps even better, ways to express the message of each essay. You will also learn to read your own work with a more critical eye.

Qualities of Effective Writing

Reading the work of some professional writers, you may have developed the idea that the best writing is writing that is difficult to understand, writing that sends the reader to the dictionary with every sentence, or writing that uses many technical or specialized terms. Often, we think something difficult to read must be well written. Although it is sometimes difficult to read about topics that are new to us because we're learning new vocabulary and struggling with complex ideas, it simply is not true that the best writing is hard to read. Indeed, the most effective writing, the kind of writing you want to produce in your classes, is simple, concise, and direct.

Keep It Simple

Simple means "unadorned" or "not ornate." *Writing simply* means saying something in common, concrete

William Safire's Rules for Writing

William Safire, long-time language enthusiast, political columnist, and contributor to "On Language" in the *New York Times Magazine*, has a little fun with grammar rules and myths.

- Remember to never split an infinitive.
- The passive voice should never be used.
- Do not put statements in the negative form.
- Verbs has to agree with their subjects.
- Proofread carefully to see if you words out.
- If you reread your work, you will find on rereading a great deal of repetition can be avoided by rereading and editing.
- A writer must not shift your point of view.
- And don't start a sentence with a conjunction. (Remember, too, a preposition is a terrible word to end a sentence with.)
- Don't overuse exclamation marks!!
- Place pronouns as close as possible, especially in long sentences, as of 10 or more words, to their antecedents.
- Writing carefully, dangling participles must be avoided.
- If any word is improper at the end of a sentence, a linking verb is.
- Take the bull by the hand and avoid mixing metaphors.
- Avoid trendy locutions that sound flaky.
- Everyone should be careful to use a singular pronoun with singular nouns in their writing.
- Always pick on the correct idiom.
- The adverb always follows the verb.
- Last but not least, avoid clichés like the plague; seek viable alternatives.

language without too much complication in the sentence structure. Writing simply doesn't mean you have to use only short or easy words. It doesn't mean that all your sentences will be simple sentences. It doesn't mean that you can't use figures of speech or intricate details. Simple writing means that you try to get your point across in a direct and interesting way. You aren't trying to hide your ideas. Instead, you are trying to amplify those ideas and begin an intelligible conversation with your reader.

Rely on Everyday Words

When writing about computers or other technical subjects, it's tempting to use **jargon** or specialized words you might use when talking to others with the same knowledge, interest, and background. When writing for a limited audience whose members are familiar with technical terms, a bit of jargon might be acceptable. However, most of the writing you will do in college and later in the workplace will address a larger audience. You will want to avoid the use of highly technical terms, acronyms, and abbreviations.

If it seems that the writers in this text use many big words or technical terms, stop for a minute to consider the original audience for each of the essays. Consider how your vocabulary grows each year as you read, discuss, and consider new ideas. The everyday words of a tenth grade student will probably be fewer in number than the everyday words of a junior in college. Similarly, the everyday words of a college freshman will be different from the everyday words of a computer professional with three years of work experience. Use words that are comfortable and familiar to you and your readers when you write, and you will write clear, effective essays.

Use Precise Words

We sometimes assume that the reader will know what we mean when we use adjectives like "beautiful," "quiet," or "slow." However, the reader has only his or her own ideas of those adjectives. You can make your writing more interesting and effective by adding concrete details to give the reader an image that uses at least two of the five senses.

You can use details from all of the senses to make your writing even more concrete and precise. What are some of the sensual qualities of the experience or thing? Can you compare it to another thing that your readers may be familiar with to help them understand it better? Can you compare it to something totally unlike it? Can you compare it to a different sense to surprise readers and help them understand the image you are trying to create?

A good way to practice your ability to write original concrete images is to expand on a cliché. A **cliché** is an overused saying or expression. Often, clichés begin as similes that help make images more concrete. They become clichéd or overused because they lose their originality or they don't contain enough detail to give us the entire picture. Choose a cliché and write a sentence that expands the cliché and uses the senses to create a clear picture of the thing described. You might try some of the following clichés:

> She is as pretty as a picture.
>
> It smelled heavenly.
>
> It was as soft as a baby's bottom.
>
> His heart is as hard as stone.
>
> It tastes as sour as a pickle.
>
> We stared at the roaring campfire.
>
> We listened to the babbling brook.

Precise details allow us to experience the world of the writer. We leave our own views and perceptions and learn how someone else sees the world. We learn what "quiet" is like for one writer and what "beautiful" means to another. Fill in the gaps between your words and ideas with vivid images and your writing will become more interesting and more effective.

Be Concise

Rid your writing of excess words and leave only that which makes your meaning clear and concrete. Becoming aware of several common problems can help you make your writing more concise. When you begin a sentence with either "it is" or "there is," you transfer all the meaning of the sentence to the end of the sentence. This is known as a **delayed construction**. You have delayed the meaning. The reader must read on to find out what "it" or "there" refer to. They don't get anything important from the beginning of the sentence.

> Examine the following sentences:
>
> > It is important to change the oil in older gasoline engines.
> >
> > There is an apple on the table.
> >
> > There isn't anything we need to fear except our own fear.

We can rewrite these sentences, making them more concise, by deleting the "there is" or the "it is" and restructuring the sentence.

Changing the oil in older gasoline engines is important.

An apple is on the table.

We have nothing to fear but fear itself.

Notice that the second group of sentences is shorter and the important information is no longer buried in the middle. Revising this type of sentence can make your writing more concise and get information to the reader more effectively.

If you think you may be guilty of using "it is" and "there is" (or "it's" and "there's") too often, you can use most word processing programs to seek these constructions out. Use the "search" or "find and replace" tool that's found in the Edit portion of your pull-down menu. Type "it is" and ask your computer to find every place you use this construction in your document. When you find a sentence that begins with "it is," revise the sentence to make it more concise. Do the same with "there is," "it's," and "there's." After you become more aware of these errors by correcting them, you'll find that you notice the errors before or as you make them. You will begin to write more concisely, and you'll have fewer delayed constructions to revise.

You can also make your writing more concise by avoiding common wordy expressions. Sometimes when we're nervous about writing or insecure about our knowledge of a topic, we try to hide that insecurity behind a wall of meaningless words, such as in the following sentence:

At this point in time, you may not have the ability to create a web page due to the fact that you've avoided using computers for anything other than playing Solitaire.

This sentence is full of deadwood phrases that add no meaning to the sentence. If we take out the unneeded words, we have this sentence:

You may not be able to create a web page because you've only used your computer to play Solitaire.

Your computer may have a grammar checker that will identify some commonly used wordy expressions. If your computer doesn't have a grammar checker, or if your instructor has asked you not to use the grammar checker in your computer, you can still learn to revise the wordiness out of your paragraphs. Use the computer to separate a paragraph of your writing into sentences. As you scroll through the paragraph, hit the hard return or "Enter" key on your keyboard twice every time you find a period. Once you have separated the sentences, look at each sentence. What is the important idea in the sentence? What words are used to convey that idea? What words don't add any meaning to the sentence? Delete words that don't convey meaning, and revise the sentence to make it more concise.

Use Action Verbs

Action verbs are words that convey the action of a sentence. They carry much of our language's nuance and meaning. Many inexperienced writers use only "to be" verbs: *am, is, are, was, were, be, been,* and *being.* If you use too many of these verbs, you risk losing much of the power of language. If I say someone is coming through the door, I've created a picture of a body and a doorway. If I say someone marches or slinks through the door, I've added information not only about movement but also about the quality of that movement. I've given my subject the attitude of a soldier or a cat. For example, consider this sentence written by Howard Rheingold:

> Thirty thousand years ago, outside a deceptively small hole in a limestone formation in the area now known as southern France, several adolescents shivered in the dark, awaiting initiation into the cult of toolmakers.

By using the verb "shivered," especially when accompanied by the words "in the dark," Rheingold paints a word picture much more vivid than he would have conveyed with the use of a "to be" verb. Using interesting verbs can enliven your writing.

If you want to focus upon using more action verbs, skim through your essay and circle all the "to be" verbs. Read the sentences with circled "to be" verbs more closely, and choose several to rewrite using active verbs in place of the "to be" verbs. You won't be able to do this for every sentence, but replace them where you can and your writing will become more lively, more concise, and more effective.

Fill in the Gaps

When we write, we sometimes forget that we are writing to an audience other than ourselves. We expect that our readers are people just like us, with our experiences, memories, and tastes. Because we have assumed they're so much like us, we expect our readers to be able to read more than what we've written on the page. We expect them to read our minds. We may leave large gaps in our essays, hoping the reader will fill in exactly the information we would have included.

If I'm writing an essay about my childhood in the South and I say it was always so hot in the summer that I hated to go outside, I might think my reader knows what I mean by hot. However, there are many different ways to be "hot." In east Texas where I grew up, the hot was a sticky hot. Eighty degrees made me long for a big glass of sweetened iced tea with lots of ice. The heat made my clothes cling. Sweating didn't help because the sweat didn't dry. I spent the day feeling as if I'd never dried off after my morning shower. In New Mexico, I never really felt hot unless the temperature got above 110 degrees. At that point, the heat would rush at me, making it difficult to breathe. I would open the door to leave the house, and it felt as if I had opened the oven door to check on a cake. If I say I was hot in the summer without describing how heat felt to me, my reader may not get the message I'm trying to convey. Don't expect your reader to know what you mean by "hot" or by any other general description. Instead, take a minute to add details that will fill in the gaps for the reader.

Speak Directly

To *speak directly* is to say, up front, who is doing what. Sometimes we don't tell the reader who is completing the action or we tell them too late. Let's look at the following sentences:

> The steak was stolen from the grill.

> The decisive battle was fought between the Confederate and the Union armies in Vicksburg, Mississippi.

> The red truck has been driven into the side of the green car.

Although we might be able to guess who the actors are in each of the sentences, the first and last sentences don't tell us directly. Even if the reader can guess that it was a dog who stole the steak from the grill or my neighbor who drove the red truck into the side of the green car, the reader has to stop and figure out who is doing what before he or she can read on. This slows the reader down and diminishes the effectiveness of your writing.

Language professionals call this **passive voice**. The action comes before the actor. Note that sometimes, as in the first and last sentences above, the writer doesn't mention the actor at all. To identify passive verbs in your writing, look for verbs coupled with another action word that ends in "-ed" or "-en" such as "was stolen" or "was forgotten."

Find the action and the actor in the sentence to make sure that they are in the most effective order. The most effective sentence order is actor first, then action. If the sentence does not specify the actor but leaves it implied, chances are that it is a passive sentence. For example, read this sentence: "The red truck was driven into the green car." It does not say who the driver was, and thus it is a passive sentence.

Rewriting some of your sentences to eliminate use of the passive voice will make your writing stronger and more interesting.

President Barack Obama has won high marks for his verbal eloquence, as illustrated by this cartoon published in the *International Herald Tribune*. His 2004 Keynote Speech at the Democratic National Convention and his best-selling book, *The Audacity of Hope*, helped propel him to national prominence.

Activity 6.1 **When You Reeeaaallly Want to Describe Something**

This activity requires a thesaurus or access to the Visual Thesaurus website (http://www.visualthesaurus.com).

1. Strunk and White's *The Elements of Style,* in an entry on "Misused Words and Expressions," says,

   "*Very.* Use this word sparingly. Where emphasis is necessary, use words strong in themselves."

   With a partner, paraphrase and discuss this Strunk and White writing tip.

2. To demonstrate Strunk and White's advice in (1) above, revise the following sentence, getting rid of the adverb "very."

   Julie is very pretty.

   No, don't say, "Julie is beautiful." Make a list of more precise and vivid words that could be used instead. Refer to a thesaurus (or the Visual Thesaurus website) to find words such as "stunning" and so on.

3. As a class, brainstorm other intensifying adverbs such as "awfully" or "extremely" that you tend to use as words of emphasis (in writing or in everyday speech) and list those words on the board.

4. In pairs again, compose a short paragraph of two or three sentences about a subject or event (e.g., a tornado, a celebrity sighting, a sports event, a news event, a concert, etc.) and intentionally use as many common or trite intensifying words as possible.

5. Exchange the short paragraph you composed in (4) above with another pair of classmates. Revise the other partnership's dialogue with the use of a thesaurus. The revised dialogue should not contain any "intensifiers" or trite words of emphasis. Replace such words and phrases with more powerful and concise language. For example, "I was really happy to see the Hornets win. They totally beat the Giants," could be revised to read (with the help of more concise and powerful words): "I was euphoric to see the Hornets thrash the Giants."

6. Read your "before" and "after" dialogues to the class. Afterward, discuss which words were eliminated and how the words that replaced those intensifiers changed the tone and/or meaning of the dialogue.

Source: Adapted from a lesson plan, "When You Reeeaaallly Want to Say Something," from the Visual Thesaurus website, http://www.visualthesaurus .com/cm/lessons/1450.

Remember to Proofread

It is understandably difficult to find the errors in an essay you have been working on for days. A few tricks used by professional writers might help you see errors in your essay more clearly.

1. With pencil in hand, read the essay aloud, slowly—and preferably to an audience. When you are reading aloud, it is more difficult to add or change words, so you tend to catch errors you would not see reading silently to yourself. Plus the reactions of your audience may point out areas where future readers may become confused or lose interest.

2. Another trick is to read the essay backwards, sentence by sentence. This forces you to look at sentence structure and not at the overall content of the essay. If you are working on a computer, another way to accomplish this is to create a final edit file in which you hit the hard return twice at the end of every question or statement. You might even go so far as to number the sentences so they look more like grammar exercises. Then look at each sentence individually.

Reading 6.1

Grammar Girl's Top Ten Grammar Myths
by Mignon Fogarty, quickanddirtytips.com

In this blog entry by Mignon Fogarty, she offers her top-ten list of grammar mistakes and misunderstandings.

10. **A run-on sentence is a really long sentence.** Wrong! They can actually be quite short. In a run-on sentence, independent clauses are squished together without the help of punctuation or a conjunction. If you write "I am short he is tall," as one sentence without a semicolon, colon, or dash between the two independent clauses, it's a run-on sentence even though it only has six words.

9. **You shouldn't start a sentence with the word "however."** Wrong! It's fine to start a sentence with "however" so long as you use a comma after it when it means "nevertheless."

8. **"Irregardless" is not a word. Wrong!** "Irregardless" is a bad word and a word you shouldn't use, but it is a word. "Floogetyflop" isn't a word—I just made it up and you have no idea what it means. "Irregardless," on the other hand, is in almost every dictionary labeled as nonstandard. You shouldn't use it if you want to be taken seriously, but it has gained wide enough use to qualify as a word.

7. **There is only one way to write the possessive form of a word that ends in "s." Wrong!** It's a style choice. For example, in the phrase "Kansas's statute," you can put just an apostrophe at the end of "Kansas" or you can put an apostrophe "s" at the end of "Kansas." Both ways are acceptable.

6. **Passive voice is always wrong. Wrong!** Passive voice is when you don't name the person who's responsible for the action. An example is the sentence "Mistakes were made," because it doesn't say who made the mistakes. If you don't know who is responsible for an action, passive voice can be the best choice.

5. **"i.e." and "e.g." mean the same thing. Wrong!** "e.g." means "for example," and "i.e." means roughly "in other words." You use "e.g." to provide a list of incomplete examples, and you use "i.e." to provide a complete clarifying list or statement.

4. **You use "a" before words that start with consonants and "an" before words that start with vowels. Wrong!** You use "a" before words that start with consonant sounds and "an" before words that start with vowel sounds. So, you'd write that someone has an MBA instead of a MBA, because even though "MBA" starts with "m," which is a consonant, it starts with the sound of the vowel "e"—MBA.

3. **It's incorrect to answer the question "How are you?" with the statement "I'm good." Wrong!** "Am" is a linking verb and linking verbs should be modified by adjectives such as "good." Because "well" can also act as an adjective, it's also fine to answer "I'm well," but some grammarians believe "I'm well" should be used to talk about your health and not your general disposition.

2. **You shouldn't split infinitives. Wrong!** Nearly all grammarians want to boldly tell you it's OK to split infinitives. An infinitive is a two-word form of a verb. An example is "to tell." In a split infinitive, another word separates the two parts of the verb. "To boldly tell" is a split infinitive because "boldly" separates "to" from "tell."

1. **You shouldn't end a sentence with a preposition. Wrong!** You shouldn't end a sentence with a preposition when the sentence would mean the same thing if you left off the preposition. That means "Where are you at?" is wrong because "Where are you?" means the same thing. But there are many sentences where the final preposition is part of a phrasal verb or is necessary to keep from making stuffy, stilted sentences: "I'm going to throw up," "Let's kiss and make up," and "What are you waiting for" are just a few examples.

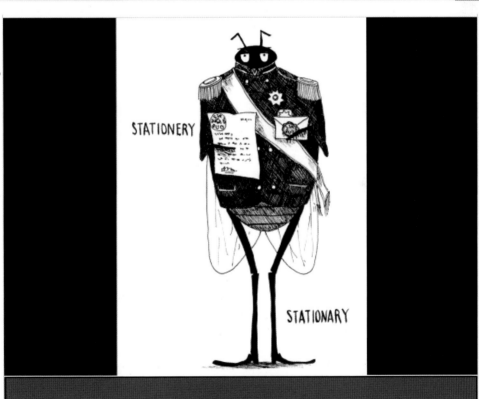

STATIONERY

STATIONARY

Stationary means "fixed in place, unable to move;" ***stationery*** is letterhead or other special writing paper. (Hint: ***Station<u>e</u>ry*** with an **e** comes with an **e**nvelope.) Examples: Evan worked out on his ***stationary*** bike. The duke's initials and crest appeared atop his personal ***stationery***.

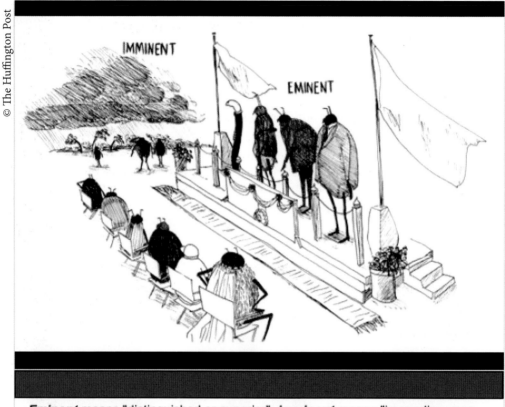

Eminent means "distinguished or superior"; *imminent* means "impending, sure to happen." Also, *eminent* domain is the right of a government to take over private property for public use. Examples: The rain was *imminent*; it would arrive soon, soaking the *eminent* dignitaries on the stage. (Think of *imminent* and *impending*, which both begin with the same letters.)

Reading 6.2

Top Ten Distractions for Writers, or Any Job Really

by Sam Scham

The following list, "Top Ten Distractions for Writers, or Any Job Really," by Sam Scham, was published in the Yahoo Contributor Network.

When you have a set goal in mind, whether it is for personal or work reasons, so many other things can become easy distractions. For writers in particular, life seems to get in the way. There are other pressing matters that we have to worry about.

1. The Internet

The Internet is a very huge distraction these days. For writers who do research online for their great idea, it is easy to stumble upon different links and steer away from the main point in focus. If you find yourself doing this, try to limit the time you do research therefore getting off the Internet earlier and allow more time for writing.

2. The Radio

Music can help a writer generate ideas and feelings. Listening to the radio can be a distraction if you leave it on for too long. If you are like me, you are able to write the best in silence. You need to be able to hear yourself think. If you are listening to the radio and it is hard to turn away from it, listen to it in segments. Listen to some music and when a commercial comes on, mute the radio and start writing. Maybe, before you know it, you will forget that you were ever listening to the radio.

3. The Television

The television and the radio are similar in many ways. For one, it is hard to turn off, especially if you are in the middle of a show that you want to finish. But then, you see a commercial for what is coming up next and you are intrigued to watch it. At the end of the current show, turn off the TV and get writing. Soon, you will not notice the absence of the picture box.

4. Own Procrastination

You want to sit down and write, but at the same time you don't, you have no motivation. The solution is to take a day off, do not think of it at all. Work on any other pressing matters like home chores or calling up an old friend that you've been meaning to catch up with. On the next day, wake up and get writing. Just jump right into it and it will be like you never took a break.

5. Other People

Especially if you live with family or friends other people always being around can be a huge distraction. In order to solve this, find out when everyone will be out and fit in time to write while they are gone. If that just doesn't work with your everyday schedule, find a nice place outside or at the local library where you can work in peace without other people bugging you.

6. Other Responsibilities

Work, chores, walking the dog; these everyday responsibilities are tiring and at the end of the day you just cannot get the energy to write. Try writing in the morning, even if it is just for a few minutes. Get the best out of what you got and do not get discouraged.

7. Telephones

With cell phones these days, you can be getting texts at every minute either from friends or social networks. When you are writing, the best way to refrain from your cell phone is by turning it completely off and leaving it somewhere out of sight so that you are not tempted to check it.

8. Outdoor Activities

Especially on a really nice day, you may want to forget the writing and spend some time outdoors. That is completely fine. Enjoy life to the fullest. If you end up not writing for the day, remember that there is always tomorrow. But be careful not to put it off for too long and too often. If you really want to spend time outside, take the writing with you and kill two birds with one stone.

9. Everyday Needs

You need to eat sometime and when you work and do everything else, cooking can really tire you out and make you not want to write. On those days, try to make simple meals if you absolutely do not want to order out. There is nothing wrong with having a bowl of cereal for dinner.

10. Being Bored

We all get bored sometimes, even of our own writing. Take a break. Do not work on writing your big project, but work on something else. A day or two later go back to that big project and start working on writing it again and if you are still bored, put it to the side again. At least you cannot say that you did not try.

Activity 6.2 Write a List of Your Writing Habits

As you write an essay assigned by your instructor, keep notes about your writing process. What distracts or keeps you from writing? What works well when you write? What kind of prewriting do you do? What are the best (or worst) conditions for you when you write?

Organize your notes about your writing process into a theme such as "Best Places to Write" or "Ways to Avoid Procrastinating." As Sam Scham does, write two or three sentences about each of your writing habits.

Gain Feedback by Peer Editing

Your instructor may schedule class periods for peer workshops. These workshops are opportunities for you to get responses from your readers. Often, you will be divided into groups of three or four students and you will be given a list of questions to answer about your peers' essays. Your peers will get copies of your essay, and they will give you comments as well. The first peer workshop can be a difficult experience. It is never easy to take criticism, constructive or not. Taking criticism in a small group is even more difficult. There are several things you can do to make your peer groups more productive.

When Your Essay Is Being Reviewed

1. Write down everything the reviewers say. You think you will remember it later, but often you will forget just that piece of advice you need. More importantly, writing while the reviewers speak is an effective way to keep the channels of communication open. It is hard to come up with a defense for your paper if you are busy writing.

2. Save your comments until all the reviewers are done. If you have specific questions, write them in the margins of your notes. If they ask you questions, make a note to answer them when everyone is done. If you allow yourself to speak, you will be tempted to start defending your essay. Once you start defending your essay, two things happen. First, you stop listening to the comments. Second, you offend your reviewers, making it less likely that they will give you honest criticism in the future.

3. The first comment you should make to your reviewers is "Thank you." The second comment can be anything but a defense. Your readers are only telling you how they have interpreted your essay. They are giving you their opinions; you do not have to make the changes they suggest.

4. Save all the comments you get on your essay. Set them aside for a day or so. Then make the changes that you think will make your essay better.

When You Are the Reviewer

1. Read an essay through, at least one time, just to browse the content of the essay. Appreciate the essay for what it does well. Try to ignore any problems for now. You will get back to them the second time you read and begin your comments in the margins. Every essay will have at least one thing about it that is good.

2. Always begin your comments with a sincere discussion of what you like about the essay.

3. Be specific in your comments. Your peers will probably understand you better if you say, "The topic sentence in paragraph four really sets the reader up for what the essay accomplishes in paragraph four. But I can't really find a topic sentence for paragraph six, and the topic sentences in paragraphs two and three could be improved." Note how this statement gives a positive response and then identifies specific places where the author can improve the essay. This works much better than a generalized statement like, "Topic sentences need work."

4. Be descriptive in your comments. It is often helpful for students to hear how you are reading their essays. "Paragraph five seems to be telling me . . . " or "I got the feeling the essay's overall message is . . . " are good ways to start descriptive sentences.

5. Realize that you are analyzing a paper and not a person. Directing your comments toward the essay, "Paragraph nine doesn't really have anything new to add, does the paper need it?" sounds better to the listener than "You repeat yourself in paragraph nine. Do you really need it?"

Independent Reviewing

If your instructor does not require peer editing, you can ask someone to review your essay. Choose someone you trust to give you an honest opinion. It might not be effective to ask a parent, spouse, or girlfriend/boyfriend to give you a critique if you know they are going to like anything you write, just because you wrote it. It might be better to ask another student who has recently had an English class or one of your current classmates. In exchange, you might offer to look over their work. Remember, you learn to read your own essays better by reading other peoples' essays more critically.

Sample Questions for Peer Review

When you have revised your paper several times, have someone answer these questions regarding its overall content, paragraph development, and word choice and sentence structure.

Overall Content

1. What is the thesis or main point of the essay? Where does the writer state this main point? If the main point is implied rather than stated, express it in a sentence. Does the main point give a subject and an opinion about the subject? How might the writer improve his/her thesis?

2. What is the purpose of this essay? What are the characteristics of the audience the writer seems to be addressing (formal, fun-loving, serious, cynical, laid-back, etc.)?

Paragraph Development

1. Do each of the paragraphs in the essay work to support the main point of the essay? Which paragraphs seem to wander from that main point? What other information needs to be added to develop the main point?

2. List two places in the essay where the writer uses vivid sensory details. How effective are those details? Are they used to support the thesis of the essay? Identify two places in the essay where the writer needs more effective details. What kind of details might he or she include?

3. What grade would you give the introduction? How does it draw the reader into the essay? What specific things can the writer do to make the introduction more inviting?

4. Which paragraph do you like the best? Why? Which paragraph in the essay do you like the least? Why? What can the writer do to improve his/her paragraphs?

5. What grade would you give the conclusion? How does it provide closure for the essay? What specific things can the writer do to make the conclusion more effective?

Word Choice and Sentence Structure

1. Are adequate transitions used between the paragraphs? Find an effective paragraph transition and identify it. Why does it work? Find two places between paragraphs that need more or better transitions. What can the writer do to improve these transitions?

2. Are a variety of sentences used? Where might the writer vary the sentence structure for better effect? What two sentences in the essay did you find most effective? Why?

3. Are there any words that seem misused or out of place? What positive or negative trigger words are used? Do they enhance the message of the essay or detract from it?

Activity 6.3 Peer Editing of Sample Student Essay

As your instructor directs, either individually or in groups, peer edit one of the following sample student papers and then answer the questions regarding overall content, paragraph development, and word choice and sentence structure listed in the above section, Sample Questions for Peer Review. Then discuss your peer editing in your small groups, comparing your answers to those of others in your group.

Sample Student Essay for Peer Editing, Profile Assignment

Longing for Better Days

As she sits in her cramped room in Amman, Jordan, watching the recent news, Aysha Mustafa, 92, is saddened by the world she lives in today. As she places her wrinkled hands on her lap and begins to recall a time when things were pleasant, tears begin to flow down her cheeks. Those times are long gone she says. Aysha moved from Palestine to Jordan after the sudden death of her husband in 1995. Moving here was tough she says, "It was hard to leave my country." Aysha's story goes back 60 years ago, where she lived in her homeland Palestine. She recalls her childhood as being peaceful and joyous. She smiles as she describes memories of her and her brother riding in the back of her father's wagon. "Life was good," she says. Although her family had very little to live on, she was still happy.

Like many Palestinians, Aysha still dreams to one day return back and live in her homeland Palestine, where she longs to rekindle sweet memories there. "Jordan is fine she says but I rather live on the land that is mine." As we sit in the living room watching the crisis in Gaza in January 2009, Aysha begins to wipe the tears from her sad yet hopeful eyes, and reiterates with a sigh in her voice, "May God be with them." The appalling images of young children being killed by Israeli rockets leave 92 year old Aysha in distress. How many more men, women and children will die before both sides reach an agreement she questions? As her grandson flips through the channels, he crosses upon the Al-Jazeera news that announces that the number killed in Gaza has reached the disturbing number of 781. She suddenly lowers her head and gazes into space. . "It kills me to see my people getting killed like this," she stutters trying to hold back tears. The Israeli and Palestinian conflict has been going on for more than 60 years now. Many innocent civilians of both sides have been killed due to this grotesque war.

Despite all of this, it is people like Aysha that still carry hope that one day they will return back to their homeland and live in peace and harmony. Aysha's wish like many others is for all Palestinians to live a life of security and freedom, freedom to make their own choices and decisions on their own land. Aysha struggles to explain how as a child she used to run around in the fields freely, fearing no one or anything. "The feeling of freedom is indescribable," she says. "I was free to walk and go as I pleased, with no blockades to hold me back."

Today however, boys and girls in Palestine do not share the same luxury that Aysha experienced before the occupation. It is heart breaking watching this old yet strong willed woman recalling her childhood memories. Suddenly, Aysha begins to hold her chest and breathe heavily; her grandson approaches her and gives her her heart medicine. He explains that talking about such a personal and stressful topic leaves his grandmother feeling tired and overwhelmed. She has a weak heart, "My days are getting shorter," she says. Aysha is an inspiration, throughout this interview she kept calm and never wavered or seemed weak. One would think she would be vulnerable to everything surrounding her, but on the contrary she was full of wisdom. When asked what she hoped for, she said with a confident tone, "My people will see better days than this; I know this for a fact. They will be happy again; mothers will no longer be forced to bury their children. The day of justice and freedom is near, I can feel it." As she said this, Aysha seemed certain that this war will not last very long. Many Palestinians have the same hopes as Aysha, they too are confident that the day will come when their people will believe in security again.

Aysha is one of many Palestinians who shares the same dream as millions, which is a liberated and a prosperous Palestine. As she stands up and leans on her cane she says, "We want our rights, we want justice, we want freedom on our land, and we want Palestine."

Aysha's final words were that she prays that once her soul rests, she hopes to be buried next to her husband's grave on the holy land of Palestine.

Sample Student Essay for Peer Editing, Rhetorical Analysis Assignment

Rhetorical Analysis of President Reagan's "Challenger Speech"

FIVE, FOUR, THREE, TWO, ONE, WE HAVE LIFT OFF! THE SPACE SHUTTLE CHALLENGER HAS CLEARED THE LAUNCH PAD. This was supposed to be a glorious day in American history, a mile stone in the United States Space Program. Instead this day quickly turned into one of the most horrific scenes witnessed live by the American public, which included thousands of school children, who watched from the comfort and safety of their classrooms.

On January 28, 1986, the space shuttle Challenger was scheduled for launch in Florida. It would mark the second flight by the United States Space program and it was the first educational launch program. On this particular flight there was to be a teacher on board, she was the first teacher on a space shuttle as a result of a special program from NASA. Although there were some clear concerns regarding whether the shuttle should launch, NASA officials gave the green light and the mission moved forward. Within seconds of lift off, the space shuttle Challenger burst into flames and disintegrated in mid flight, instantly killing all seven passengers aboard. The nation was shocked, especially thousands of young children who eagerly watched the live coverage on television. Within hours of the explosion President Ronald Reagan went on live television and addressed the nation from the White House. President Reagan was scheduled to address the nation on that particular day to report on the state of the Union, instead he went on television and paid tribute to the Challenger Seven. President Reagan delivered one of the most inspirational, and motivational speeches of his tenure as the President of the United States. It is a speech, like all great speeches, that would out live his presidency, and be regarded as one of the great speeches of our time.

The nation stood still, not knowing what to make of the days events. In such times of sorrow people tend to need support, guidance, and reassurance. The American people needed someone to follow, a shoulder to lean on, a vision of the future, a leader. President Reagan went on live television and paid tribute to the "Challenger Seven" in a speech from the White House. President Reagan sat alone behind a large desk surrounded in the background by family pictures. President Reagan used his ethos as a credible individual; he was the leader of the free Nation. He gave the speech from the White House, which is clearly recognized by the American public as a symbol of power and security. The image of him sitting behind a great desk flanked by pictures of family and loved ones borrowing once again from their ethos. This was a not only the President of the United States delivering this speech, this was a husband, a father, and a son too.

The occasion for the speech was obvious: The Nation had just witnessed seven brave individuals perish before their very eyes. These brave souls were, husbands, sons, daughters, fathers, and they had paid the ultimate sacrifice for mankind. President Reagan portrayed all of these different roles played by each of the "Challenger Seven" from behind that desk. As the speech proceeded, President Reagan was careful to not down play the Challenger incident, but he appealed to logos, or logic, by saying "But we have never lost an astronaut in flight. We've never had a tragedy like this one." Here he used pathos to emphasize the severity of the incident while at the same time letting the nation know that there have been other brave astronauts who have also paid the ultimate price for the visions and progress of mankind. President Reagan throughout his speech used his words very carefully and with great insight. His words and the double meaning or relation to the events of the day made a huge impact on the delivery and acceptance of his speech by the American public. As he stated "Your loved ones were daring and brave, and they had that special grace, that spirit that says, Give me a challenge, and I'll meet it with joy." As one can see, President Reagan is using the word challenge here, this is a direct reference to the space shuttle Challenger.

President Reagan goes on to address the thousands of children who also witnessed the event, addressing the emotion or pathos of the occasion. He states, "And I want to say something to the schoolchildren of America who were watching the live coverage of the shuttle's take-off. I know it's hard to understand, but sometimes painful things like this happen. It's all part of the process of exploration and discovery. It is all part of taking a chance and expanding man's horizons. The future doesn't belong to the fainthearted; it belongs to the brave. The Challenger crew was pulling us into the future, and we'll continue to follow them." Here President Reagan's audience is the children, who in turn are the future of the nation. By saying that the Challenger was taking them towards the future, he is saying what everybody already knows. The children are the future of the nation and he is telling them that they must continue to move forward, for one day they will be the leaders of the country.

President Reagan's message is very clear: This was a tragedy, yet we as a nation must continue to move forward in order to honor the memory of the "Challenger Seven." President Reagan, utilizing logos, then mentions the

NASA employees in his speech. Here he does not blame or degrade the space program or its employees. Instead he praises there hard work and dedication to the American people and the space program. He does not speculate on the cause of the explosion nor does he address any issues related to who is to blame. He completely omits any negative or accusatory comments in his speech. This was a very tactful and extremely intelligent move by Reagan. He knew the American public had many questions regarding the explosion. He also knew that those questions needed to be answered and that it was his responsibility to provide those answers to the nation. Yet on this day, and in this speech, it was not the right time to do so.

President Reagan in closing his speech borrows from the ethos of the past when he stated "There's a coincidence today. On this day three hundred and ninety years ago, the great explorer Sir Francis Drake died aboard ship off the coast of Panama… a historian later said, He lived by the sea, died on it, and was buried in it. Well, today, we can say of the Challenger crew: their dedication was, like Drake's complete."

President Reagan's speech on the space shuttle Challenger served several purposes. First, it paid tribute to the seven astronauts who lost their lives in the explosion. Second, it provided the nation with a much needed reassurance that everything was going to be all right. And although this was terrible accident and set back for our country, he also left no doubt that the Nations commitment to NASA and the space program would not only survive, but continue to advance forward into the future.

Sample Student Essay for Peer Editing, Short Op-Ed Argument

Women in Combat

It is without a doubt that most of us have seen, read, or even heard about women in foreign countries, specifically the Middle East, being victims of sexual discrimination in male dominated work. But, would anyone possibly imagine, that even at a smaller scale, it occurs right here right now. This op-ed piece focuses on women in combat. While some countries do allow women to fight in combat, it seems archaic that the leader of the free world and by many referred as the #1 nation in the world, that we still bar women from certain roles in the military.

The most common fallacies believed by many include, women's enervated strength. Or, there psychological structure is so that they are considered nurturers not murderers. The most archaic mentality yet is that women are a distraction to men. The list can go on, but the above seems to be the most common misconceptions.

The case against the strength of a woman seems irrefutable. No one can argue that in general men are stronger than women. But there are many factors to be considered in arguing the rebuttal. For instance, the double standards set by our military. The annual Physical fitness test clearly subordinates the female's potential physical ability. A study conducted in Great Britain by the Ministry of Defense concluded that "women can be built to the same levels of physical fitness as men of the same size and build" (Shepard, 2007). How can we expect a woman to perform closer to a man's standards when we delude her understanding of what it really takes to achieve physical fitness? Would it be any different if we took a male chef and only taught him how to cook appetizers, then graded him for the entire meal including entre and desert?

Psychological structure is also a hot topic. Women are nurturers, not murderers. Kingsley Browne, author of Co-Ed Combat, The New Evidence Why Women shouldn't Fight the Nation's Wars, made a diluted attempt to answer this question by stating "There are large differences in men and women and willingness to take Physical risks. For example something like 93% of work place deaths are men" (Traders Nation, 2007). While men seem quite capable to murdering, Browne failed to cite that women are also capable of committing heinous crimes, as evidenced by the 2.1 million women serving sentences in American Prisons for violent crimes (Shepard, 2007).

Psychological Structure is an important factor in wars, as Browne reiterates. "Women's greater fear of death and injury and greater aversion to physical risks are likely to affect their combat performance negatively" (Arron, 2007). Clearly not all women are cut out for combat. But if we use this formula, it is also evidenced that not all men are cut out for combat. It is said that over 100,000 men panicked at the thought of going to the Vietnam War and fled the country to avoid the draft (Shepard, 2007). Surely any veteran of any War would consider this a perfect paradigm of a coward?

Another myth is that, women are a distraction to men. While the idea may rain ring true one could also conclude that any soldier, male or female, that is so easily distracted may be a danger not only to themselves but also to the unit they serve. While this conclusion does not rectify that argument, it does show the weak rationales that women face. Furthermore this mentality sends society the message that it's acceptable to punish/exclude women from full participation due to men's personal failings. Since World War One female nurses have served on the front line, and it has never been documented that women distract men (Jericho, 2008, p. 8).

This topic clearly incites emotions from opponents and proponents of women in combat. Women deserve attention to the matter starting with the Pentagon ensuring our women are properly trained and given the tools to succeed. But the story doesn't begin there, it begins at home. If we cannot treat a boy and a girl the same when growing up, why should we expect anyone to treat them any different as adults. How many times do we see a girl with a dole while the father teaches the son to hunt? Or watch a father rough house with his son, while the mother teaches her daughter how to apply makeup? Give your sister the tools and she will build you a bridge.

References

Arron. (2007) The Clock Stopped. Retrieved from: http://thestoppedclock. blogspot.com/2007/12/cowardly-untrustworthy-women.html

Jericho, J. (2008) Effectiveness of the Sex Discrimination Act. Retrieved from: http://www.aph.gov.au/Senate/committee/legcon_ctte/sex_ discrim/submissions/sub02.pdf

Sheppard, c. (2007) Women in Combat. Strategy Research Project. Retreived from: http://www.carlisle.army.mil/usawc/Registar/ policies.cfm

Traders Nation. (2007) Retrevied from: http://www.youtube.com/ watch?v=1VgAd3WdaD0

Activity 6.4 **Write on Your Blog**

Choose one of your previous blog postings, and revise it using the suggestions provided in this chapter.

Activity 6.5 **Write in Your Commonplace Book**

Choose one of the readings in this chapter that you think could be improved, and write in your commonplace book about how it could be changed. Give specific examples.

7
RESEARCHING RHETORICALLY

Praxis in Action

How I Do Research by Jane Concha

You have your topic and you're ready to go. But now you think, "Where do I go from here?" I have definitely been there. Sometimes, I am so nervous that I don't even research until the last minute, thinking that the Internet would grant me some great sources. Unfortunately, that *never* works.

What I have now realized is that research takes time; with patience and a clear path, I have always managed to find sources that are geared to my topic and add depth to my paper.

To start, I brainstorm ideas of where I want to go with my research. Sometimes, a quick search on Google can help give me some hints on where to start. For example, if I choose to write on the desert in El Paso, a quick search can help me find the name of the desert, the type of climate, and the habitat. From there, I could easily go on the library database and search the keywords I have based on my online search.

I like to use online databases from my library website like Jstor and Academic Search Complete (EBSCO) because I can access print articles from my computer, and that satisfies professors who require that you have a certain number of print sources.

However, I'd recommend to fellow students that it's a good idea to get over their fear of actually going to the library in person except to use the computers or have study dates. Yes, you may be able to access articles and even books (Google Books, etc.) from your computer, but the library does have one great advantage— the research ninjas called librarians. These are people to cultivate, not once but throughout your academic career. They can help you find sources you wouldn't have thought of and can be invaluable when you can't find that essential bit of information.

Jane Concha uses the Internet, online databases, and librarians when conducting research for a paper.

Even when websites look useful, I'm careful with a *.com* website because those sites usually get their information from research that is easily accessible on a database or information that is slanted toward a certain point of view. However, I do like *.gov* websites because they usually have great statistics I can add to my paper.

Once I find my sources, I pick out the ones that I don't want and discard them. I usually don't look at anything over five years old. I also reject information that pertains to my topic, but is too boring to be interesting to my reader.

Once I'm done finding great sources, it is a lot easier to write my paper.

Research Provides Inartistic Proofs

As discussed in Chapter 4, ancient Greeks began the writing process with invention, a stage in which they searched their memories for data related to the topic at hand. This information constituted artistic proofs, knowledge that rhetors invented from their own minds, emotions, and observation. However, rhetors also supplemented their invented proofs with information that was gleaned from other sources such as the testimony of witnesses, evidence given under torture, and written contracts. Yes, evidence given under torture was considered a legitimate proof. None of these inartistic proofs were generated from the rhetor's mind or "invented." As such, the Greeks considered these sources of information to be inartistic proofs.

Today, the range of inartistic proofs available to writers and speakers is vastly expanded—scientific studies, opinions from authorities, videotapes of events, government documents, and so on. You can locate these in the traditional way—library books and print periodicals—but more likely you will begin your search with the Internet, a resource the ancients could not have imagined. However, as in ancient times, it is still the task of today's rhetor to locate available resources, sift through them to locate those that are relevant, evaluate their reliability and validity, and incorporate them into a text to support an argument.

Researching rhetorically, the title of this chapter, refers to making use of your ethos or credibility as a writer by incorporating your expert knowledge because of everyday experiences and the subjects you have studied. It also involves maximizing as well as "borrowing" the credibility of source materials you quote or paraphrase in your text. When you quote or paraphrase an expert, your paper gains authority that it would not otherwise have. For example, if you are the parent of a child with attention deficit hyperactivity disorder (ADHD), your experiences caring for that child and interacting with the health care and educational systems, as well as the reading you have done to seek out effective treatment, qualifies you to speak with authority about what it is like to raise such as child. If you are writing a paper about educational options for children with ADHD, you can cite some of your own experiences, but you will also want to quote or paraphrase opinions of authorities about the best ways to provide a quality educational environment for these children. These opinions of experts can be found in books, periodicals, and possibly government documents, and including them will increase your power to convince an audience.

You Do Research Every Day

Although the words "research paper" sound imposing to many students, research is really a natural part of your experience. You do research every day, often without being aware of the process, whether it is determining the calorie count of a serving of sugar-free ice cream or calculating the dollar amount you will spend on gasoline for a weekend trip. The information-gathering you do for a research paper builds on the informal research skills you already have by adding additional places to look for information and additional tools to use in that search.

How do you go about finding the best reference sources to support your general knowledge? A key factor to keep in mind is the credibility of each of the sources you choose. Citing information from a source written in the last three years is generally more credible than a source published ten years ago because the information is obviously more current. Peer-reviewed journals and books published by reputable publishers are probably the most credible sources. Information from news magazines such as *Time* or *Newsweek* has more credence than material found in popular magazines such as *Glamour* or *People,* which are designed for entertainment rather than covering the news. Indeed, many instructors will forbid the use of Wikipedia as a source, not because all the information is inaccurate (because it is not) but because the reader has no way of evaluating whether information is correct or not since the entries were written by volunteers and the content has not been vetted by a reputable publisher or other authoritative organization.

Don't be reluctant to ask for help. Your instructor may be willing to suggest resources on your topic, as will librarians. Instructors may refer you to specific books or authors. Others may demonstrate a journal search for you, in the process finding you valuable sources. As noted by Concha in the chapter opener, librarians can be valuable allies in your search, as their job is to serve your needs as a library patron. If you ask for help, a librarian will often run a search for you in the online catalog or may even walk with you into the stacks to find appropriate source materials.

Primary and Secondary Research

If you've ever purchased a major consumer product, say a computer, chances are you already knew quite a bit about what was available before you took out your charge card. For example, many of your friends probably have computers as well as definite opinions about what brands and models are preferable. Perhaps you already own a computer and like it so much that you want to upgrade to the next model or maybe you have complaints about its performance. Still, before you made your purchase, you probably did some research on the Internet, reading product specifications and reviews. Maybe you tried out a computer or two at the local Apple Store or another retailer. If you went through this sort of process before buying a computer or another consumer product, you already know the basics about primary and secondary research.

Primary research involves personal interaction with your subject. Interviews with people on the scene of an event and questionnaires are all primary sources. Novels, poems, diaries, and fictional films are also primary sources because they stand alone and are not interpreting anything else. To return to the computer purchase analogy, when you visited the Apple Store or other retailers to examine computers, you were doing primary research. When you looked at product reviews in magazines, you were doing secondary research. Similarly, when you read a *Time* magazine article that analyzes climate change and quotes prominent experts in the field, you are conducting secondary research.

A little later in this chapter, Activity 7.1 asks you to interview someone who has had an unusual life experience and write a profile of that person. You may be able to gather all the information you need for this assignment by doing an interview, though it might be a good idea to revisit the observation exercise (Activity 4.10) in Chapter 4. If you know the person personally, you can also utilize that prior knowledge.

Other writing assignments ask you to combine your own experience or primary research with information gained from secondary research in books or periodicals. For example, you might be asked to write an essay about recycling. You can include your own experience with recycling or visit a recycling center in your community and report what you see. You can also support this primary research with secondary research in books or periodicals in which authorities offer facts and opinions about the effectiveness of recycling. In addition, you can interview an authority on recycling, perhaps a professor or chairperson of a community committee, as an additional secondary source.

You may notice that many magazine articles or books refer to other books, statistical studies, or additional evidence but do not document sources in the text or give a bibliography. In this course, however, your instructor will probably ask you to document outside references following the Modern Language Association (MLA) or American Psychological Association (APA) format. The purpose is to train you in academic writing, which differs from journalism or popular writing in that all sources are credited both in the text and in a works cited page. Documentation also benefits those who read your essays and might want to use the same sources for additional research of their own. It is, therefore, not a check against plagiarism but an important tool for other researchers.

Reading 7.1

Bringing History to Life with Primary Sources
by Alexander A. Aimes

In this article, Alexander A. Aimes argues that primary sources add depth and help bring a research topic to life.

History sometimes bores because of the way it is taught. Often, educators merely present students with information they are supposed to remember, rather than encourage students to explore historic documents and draw conclusions. As a Museum Studies intern at Mystic Seaport, a maritime history museum in Mystic, Connecticut, I worked with other interns to create history education programs targeted at high school audiences. We presented students with primary sources and asked them to think critically about the documents, to develop their own ideas about history.

My favorite program we developed related to the Temperance Movement, a mid-nineteenth century social reform movement that aimed to put an end to alcohol consumption. Members of the Greenman family, prominent shipbuilders and storeowners who lived in Mystic, became involved in Temperance as the movement gained national momentum. We traced the development of their beliefs through historic documents relating to their business and civic activities. For example, we showed students pages from the 1840s account books of the family-owned Greenman General Store that had frequent references to the sale of alcohol. By the 1850s, those references had vanished. Also, we gave students newspaper articles from the 1870s in which the Greenmans publicly stated their support of Temperance, indicating the passion with which the Greenmans advocated against alcohol. The text of the education program encouraged students to discover the Greenmans apparently stopped selling alcohol, a decision that affected the company's profits, *before* their public announcement of their change in attitude toward alcohol.

Students going through the educational program realized they would not know this fascinating detail, which hints the Greenmans were willing to lose company revenue in support of their beliefs, if they had not scrutinized account books from the 19th century. Moreover, we asked students to think about whether they could cite negative evidence—that is, the *absence* of liquor sales in the 1850s account books—as sufficient grounds for assuming the Greenmans changed their business practices by that decade? What other evidence would help support this conclusion—an open ended question students can answer in a variety of ways.

Focusing on historical evidence allows us to ask deeper questions about our conclusions. The questions we encouraged the students at Mystic Seaport to think about show the debatable nature of historical conclusions based on primary sources. While applied here to a museum activity, this strategy of poring over primary sources can be used in almost any research context. Original documents get us as close as possible to whatever subject we are studying. They also add depth to our interpretations by encouraging critical analysis of sources.

Interviews

Depending on your topic, your community probably has some excellent sources sitting behind desks at the nearest college, city hall, or federal office building. If you are looking into the environment, you could contact the Environmental Protection Agency, an attorney who specializes in environmental law, a professional employee of the park system or the Bureau of Land Management, a college professor who works in the natural sciences, or a group in your area dedicated to beautification and restoration efforts.

If you don't know anyone connected with these organizations, a look in the yellow pages or blue government pages of the phone book should give you the information you need.

When you contact the person you'd like to interview, identify yourself and your reason for wanting to speak with him or her. Most people are happy to assist college students in their research, and almost everyone is flattered by the attention. If your first choice refuses, ask him or her if they know anyone who might be knowledgeable about your topic and available for an interview. When you get a positive response, arrange an hour and a location convenient for both of you. If the interview is scheduled more than a week from the initial contact, you can write a letter confirming your appointment, or you can call the day before the scheduled interview to confirm the time and location.

Once you've scheduled the interview, make a list of questions you will ask your interview subject. There are two types of questions you can ask your subject: open and closed. **Open questions** such as the following leave room for extended discussion because they don't have a yes, no, or specific answer:

> Could you tell me about the most positive experience you've had with [topic]?
>
> When did you decide to study [topic]?
>
> What's the most negative experience you've had with [topic]?

Questions like these allow for extended discussions. Even if it seems your subject has finished his or her response to the question, let a few moments of silence pass before you ask another question. Silence can be uncomfortable for some people, and he or she might feel compelled to expand on the response to your question in interesting ways.

Closed questions are useful for gathering specific information. Questions such as "When did you graduate?" and "How long have you been involved in [topic]?" are closed questions. Although closed questions are important to an interview, be sure they're balanced by questions that allow your subject room to talk and expand on his or her ideas.

Before the interview, confirm the exact location of your appointment. If you are unfamiliar with the planned meeting place, go by the day before to make sure you can find it. Take several pens or pencils with you to the interview in addition to a writing tablet with a stiff back. If possible, use a recorder to record the interview, but be sure to ask your subject if it is okay. Most people will allow recording, if you assure them that the recording is only for your use in collecting information for your research paper. If you are using a recorder, test its operation before you get to the interview location so you won't have any surprises when you're with your subject or discover later that the machine was not working.

Although you've prepared a list of questions to follow, don't be afraid to ask a question that isn't on your list. If your subject mentions briefly an experience that seems relevant to your topic, you might want to ask him or her more about that experience, even though it isn't on your list of questions. Indeed, the best way to interview may be to read over your questions just before you meet your subject, then not refer to them during the interview. Before you leave, however, look over your list to see if you have missed any questions of importance.

Remember to let lulls in the conversation work for you by drawing your interview subject into further explanations or illustrations of previous comments. If you interview a talkative person who strays from the topic, try to steer him or her back to the questions you've prepared, but if you can't, don't worry. You'll probably get useful information anyway. Be courteous and attentive. Even if you're recording the interview, take notes. It makes both the subject and the interviewer feel more comfortable and serves as a backup, should your recording not work.

Within 15 minutes after leaving the interview, jot down some notes about your subject's appearance; the sights, sounds, and smells of the place where you conducted the interview; and any overall impressions of the meeting. Make sure you have the date and location of the interview in your notes because you will need it for documentation on your works cited page.

Activity 7.1 **Write a Profile of a Person**

Write a profile of a person that is unusual in some way. Your profile should include description, quotes, and whatever background explanations are needed to provide a context, so that the story flows logically from one element to another. The length should be approximately 750 to 1,000 words. Answering the following questions will help you elicit information you need to write your profile.

1. **History**—What is the history of the person? Does the history affect the present?

2. **Qualities**—What qualities make this person worth writing about? Can you give examples that *show* the qualities?

3. **Values and standards**—What does the subject believe in most strongly? How does this shape his/her actions? Can you give specific examples?

4. **Impact**—How does the subject affect those around him or her? This may include both positives and negatives. Give examples.

5. **Description**—Write a physical description of the person, including any unusual aspects that make the person stand out in a crowd. Describe the setting where you interviewed the person or where the person works or lives.

Secondary Research Sources Expected by Professors

You have been assigned a research paper or project. What does your professor expect? First of all, you need to understand the assignment: What specifically does your professor want you to research? Do you have instructions about what kinds of sources your professor wants? Are restrictions put on what Internet or database sources you can use? Possibly, your instructor has specified that you need to use books, journals, major magazines and newspapers, and certain web-based information. This means that you are to use reputable sources to obtain a balanced, impartial viewpoint about your topic. So, how do you find these sources?

Neither you nor your professor should be surprised that you can find enough material for your research paper through the Internet, even if your professor says you can use only print sources. Your library has full-text databases such as Jstor and Academic Search Complete (EBSCO) that will provide you with PDF images of actual journal pages, not web pages. Moreover, Google and other online libraries have the full-text versions of many book chapters or entire books.

However, in many cases the latest books in a field are not online, so you need to venture into the actual library building to find some of the best sources for your research. This is also true of primary sources such as letters and maps. Moreover, librarians can aid you in finding the research materials you need.

Consider the following secondary research sources:

Books: In these days of easy-to-find resources on the Internet, students may wonder why they should bother with books at all. However, scholarly books treat academic topics with in-depth discussion and careful documentation of evidence. College libraries collect scholarly books that are carefully researched and reviewed by authorities in the book's field. Look for recently published books rather than older books, even if they are on your topic. Academic books or well-researched popular books often have bibliographies or lists of additional references at the end of the book. These lists are useful for two reasons: First, if such lists of books are present, it is a good clue this is a well-researched book, and, second, it gives you a ready list of other possible resources you can consult for your research project.

Scholarly journals: Just having the word "journal" in the title does not mean it is a journal. *Ladies Home Journal,* or *The Wall Street Journal,* for example, are not journals. Your instructor means peer-reviewed journals in which the authors have documented their sources. Peer-reviewed means that articles have been reviewed by experts in the field for reliability and relevance before being published. Your library should have print indexes to journals in which you can look up your topic. You may also be able to find journal articles—sometimes in full text—through the online databases offered by your college library.

Major magazines and newspapers: These publications report the news based on the actual observation of events and interviews with experts and also present informed editorial opinions. Examples are magazines such as *Time* and *Newsweek* and newspapers such as *The New York Times,* the *Boston Globe, The Wall Street Journal,* and the *Washington Post.* You can locate full-text articles directly from the online versions of major print magazines and newspapers. Often, these publications charge a fee for articles not published recently. However, you can often find the same articles free through one of your library databases.

Special interest publications: These are periodicals that focus on a specific topic but are written for a wider audience than scholarly journals. Authors of articles base their articles on interviews with experts, recent scholarly books and journals, and other reputable sources. Examples include *Psychology Today* and *Scientific American*.

Government documents: Government documents present a wealth of information for many contemporary events and issues. Your library may be a federal depository, which means that users can locate many federal documents onsite. If so, you can look up government sources in the online library catalog. Government documents are also available through online databases.

Encyclopedias: Encyclopedias can be useful to browse when you are looking for topics. They are also helpful for providing background information such as dates when events occurred. However, most instructors prefer that you do not use encyclopedias as sources in your paper. This is particularly true for Wikipedia, the online encyclopedia that is assembled by volunteers who have specialized knowledge on topics and, thus, has no systematic vetting of the contents. However, Wikipedia entries often include bibliographies which can be useful in pointing you to books, articles, or other websites that can be used as references.

Web pages: The problem with web-based information is that anyone with some knowledge of computers can put up a website on the Internet. Thus, information from websites must be carefully evaluated as to author, publishing organization, etc. One way to deal with this problem is to find web information through librarian-generated indexes and search engines that are designed to screen websites for credibility (see the section titled "Find Internet Information," which appears later in this chapter).

As you use the categories above to find secondary sources for your paper or project, realize that your topic influences your choice of reference materials. If you are writing about a literary topic such as Shakespeare's *Othello*, you will find a number of relevant books and journal articles. If your topic is more contemporary, such as the current status of the country's housing market, you may be able to find some books or journal articles for background information, but you will need to use recent magazine and newspaper articles to find the latest information.

As you examine your sources, remember that gathering the information should help you discover what you think about your topic, not just what others think. This will enable you to create a paper based on *your* ideas and opinions, with source materials supporting your position.

Employ Computerized Library Catalogs

Public Access Catalogs (PACs) or computerized catalogs, accessed through the Internet, have replaced card catalogs. A library computerized catalog provides bibliographical information about the library's collection, including thousands of books, photos, videos, journals, and other items. Generally, catalogs can be accessed by any of the following methods: keyword, subject, author, title, or call number. You may also find books that are available in digital form through the catalog. In addition, on the library home page, you will find links to other information and services such as database searches, interlibrary loans, and course reserves.

Types of Computerized Searches

Conducting a computerized search involves accessing the library's catalog using one of the following search methods:

- *Keyword*—Unless you know the author or title of a book, keyword is the best type of search because it finds the search word or words anywhere in the bibliographical citation.

     Example: water quality

- *Title*—Type the exact order of words in the title.

     Example: History of the United Kingdom

- *Author*—Type the author's name, putting the last name first. You don't need to include a comma.

     Example: Miller Henry J.

- *Subject*—Type the exact Library of Congress subject heading.

     Example: Spanish language—Grammar, Historical

- *Call Number*—Type the exact call number.

     Example: B851.P49 2004

If you have a general topic, you probably want to use the keyword search, for subject search actually refers to the exact Library of Congress subject-search designations, and, unless you use the precise search terms specified by that classification system, you may not get the results you want. The use of keywords, however, will lead you to hits on your topic. Then, once you have found one book that is in your topic area, you can examine the screen for Library of Congress subject headings and click on those to browse for more books.

An invaluable resource of any library is the Interlibrary Loan department. Here you can request books your library does not own, as well as journal articles from periodicals not in the library's collection or obtainable through the library's databases. Books and articles are obtained for you by the staff on a minimal or no-fee basis. This is extremely helpful because you can request books you find in bibliographies. However, it generally takes seven to ten days to obtain books through an interlibrary loan, so you need to plan well in advance. To request an item, you simply go to the Interlibrary Loan department in your library or fill out a form on the library's website.

Explore

Activity 7.2 Locate Books on Your Topic

Using the online card catalog at the library, locate three books about your topic. Write down the titles, authors, publishers, dates of publication, and catalog numbers. Now, go to the stacks and find the books. While you are there, find two other books nearby on the same topic. Check the table of contents and index to see if they contain information you can use.

Utilize Electronic Library Resources

College and university libraries increasingly rely on databases to provide digital versions of articles published in journals, magazines, newspapers, and government documents, as well as other publications and materials. Generally, the databases are available to students and faculty through the Internet via the library home page, though a library card and a password may be required for off-campus access.

Library databases make use of online forms similar to those of a library computerized catalog. Searches are by subject, title, author, and name of publication. Advanced search features are available. Some databases provide the full-text versions of articles published in newspapers, journals, and magazines. Others give publication information only, such as title, author, publication, date of publication, and an abstract of the article. Popular databases include Lexis-Nexis, Academic Search Complete, Periodical Archive Online (ProQuest), Project Muse, and JSTOR.

Academic Search Complete is one of EBSCO's popular online databases that can be accessed by students through their library's website. The database indexes full-text articles on a wide variety of topics.

Activity 7.3 **Locate Newspaper and Magazine Articles**

Go to your library's online databases and choose one that relates to your topic. Then access it and type in your topic. Try using various key words. Jot down titles, authors, and publication information concerning any articles that look interesting. If full-text versions are available, save them to your computer or disk drive or e-mail them to yourself. If not, find out if your library has a hard copy version or microfilm of the articles.

Find Internet Information

The World Wide Web is an incredible resource for research. Through it, you can find full texts of pending legislation, searchable online editions of Shakespeare's plays, environmental impact statements, stock quotes, and much, much more. Finding credible research sources is not always easy. Anyone with an Internet connection and a little knowledge can put up a web page and claim to be an expert on a chosen topic. Therefore, information from the Internet must be scrutinized with even more diligence than print sources. For example, if you enter the word "environment" in one of the keyword search engines, you may receive thousands of "hits," or sites that relate to that topic from all over the world. How do you sift through all of that feedback in order to find information relevant to your topic? It is a problem that has not been completely solved on the Internet.

However, the search engine Google now provides Google Books, http://books.google.com, which offers the full-text versions of millions of books, though usually not the full text of the entire book unless the book is no longer copyrighted. Also, Google Scholar, http://scholar.google.com, provides access to scholarly papers, though if your library has computerized databases, it will likely have a more extensive collection available to you. Also, the Directory of Online Open Access Journals, http://www.doaj.org, enables you to search online journals that offer free access.

Click on the menu bar on the left side of the Google.com search page to find links to Google Books and Google Scholar. Google Books offers the full-text versions of millions of books, though usually not the full text of the entire book unless the book is no longer copyrighted. Also, Google Scholar, at http://scholar.google.com, provides access to scholarly papers, though not always full text.

One of the best ways for students to find Internet resources is through indexing projects sponsored by major libraries. In the case of each directory/search tool, librarians have personally reviewed and selected websites that are of value to academic researchers, including both students and faculty. These indexing websites may be organized by subject area, in addition to having keyword search engines. Thus, you might quickly locate the most authoritative websites without having to wade through masses of sites looking for the reliable ones. The following websites offer links to a variety of reputable sources:

IPL2: Information You Can Trust, http://www.ipl.org

Infomine, http://infomine.ucr.edu

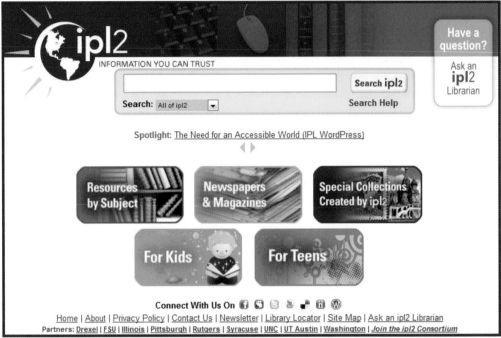

IPL2: Information You Can Trust is a public library on the Internet. It offers links to resources by subject, newspapers and magazines, and special collections created by the Internet Public Library.

Government documents also can be found easily through the Internet and are indexed at a variety of sites, including these:

> FirstGov, http://www.firstgov.gov
>
> Thomas Legislative Information, http://thomas.loc.gov
>
> Federal Citizen Information Center, http://www.pueblo.gsa.gov/
>
> FedWorld.Gov, http://www.fedworld.gov/

Activity 7.4 **Find a Journal Article in Google Scholar**

Go to Google Scholar either through Google.com or directly at http://scholar.google.com and search for a journal article on your chosen topic. If the Google link does not offer you full text, then go to the index of electronic journals on your college library website and search for the journal. Likely, your library will offer a database that provides full text for the article. Note: The advantage of this method of finding journal articles is that Google Scholar indexes articles from journals available in many different databases.

Evaluate Sources

Many people tend to believe what they see in print. They may think that if information is in a book or a news magazine, it must be true. If you read critically, however, you know that all sources must be evaluated. With the Internet, perhaps even more than with print texts, it is important to evaluate your sources. Here are some guidelines to consider when evaluating sources.

- **Who is the author?** This question is equally important, whether the source in question is a book, a magazine, or a website. If you have the dust jacket of the book, the back flap will quickly provide you with essential information to screen the author. In the short biographical sketch, usually included along with a photo, you can learn the author's academic credentials and university affiliation, what previous books the author has published, and other qualifications that the publisher thinks qualifies the author to write this particular book. If there is no dust jacket (as is often true with library books), you can try to find information about the author through an Internet search engine or a reference text such as *Contemporary Authors.* A magazine or journal will often provide brief biographical information at the end of the article or on a separate authors' page. If the text is on a website, determining the authorship is more complex, as authors often are not named. In that case, you are forced to rely on the credibility of the entity publishing the website. Many websites have a link called something like "About Us" or "Mission Statement," and that page will give you some idea about the motivations of the entity sponsoring the site. Is it selling something? Is it part of an organization that has a political agenda? These are things to keep in mind when considering the bias of the site's content.

- **For what audience is the text written?** Determining this may require some detective work. In the case of a book, the preface or introduction may give you some clues. With magazines and journals, consider the demographics of the readership. With a website, a little clicking around in the site and a look at the kind of texts, graphics, and advertising used (if any) should tell you what readers the site is designed for.

- **What sources does the author rely upon?** If you are working with an academic text, the sources should be clearly cited in the text by author and page number, footnotes, or endnotes. If it is a more popular book or article, sources are acknowledged less formally; however, a credible author will still make an effort to credit sources. For example, an article might say, "According to the March issue of the *New England Journal of Medicine.* . . . "

■ **Does the text have an obvious bias?** Ask yourself if the argument is logical and if sources are mentioned for any statistics or other evidence. Are any opposing viewpoints discussed fairly? Does the author engage in name calling (a clear sign of bias)? Are there obvious holes or contradictions in the argument? For most purposes, you are looking for texts which do not appear to have been written with a biased agenda. However, in some cases, the opposite is true. If you are looking for a political candidate's position on a certain issue, then reading the candidate's book or going to the candidate's website will provide you with a biased viewpoint but one which you can analyze for the purposes of your paper. When dealing with information from sources with an obvious agenda, though, you must be careful not to represent the material as unbiased in your text.

■ **What do others think of the text?** For a book, you can look for a review in *Book Review Digest* or *Book Review Index*, two publications you can find in the reference section of the library. Also, *The New York Times* and other newspapers review prominent popular books. Most magazines and newspapers print letters to the editor, which may offer comments on controversial articles. The Scout Report, which can be found at the *Scout Project*, http://scout.wisc.edu, reviews selected websites. If you locate a review of your text, you can cite the review in your research paper to provide additional evidence of the text's credibility.

Activity 7.5 **Locate and Evaluate a Source**

Locate one source (book, magazine or newspaper article, or website page) which you think would be a credible source for a research paper. For that source, answer the questions in the Evaluate Sources section above.

Activity 7.6 **Evaluate a Website**

Go to the Internet and look up a website related to a topic you are researching. Answer these questions as fully as you can.

1. Who is the author of this source? Is the author credible on this topic? Why or why not?

2. What does the text focus on? Is it thoughtful and balanced, or does it seem one-sided? What gives you that impression?

3. When was the website last updated?

4. What is the purpose of this site? Is it to provide information? Or is it trying to persuade readers to accept a particular point of view?

5. How professional is the tone, and how well-designed is the site? How carefully has it been edited and proofread? Are there any grammatical and spelling errors that compromise its credibility?

6. What kinds of links does the site provide? Do they add to the website's credibility or detract from it?

Avoid Plagiarism

Plagiarism is defined as follows by the Writing Program Administrators (WPA), a group of English professors who direct college composition programs: "In an instructional setting, plagiarism occurs when a writer deliberately uses someone else's language, ideas, or other original (not common-knowledge) material without acknowledging its source." A keyword here is "deliberately." Instructors, however, may have difficulty distinguishing between accidental and deliberate plagiarism. The burden is upon you as the writer to give credit where credit is due. These are some examples of plagiarism:

- Turning in a paper that was written by someone else as your own. This includes obtaining a paper from an Internet term paper mill.

- Copying a paper or any part of a paper from a source without acknowledging the source in the proper format.

- Paraphrasing materials from a source without documentation.

- Copying materials from a text but treating it as your own, leaving out quotation marks and acknowledgement.

The guidelines provided in the following table can help you identify when it is appropriate to give credit to others in your writing.

Choosing When to Give Credit

Need to Document	No Need to Document
• When you are using or referring to somebody else's words or ideas from a magazine, book, newpaper, song, TV program, movie, web page, computer program, letter, advertisement, or any other medium. • When you use information gained through interviewing another person. • When you copy the exact words or a "unique phrase" from somewhere. • When you reprint any diagrams, illustrations, charts, and pictures. • When you use ideas given to you by others, whether in conversation or through e-mail.	• When you are writing your own experiences, your own observations, your own insights, your own thoughts, or your own conclusions about a subject. • When you are using "common knowledge"—folklore, common-sense observations, or shared information within your field of study or cultural group. • When you are compiling generally accepted facts. • When you are writing up your own experimental results.

The Online Writing Lab (OWL) at Purdue University provides an excellent handout on avoiding plagiarism, including the information about when to give credit to sources in the table above. See http://owl.english.purdue.edu.

Activity 7.7 **Plagiarism Exercise**

Collaborate

In this exercise you will intentionally plagiarize a text. Then you will collaborate with a partner to produce a text that paraphrases and cites sources.

1. With a partner, choose a public figure currently in the news. On your own, write a brief bio of the individual you have both chosen, intentionally quoting extensively from one source without using quotation marks or citing the source.

2. Exchange your text with your partner by e-mail. Now, paste into Google or another search engine a sentence or long phrase copied in your partner's text, putting the copied text in quotation marks. Search. Repeat until you are able to identify the source of the text that your partner has intentionally plagiarized. Your partner should follow the same exercise using your text.

3. Finally, back in class, work with your partner to compose a brief bio of the individual that paraphrases these texts (and others, if needed).

4. Turn in the final version, along with the plagiarized versions. Describe your experience in trying to locate the source of your partner's plagiarized text.

Reading 7.2

Anatomy of a Fake Quotation
by Megan McArdle

In this article, originally published in *The Atlantic*, Megan McArdle tells the story of how a fake Martin Luther King, Jr. quote was created and posted on the Internet.

Yesterday, I saw a quote from Martin Luther King Jr. fly across my Twitter feed: "I mourn the loss of thousands of precious lives, but I will not rejoice in the death of one, not even an enemy."—Martin Luther King, Jr. I was about to retweet it, but I hesitated. It didn't sound right. After some Googling, I determined that it was probably fake, which I blogged about last night.

Here's the story of how that quote was created.

It turns out I was far too uncharitable in my search for a motive behind the fake quote. I assumed that someone had made it up on purpose. I was wrong.

Had I seen the quote on Facebook, rather than Twitter, I might have guessed at the truth. On the other hand, had I seen it on Facebook, I might not have realized it was fake, because it was appended to a long string of genuine speech from MLK Jr. Here's the quote as most people on Facebook saw it:

> I will mourn the loss of thousands of precious lives, but I will not rejoice in the death of one, not even an enemy. Returning hate for hate multiplies hate, adding deeper darkness to a night already devoid of stars. Darkness cannot drive out darkness; only light can do that. Hate cannot drive out hate, only love can do that.

Everything except the first sentence is found in King's book, *Strength to Love*, and seems to have been said originally in a 1957 sermon he gave on loving your enemies. Unlike the first quotation, it does sound like King, and it was easy to assume that the whole thing came from him.

So how did they get mixed together?

Thanks to Jessica Dovey, a Facebook user, that's how. And contrary to my initial assumption, it wasn't malicious. Ms. Dovey, a 24-year-old Penn State graduate who now teaches English to middle schoolers in Kobe, Japan, posted a very timely and moving thought on her Facebook status, and then followed it up with the Martin Luther King, Jr., quote.

> I will mourn the loss of thousands of precious lives, but I will not rejoice in the death of one, not even an enemy. "Returning hate for hate multiplies hate, adding deeper darkness to a night already devoid of stars. Darkness cannot drive out darkness; only light can do that. Hate cannot drive out hate, only love can do that." MLK Jr.

At some point, someone cut and pasted the quote, and—for reasons that I, appropriately chastened, will not speculate on—stripped out the quotation marks. Eventually, the mangled quotation somehow came to the attention of Penn Jillette, of Penn and Teller fame. He tweeted it to his 1.6 million Facebook followers, and the rest was Internet history. Twenty-four hours later, the quote brought back over 9,000 hits on Google.

The quote also went viral on Twitter, and since the 140-character limit precluded quoting the whole thing, people stripped it down to the most timely and appropriate part: the fake quote. That's where I saw it.

The speed of dissemination is breathtaking: mangled to meme in less than two days. Also remarkable is how defensive people got about the quote—though admirably, not Penn Jillette, who posted an update as soon as it was called to his attention. The thread for my post now has over 600 comments, and by my rough estimate, at least a third of them are people posting that I need to print a retraction, because of the nonfake part of the quotation. But I didn't quote that part; I was only interested in the too-timely bit I'd seen twittered.

Even more bizarrely, several of these readers, who clearly hadn't read too closely, started claiming that I had retroactively edited the post to make them look like idiots, even going so far as to scrub all the versions in RSS readers so that they, too, showed that I was talking about the truncated version. Even if you think I am the sort of low scoundrel who would do such a thing, this seems like a lot of work for not much reward. I'm not sure whether it's even possible to completely scrub an RSS feed, but even if it were, I'd have had to notify my bosses, who tend to frown on retroactive editing.

Meanwhile, several other people began confabulating a provenance for it. *Obviously*, he was talking about Vietnam, and what sort of moral midget couldn't understand that? This even though the latest citation for the true part of the quote was a book published in 1967, which would have been written earlier than that, when U.S. casualties in Vietnam were still relatively low. Moreover, the ambiguity with which the antiwar movement viewed the North Vietnamese makes "enemy" a hard fit.

It is, of course, not strange that people might look for possible confirming facts. What's strange is that they were sure enough of themselves to make fun of anyone who disagreed. Yet several other people on the comment thread had linked to a version of the quotation from 1957. I am second to no one in my admiration for Dr. King. But I do not think that he prefigured Vietnam by seven years.

Which only illustrates why fake quotes are so widely dispersed. Though one commenter accused me of trying to make people feel stupid for having propagated the quote, that was hardly my intention—we've all probably repeated more fake quotations than real ones. Fake quotations are pithier, more dramatic, more on point, than the things people usually say in real life. It's not surprising that they are often the survivors of the evolutionary battle for mindshare. One person actually posted a passage which integrated the fake quotation into the larger section of the book from which the original MLK words were drawn.

We become invested in these quotes because they say something important about us—and they let us feel that those emotions were shared by great figures in history. We naturally search for reasons that they could have said it—that they could have felt like us—rather than looking for reasons to disbelieve. If we'd put the same moving words in Hitler's mouth, everyone would have been a lot more skeptical. But while this might be a lesson about the need to be skeptical, I don't think there's anything stupid about wanting to be more like Dr. King.

Ms. Dovey's status now reads: "has apparently gone back in time and put her words into one of MLK's sermons. I'm somewhere between nervous and embarrassed and honored . . . I really hope I haven't said anything he wouldn't agree with . . . Only what I feel in my heart."

A lot of us were feeling the same thing—and I think it's clear from his writings that MLK would have too. There's no reason to be embarrassed about that.

Activity 7.8 Discuss "Anatomy of a Fake Quotation"

1. How was the fake quotation created? How did it spread on the Internet?

2. Note the speed and the reach of the fake quote. What does Megan McArdle suggest the story of this fake quote says about why fake quotes can become so widely disbursed?

3. What is your reaction to this story of the fake quotation?

Activity 7.9 Prepare an Annotated Bibliography

An annotated bibliography is a list of bibliographical citations with a few sentences or a paragraph for each entry that offers explanatory information or critical commentary about the source. Many instructors request an annotated bibliography as a step in writing a research paper because it is an indication of the scope and direction of your research.

1. Select 10 quality sources about your topic. These should be, as your instructor directs, a mix of books, scholarly journal and magazine articles, government documents, and selected texts from websites.

2. Skim the text of each source and read portions more closely that seem relevant to your topic.

3. Write a bibliographical citation for each source in MLA style. (See the appendix that follows this chapter for MLA style samples.)

4. Write a few sentences for each source in which you do the following:
   (a) Summarize the content and purpose of the source.
   (b) Explain how you might use the source in your research paper.

Sample Annotated Bibliography on the Federal Aviation Administration User Fees

Horne, T. A. (2007, February). User Fee Debate. *AOPA Pilot Magazine, 50,* 27.

The author of this article is an experienced, commercial rated pilot that has flown for over 30 years. He also sits on the Aircraft Owners and Pilots Association (AOPA) board. This article explains what the Federal Aviation

Administration (FAA) has proposed and what it means to pilots. Congress is cutting the budget for the FAA and in turn wants to impose fees for anyone who flies into a controlled airspace. This would have a very tragic effect on general aviation. This is huge because if anyone is flying anywhere around a decent-sized city, they are going to fly through these airspaces. Also, the FAA wants to charge for approaches into airports and landing on airport runways. This is bad because all of these charges would add up to more than $200. This would discourage people from flying, making them sell their aircraft. This would slowly dissolve the general aviation industry. I can use this article to explain what is going on and why the government wants to charge these fees.

Boyer, P. (Director) (2007, October 6). AOPA's Reasonable Analysis of User Fee Issues at AOPA Expo. *AOPA Expo 2007*. Lecture conducted from AOPA, Hartford, CT.

This lecture was given by the president of AOPA, Phil Boyer. He spoke of the fees that the FAA is trying to impose and what they would mean for general aviation pilots. He explains that the fees that the FAA wants are directed toward general aviation and not toward the airlines. He also gave some examples of what would be better for everyone, if the FAA really is in a crisis. This source is important because it provides an explanation and breakdown of these user fees and gives some examples of what could be put in place of these proposed fees.

Fact Sheet—Impact of Administration's Financing Proposal on General Aviation. (2007, April 23). *FAA: Home*. Retrieved March 2, 2011, from http://www.faa.gov/news/fact_sheets/news_story .cfm?newsid=8747.

This website is the official FAA website that has all of its information. This one fact sheet lists all the facts and myths related to this issue. It goes over what the FAA wants to put into place and where and when it will happen. It brings up all of the more important issues regarding the topic, but leaves some out as well. For example, nowhere in the sheet does it say anything about controlled airspace fees, which is one of the biggest fees it would implement. It does mention another, which is the fuel tax hike. This would weaken general aviation because a lot of pilots cannot afford higher fuel prices. This will be important to have a government agency's point of view on the topic.

AOPA Online: What's the FAA's user fee proposal? (2006, November
        30). *AOPA Online: Aircraft Owners and Pilots Association*.
        Retrieved March 2, 2011, from http://www.aopa.org/whatsnew/
        newsitems/2006/061130userfees.html.

This website is the official website for AOPA, which is a foundation that
protects flying and everything related to aviation. This article goes over what
the user fees would be, but it goes into greater detail about what the fuel
prices would be after the legislation is put into place. Fuel is needed for
all flights and is already expensive. What the government wants to do in
addition to implementing user fees is to put more tax on fuel. This would
make it much harder for the average pilot to afford flying his/her aircraft.
This is beneficial to the argument because it focuses on one of the major fees
that the FAA would implement: the fuel hikes.

User Fees—NBAA Calls Proposed FAA Budget a 'Sweetheart Deal' For
        the Airlines. (2006, November 30). *California Pilots Association*.
        Retrieved March 2, 2011, from http://www.calpilots.org/index
        .php?option=com_content&view=article&id=1141&catid=45:
        pre-2008-archived-articles&Itemid=81.

Cal Pilots is an organization similar to the AOPA, but it has a defined area.
It is also very concerned with this issue. The article is from the NBAA
which is the National Business Aviation Association. The article explains
that the airline industry is getting it easy with this proposal. It says that the
government is trying to move fees from the airlines to general aviation. The
problem with this is that the airline industry can handle it, general aviation
cannot. General aviation includes every aspect of aviation excluding the
airlines and the military. The majority of general aviation pilots are your
everyday, fly-for-fun kinds of people. These people cannot afford all the
fees that would be put into place. This would destroy the industry. This is
important because it ties the airline industry into the argument.

Network, A. (2009, October 12). Aero-TV: AirVenture Meet the
        Boss—Randy Babbitt Tackles User Fees. Retrieved from
        http://www.youtube.com/watch?v=J14ut3O_j3M.

This video is from AirVenture, which is a fly-in expo. Randy Babbitt is one
of the head officials for the FAA and he explains that the FAA needs money
to meet the needs of the industry. He says that the planes now are more
efficient, making them use less fuel which means that the fuel tax in effect
now is less effective. He goes on to explain that the FAA needs to make up
this deficit, but it does not know exactly where it is going to come from.

This is important because it is a government official who is explaining the situation the FAA is in and what he thinks will happen.

Wald, M. L. (2006, March 7). F.A.A. Seeks New Source of Revenue in User Fees. *The New York Times*. Retrieved March 2, 2011, from http://query.nytimes.com/gst/fullpage.html?res=9507E0D91531F93 4A35750.

Matthew L. Wald is a journalist for *The New York Times*. In the article, he interviews some very influential people in the aviation industry. Another important fact about him is that he is also a general aviation pilot. This article explains that because of the drop of airline tickets that the FAA needs to find new ways to make money because the tax implemented on tickets is not getting the job done. It says that the FAA is going to tax the users of the air traffic control system. This article is important because it gives specific numbers on how much the FAA is in debt and what the budget proposal is.

Activity 7.10 **Compare and Contrast Media**

Your instructor will select an article on a topic or event that is currently in the news. Find another article on the same subject either from the same news outlet or another major news source (*The New York Times*, *The Wall Street Journal*, *CNN*, *Time*, etc.). Compare and contrast how the reporting of the event is similar or different in the two texts. Note: You are not to write a report on the content of the articles themselves; instead, identify the author's perspective in each text and how it influences how the news is portrayed to readers.

Look for opinions, adjectives with positive or negative connotations, facts or evidence presented, the tone of the headline, and the text itself. Also consider the target audience.

Organize your observations in a one- to two-page report with a clear thesis that presents your evaluation of the two texts.

Activity 7.11 **Write on Your Blog**

In your blog, write a summary and a response to a source you might use to research your topic. Is it useful for your research? Why or why not?

Activity 7.12 **Write in Your Commonplace Book**

Copy a quote from a source that you think makes a critical point about the argument paper you are writing. Then comment about the quote— what does it mean and why is it important?

A
APPENDIX
CITING SOURCES

Praxis in Action

How I Cite by Craig Wynne

Make no mistake about it: Doing the citations can be an annoying part of the writing process. I don't know of anyone who enjoys doing citations because it is not easy to get the information in the right order, as well as put periods and commas where they are required; but citations are necessary, so your instructor knows from where you obtained your sources. If your instructor doesn't specify a format, ask if you should use MLA or APA. Also, if you are lucky enough to have an instructor who will take a look at a rough draft of your Works Cited page or bibliography, be sure to take advantage of that opportunity!

I find it can be stressful trying to put together citations at the end of a paper, as it can take a few hours trying to remember where you got your sources. I prefer to do them as I write, as it actually saves time to do that. Whenever I insert a quote or a paraphrase, I cite it immediately after I've written it. I do the internal citation, and I add the reference to my Works Cited page. I find it helps me to complete this part of the process, and it saves me time at the end having to go back through sources.

I'm also careful about using citation generators such as EasyBib and RefWorks. Many students find they can be effective time-savers, but I don't recommend relying on them entirely. Generators do a good job in setting up the order of a citation, but citations have to look a certain way, and the generators don't always get the periods and the capitals in the right places. They also won't cite inside the text. Personally, I find it easier and faster just to do the citations myself without using a citation generator. If you decide to try out EasyBib, RefWorks, or another citation generator, remember to allow yourself enough time to double-check all your citations against a handbook or handout that gives you the correct formats.

To save time and avoid undue stress, Craig Wynne prepares citations as he writes.

EasyBib is one of the citation generators available on the Internet through a keyword search. Most offer a free version, with upgraded features for a subscription fee. Note that EasyBib encourages users to double-check their entries both for content and form. Citation generators assist with documentation format, but they cannot eliminate errors.

Evolving Formats of Document Citation

The widespread use of the Internet for research is changing the way sources are cited in documents. This is certainly true of electronic sources because of the ephemeral nature of web pages. Although documents may look like print sources (often with title, author, and publication information), they also share a characteristic of live performances in that you can access them after they have occurred only if you can find a recorded version. Once web pages are removed from a website, you cannot view them unless they have been archived. Also, web pages can be updated or changed, while retaining the same appearance, which makes systematic documentation difficult.

In the past, Modern Language Association (MLA) style recommended including the URL (web address) of web page documents in the Works Cited list. However, more recently MLA has taken the position that including that information has limited value because URLs are prone to change and are cumbersome in any case. The current recommendation is that students include URLs only when the material would otherwise be difficult to locate or if the instructor requires it. If you do include a URL, enclose it with an angle bracket and follow with a period. For example, the web page for *The New York Times* would be <http://nytimes.com>.

APA style suggests including the elements of a citation in the same order as you would for a print source, adding information about electronic retrieval after the standard information. However, APA also recognizes that information such as author, publication date, publisher, or even title may be missing in an electronic source. APA suggests giving the DOI (Digital Object Identifier) a unique alphanumeric string that is a persistent link, whenever possible. If it is not available, APA recommends giving the URL of the item being cited.

Interestingly, the prevalence of Internet sources is changing the way print sources are cited. MLA style recommends adding the word "print" after printed source citation information, as you would add "web" after a source accessed on the Internet.

When You Have a Choice of Electronic Source Format, Choose a PDF

When searching for articles in online databases or web pages, you may be offered a choice of formats: HTML or PDF. If you have that choice, select the PDF because it will have page numbers. Essentially, a PDF document reproduces print documents exactly, so that reading one is just like reading the original article except that it is not surrounded by the other content of the original publication.

If you are utilizing electronic documents as sources and they are not PDFs, you may be missing several of the usual elements of document citation, such as author name, publisher or sponsoring organization, page numbers, and even a title. In this case, give as much information about these traditional elements of citation as you can, and review the examples that follow for help with format. As an easy rule of thumb, though, keep this in mind: The more of the traditional elements used to classify and place a document within the scholarly world that are missing, the less likely the text is to be credible and reliable. If readers cannot tell where the information originated, how are they to trust it?

Note that MLA and APA both specify that documents should be double-spaced. The following examples are single-spaced to save space.

MLA Style

For MLA style, you may refer to the *MLA Handbook for Writers of Research Papers* and the MLA website, http://www.mla.org. The Purdue Owl, http://owl.purdue.english.edu, is also an excellent reference.

A paper written in MLA style should be double-spaced, with margins set at one inch on all sides. Choose a standard typeface such as Times Roman in 12 pt. type.

Beginning on the first page, generate a heading on the upper right-hand side of the page that gives the page number.

Do not create a cover page unless your instructor specifies one. Instead, on the upper left-hand side of the first page, give your name, your instructor's name, the course, and the date. These items should all be flush left, double-spaced, and set on separate lines.

Double-space again and center the title. Follow the title with another double-space and indent the first line of text. Indent each paragraph.

Bibliographical Documentation

In MLA style, this is called either the Works Cited page or an Annotated Bibliography. The title, either Works Cited or Annotated Bibliography, should appear centered on the top margin of the last page of a researched essay. The Works Cited page should be double-spaced with no extra line spacing between entries. The first line of each entry begins at the margin, and all subsequent lines of a particular entry are indented 5 spaces on the left margin. All entries should be in alphabetical order. The Annotated Bibliography is formatted like the Works Cited page with the addition of an annotation or description of the source in a paragraph following the citation. The following entries are typical citations prepared according to MLA style.

Examples are offered for both print, online, and database versions, when applicable.

Book

Egan, Jennifer. *A Visit from the Goon Squad.* New York: Alfred A. Knopf, 2010. Print.

Book with Two Authors

Friedman, Thomas L. and Michael Mandelbaum. *That Used to Be Us: How America Fell behind in the World It Invented and How We Can Come Back.* New York: Farrar, Straus and Giroux, 2011. Print.

Two or More Selections from the Same Print Collection or Anthology

> **Note**: To avoid repetition on the list of works cited, cite an anthology or reader as a separate entry. Then cross-reference entries to the anthology as in the example below.

Burns, Gary. "Marilyn Manson and the Apt Pupils of Littleton." Petracca and Sorapure 284–90. Print.

Fox, Roy. "Salespeak." Petracca and Sorapure 56–72. Print.

Petracca, Michael and Madeleine Sorapure, eds. *Common Culture: Reading and Writing About American Popular Culture.* 5th ed. Upper Saddle River: Pearson, 2007. Print.

> **Note**: Alphabetize each entry among other entries on the Works Cited page. Do not group the entries from the anthology together unless they fall next to one another alphabetically. Also, remember that you will have no parenthetical citation referencing the editors Petracca and Sorapure. You should cite Burns and Fox in the parenthetical citations in your paper.

Book with Multiple Editors

Mennuti, Rosemary B., Arthur Freeman, and Ray W. Christner, eds. *Cognitive-Behavioral Interventions: A Handbook for Practice.* New York: Routledge, 2006. Print.

Online Edition of Book or Novel

James, Henry. *The American*. 1877. Fiction: *The Eserver Collection*. Web. 15 June 2008.

(This book was published before 1900, so the name and city of the publisher are not needed. For more recent books, give the print information first, then the information about web publication.)

Macfie, A. L. *Orientalism: a Reader*. New York: New York UP, 2000. *Google Books*. Web. 26 Sept. 2011.

Scholarly Article in Print Journal

Thompson, Jason. "Magic for a People Trained in Pragmatism: Kenneth Burke, and the Early 9/11 Oratory of George W. Bush." *Rhetoric Review* 30.4 (2011): 350–71. Print.

Scholarly Article Found in Online Database

Angel, R. J. "Immigrants and Welfare: The Impact of Welfare Reform on America's Newcomers." *Contemporary Sociology: A Journal of Reviews* 39.5 (2010): 568–69. Academic Search Complete. Web. 10 September 2011.

Scholarly Article from Journal Published Online

Gustafsson, Amanda. "Beware the Invisible." *Papers from the Institute of Archeology* 20 (2010): n. pag. Web. 29 Sept. 2011.

Note: MLA specifies including page numbers for scholarly publications, so if the online journal does not provide page numbers, include n. pag. (no page).

Book Review

Schneider, Robert J. Rev. of *Modern Physics and Ancient Faith*, by Stephen M. Barr. *Anglican Theological Review* 86 (2004): 506–07. Print.

Book Review Published Online

Garner, Dwight. "An Unearthed Treasure That Changed Things." Rev. of *The Swerve: How the World Became Modern*. *The New York Times*, 27 Sept. 2011. Web. 28 Sept. 2011.

An Editorial

Wolfe, Gregory. "The Operation of Grace." Editorial. *Image: A Journal of the Arts and Religion* 70 (Summer 2011): 3–4 Print.

An Editorial Published Online

"U.S. House: Members Are Not as Uncivil as They Seem." Editorial. *Nation Now. Los Angeles Times*, 28 Sept. 2011. Web. 29 Sept. 2011.

> **Note**: This editorial was published in a blog called *Nation Now* that is published by the *Los Angeles Times.*

Magazine Article

Perry, Alex. "Epidemic on the Run." *Time* 26 Sept. 2011: 46–49. Print.

Magazine Article from Online Database

Neuwirth, Robert. "Global Bazaar: Shantytowns, Favelas and Jhopadpattis Turn Out to Be Places of Surprising Innovation." *Scientific American* Sept. 2011: 56–63. *Academic Search Complete.* Web. 29 Sept. 2011.

Online Magazine Article

Leonard, Andrew. "Inside the Shadow Economy: The Growing Underwater Bazaar." *Salon*. Salon Media Group, 29 September 2011. Web. 29 September 2011.

> **Note**: The title of the magazine is followed by the publisher or sponsor of the site, a comma, and the date of publication. MLA uses this format because it does not consider online-only magazines to be periodicals. If no publisher is given, add n.p., and if no date is given, add n.d.

Interview

"Samantha Stosur, U.S. Open Champion." Interview by Cassandra Murnieks. *Time*. Time Inc., 23 Sept. 2011. Web. 29 Sept. 2011.

Online Speech

King, Jr., Martin Luther. "I Have a Dream." Speech. March on Washington for Jobs and Freedom. Lincoln Memorial, Washington, D.C. 28 Aug. 1963. *Americanrhetoric.com*. Michael E. Eidenmuller. n.d. Web. 29 Sept. 2011.

Note: The citation includes n.d. (no date) because the date when the speech was posted on the site is not given.

Page on a Website

Coe, Jennifer. "How to Refinish a Dresser." *How To*. SheKnows LLC, 3 Aug. 2011. Web. 29 Sept. 2011.

Note: The blog *How To* lists its publisher as SheKnows LLC. If the publisher were not given, then you would use n.p. (no publisher).

Image from a Website

Gogh, Vincent Van. *Cypresses*. 1889. Oil on canvas. *The Metropolitan Museum of Art*, New York. The Metropolitan Museum of Art. Web. 29 Sept. 2011.

Blog Posting

"Respect Your Audience." Web log post. *Writer's Block*. NIVA Inc., 2009. Web. 15 Sept. 2011.

Note: The blog does not list an author for the posting, so the citation begins with the title.

Government Document

"El Chamizal Dispute: Compliance with Convention of the Chamizal." 1964. *U.S. Senate Hearing*. Cleofas Calleros Papers. University of Texas at El Paso Library Special Collections. 33–9. Print.

Government Document Online

Travis, William Barret. "Letter from the Alamo, 1836." Texas State Library & Archives Commission. Web. 15 Apr. 2011.

Government Document from Online Database

"United Nations Resolutions on Operation Desert Storm." Aug–Nov 1990. Essential Documents in American History: 1492–Present. 1–17 Academic Search Premier. Web. 8 May 2011.

A Film on DVD

The Lord of the Rings: The Return of the King. Dir. Peter Jackson. New Line, 2003. DVD-ROM.

Television Program

Martin, David. "The Pentagon's Ray Gun." *60 Minutes.* CBS. New York, New York, 2 Mar. 2008. Television.

MLA Parenthetical or (In-Text) Documentation

Parenthetical documentation refers to the process of citing sources within the text. Citing sources within the text is necessary for students to indicate when they are using the words, thoughts, or ideas that are not their own and borrowed from an outside source. Whether students use a direct quote, a paraphrase, or a summary of the information, they must properly provide credit to the original author(s) of that source. Using appropriate sources for support and documenting these sources accurately adds to the credibility and value of a student's essay. The following examples provide a guideline to proper parenthetical documentation.

Direct Quote (three lines or less)

"Scientists estimate that the rangewide population of the San Joaquin kit fox prior to 1930 was 8,000 . . . " (Conover 44).

Direct Quote (more than three lines)

Conover's 2001 study of the San Joaquin kit fox found the following:

> For the most part, in the "real" world, kit foxes escape their predators and the high temperatures of their desert environment by spending the day underground in a den. In Bakersfield, they follow suit. Kit foxes move every couple of weeks to a new den.

Moving to different dens may be one reason why they have persisted; the constantly changing abodes provided new places to hide. (199)

Note: For a direct quote that is more than three lines, the passage should be indented 10 spaces and set as a block, as shown here.

Direct Quote When the Author Is Named in the Text

Hildebrand states that "generals of Alexander the Great brought news to Europe of vegetable wool which grew in tufts of trees in India" (144).

Information from Printed Source (but not a direct quote)

It is common to see an Osprey make its nest on an electric power pole (Askew 34).

Electronic Sources

Many electronic sources are not numbered with pages unless they are presented in a PDF file. If paragraphs are numbered, use numbers following the abbreviation, par. Most often the source will not have page, paragraph, section, or screen numbers. In this case, include no numbers in the parentheses. Instead, include the words that come first in the bibliographic citation.

(Coe, Jennifer. "How To")

APA Style

For APA style, you will want to refer to the *Publication Manual of the American Psychological Association* and the website provided by the American Psychological Association, http://www.apastyle.org, which offers free tutorials for APA style. The Purdue Owl also offers excellent information at http://owl.english.purdue.edu.

APA specifies that your essay should be typed in 12 pt. Times Roman type and double-spaced, with one-inch margins. In addition, APA style specifies the following general rules for formatting a paper or essay:

■ Running heads—Create running heads for your page numbers, flush left, beginning on the title page. Also, on the title page, you should have a running head that reads like this:

Running head: Title of Your Paper

with the title actually being your paper title. On succeeding pages, the flush left header should include only the title of your paper, not the words "Running Head."

■ Title page—In addition to the running heads, your title page will contain the title of the paper (one- or two-line title), followed by your name on the second line, and then the name of your college on the third line, all centered.

■ Unless your instructor specifies otherwise, the second page of your paper is a 150- to 200-word abstract that summarizes the major aspects of your paper.

■ Begin your essay on the third page, after the running head, which is the title of your paper and the centered title. Indent each paragraph and double-space.

■ At the end of your paper, include your References, which lists your sources according to APA citation style.

Bibliographical Documentation

In APA style, this is called either the References or the Annotated Bibliography. The title, either References or Annotated Bibliography, should appear centered on the top margin of the last page of a researched essay. The References or Annotated Bibliography page should be double-spaced with no extra line spacing between entries. The first line of each entry begins at the margin, and all subsequent lines of a particular entry are indented on the left margin 5 spaces for a References Page. All entries should be in alphabetical order. The Annotated Bibliography is formatted like the References page with the addition of an annotation or description of the source in a paragraph following each citation.

> **Note**: APA suggests that when you are citing a source from the web or an online database you should give the DOI (Digital Object Identifier) of the source in the References List. If the DOI is not available, you can give the URL (web address) for the

text. APA does not require that you give the date you access a source on the Internet unless you have reason to believe that the text may change or disappear from the Internet. Also note that if you cite an entire website, simply include the website address in parentheses in the text with no entry in the References page. The following entries are typical citations for APA style. Examples are offered for both print, online, and database versions, when applicable.

Book

Egan, J. (2010). *A visit from the Goon Squad.* New York: Alfred A. Knopf.

Book with Two Authors

Friedman, T. L., & Mandelbaum, M. (2011). *That used to be us: how America fell behind in the world it invented and how we can come back.* New York: Farrar, Straus & Giroux.

Book with Multiple Editors

Mennuti, R.B., Freeman, A., & Christner, R.W. (Eds.). (2006). *Cognitive-behavioral interventions in educational settings: A handbook for practice.* New York: Routledge.

Book Online Edition

James, H. (1960). The American. Retrieved from http://eserver.org/fiction /novel.html

(If the book has a DOI, then give that instead of the URL).

Online Edition of Book

Macfie, A. L. (2000). *Orientalism: a reader.* New York: New York University Press. Retrieved September 26, 2011, from Google Books.

Scholarly Article in Print Journal

Thompson, J. (2011). Magic for a people trained in pragmatism: Kenneth Burke, and the early 9/11 Oratory of George W. Bush. *Rhetoric Review, 30* (4), 350–371.

Scholarly Article Found in Online Database

Angel, R. J. (2010). Immigrants and welfare: the impact of welfare reform on America's newcomers. *Contemporary Sociology: A Journal of Reviews, 39*(5), 568–569.

> **Note:** APA does not require that you list the database where you obtained an article unless the article would be difficult to locate. Instead, use the citation format you would if it were a print source.

Scholarly Article from Journal Published Online

Gustafsson, A. (2010). Beware the invisible. *Papers from the Institute of Archeology, 20.* Retrieved September 29, 2011, doi:10.5334/pia.343.

> **Note:** This citation includes a doi (digital object identifier), which provides a permanent way to locate an article, even if databases or websites change.

Book Review

Schneider, R. J. (2004). [Review of the book *Modern physics and ancient faith*]. *Anglican Theological Review, 86,* 506–07.

Book Review Published Online

Garner, D. (2011, September 27). An unearthed treasure that changed things [Review of *The Swerve: How the world became modern*]. *The New York Times.*

An Editorial

Wolfe, G. (2011). The operation of grace [Editorial]. *Image: A Journal of the Arts and Religion, 70,* 3–4.

An Editorial Published Online

U.S. House: Members are not as uncivil as they seem [Editorial]. (2011, September 28). *Nation Now.* Retrieved September 29, 2011, from http://latimesblogs.latimes.com/nationnow/2011/09/us-house-more-civil-than-the-mid-90s-but-trouble-could-lay-ahead-.html.

Note: This editorial was published in a blog called *Nation Now* that is published by the *Los Angeles Times*.

Magazine Article

Perry, A. (2011, September 26). Epidemic on the run. *Time*, 46–49.

Magazine Article from Online Database

Neuwirth, R. (2011, September). Global bazaar: Shantytowns, favelas and jhopadpattis turn out to be places of surprising innovation. *Scientific American*, 56–63.

Note: APA does not require you to cite the database where you obtained the article unless you think the article would be difficult to find.

Online Magazine Article

Leonard, A. (2011, September 29). A growing underworld bazaar. *Salon*. Retrieved September 29, 2011, from http://www.salon.com/news/inside_the_shadow_economy/?story=/politics/feature/2011/09/29/shadowintro.

Interview

Samantha Stosur, U.S. Open Champion [Interview by C. Murnieks]. (2011, September 23). In *Time*. Retrieved September 29, 2011, from http://www.time.com/time/arts/article/0,8599,2094349,00.html.

Online Speech

King, Jr., M. L. (1963, August 28). *I have a dream*. Speech presented at March on Washington for Jobs and Freedom at the Lincoln Memorial, Washington, D.C. Retrieved September 29, 2011.

Page on a Website

Coe, J. (2011, August 3). How to refinish a dresser. *How To*. Retrieved September 29, 2011.

Image from a Website

Van Gogh, V. (1889). *Cypresses* [Painting found in The Metropolitan Museum of Art, New York]. Retrieved September 29, 2011.

Blog Posting

Respect your audience [Web log post]. (2009). Retrieved September 15, 2011, from http://www.writersblock.ca/tips/monthtip/tipjan98.htm.

Government Document

El Chamizal dispute: Compliance with convention of the Chamizal. (1964). *U.S. Senate Hearing.* Cleofas Calleros Papers. University of Texas at El Paso Library Special Collections (#33–9).

Government Document Online

Travis, W. B. (2005). Letter from the Alamo, 1836. Retrieved from Texas State Library & Archives Commission, http//www.tslstate.tx.us/treasures/republic/Alamo/travis01.gov.

A Film or DVD

Coen, E. & Coen, J. (Producers and directors). (2007). *No country for old men* [Motion picture]. United States: Paramount Vantage.

Television Program

Martin, D. (Reporter). (2008, March 2). The Pentagon's ray gun [Television series episode]. In M. Walsh (Producer) *60 Minutes.* New York, New York: CBS.

APA Parenthetical or (In-Text) Documentation

Direct Quote (three lines or less)

"Scientists estimate that the rangewide population of the San Joaquin kit fox prior to 1930 was 8,000 . . . " (Conover, 2001, p. 44).

Direct Quote (more than three lines)

Conover's 2001 study of the San Joaquin kit fox found the following:

> For the most part, in the "real" world kit foxes escape their predators and the high temperatures of their desert environment by spending the day underground in a den. In Bakersfield, they follow suit. Kit foxes move every couple of weeks to a new den. Moving to different dens may be one reason why they have persisted; the constantly changing abodes provided new places to hide. (p. 199)

> **Note**: For a direct quote that exceeds three lines, indent the passage 5 spaces and set as a block, as shown here.

Direct Quote When the Author Is Named in the Text

Hildebrand (2004) stated that "generals of Alexander the Great brought news to Europe of vegetable wool which grew in tufts of trees in India" (p. 144).

Information from Printed Source (but not a direct quote)

It is common to see an Osprey make its nest on an electric power pole (Askew, year, p. 34).

Naming the Author of a Reference in Your Text, but Not Using a Direct Quote

Thompson (2002) maintained that . . .

In 2002, Thompson discovered . . .

Electronic or Other Sources Missing Author, Date, or Page Numbers

If your source provides section notations or paragraph numbers, indicate those. Use the paragraph ¶ symbol or the abbreviation para. and number.

(Bussell, 2000, ¶ 9)

If you include a quote from a text that has neither page numbers nor paragraph or section numbers, then simply give the author and the date:

(Bussell, 2000).

If there is no author, as in an editorial, then give part of the name of the text and the date:

("Respect your audience," 2009).

If there is no date, then use n.d. If you have no date, no page number, and no author, your in-text citation will look as follows:

("The future of space," n.d.)

Works Cited

"20 Years Later, San Ysidro McDonald's Massacre Remembered." Web log post. *North County Times*. Lee Enterprises Inc., 2004. Web. 17 July 2004.

"A $300 Idea that Is Priceless." *The Economist* 28 Apr. 2011. Print.

Adams, Scott. "Dilbert." Comic Strip. *United Feature Syndicate*. Print.

Aimes, Alexander. "Bringing History to Life with Primary Sources." Student essay. Used by permission.

"Choosing When to Give Credit." *The Purdue Online Writing Lab*. Purdue University. 9 June 2009. Web. 12 Nov. 2011.

Davey, Monica M. "Meet Tim Cook." 12 August 2007. Photograph. European Pressphoto Agency, Frankfurt.

Duggan, Paul. "In Sex-Crime Cases, Credibility a Thorny Issue." *The Washington Post* 1 July 2011. Print.

Echanove, Matias, and Rahul Srivastava. "Hands Off Our Houses." *The New York Times* 1 June 2011: A27. Print.

Fogarty, Mignon. *Grammar Girl: Quick and Dirty Tips for Better Writing*. New York: St. Martin's Press, 2008. Print.

Gleiberman, Owen. "Film Review: The Hangover." Rev. of *The Hangover*, by Dir. Todd Phillips. *EW.com* 2 June 2009. Web. 15 Nov. 2010.

Govindarajan, Vijay. "The $300 House: A Hands-On Lab for Reverse Innovation?" Web log post. *HBR Blog Network*, Harvard Business School Publishing, 26 Aug. 2010. Web. 22 Oct. 2011.

Govindarajan, Vijay. "The $300 House: A Hands-On Approach to a Wicked Problem."

Web log post. *HBR Blog* Network, Harvard Business School Publishing, 7 June

2011. Web. 22 Oct. 2011.

Greene, Andy. "All Star Rockers Salute Buddy Holly." *Rolling Stone.* Straight Arrow

Publishers, 7 July 2011. Print.

Jayawardhana, Ray. "Alien Life, Coming Slowly into View." *The New York Times.*

27 March 2011: WK10. Print.

Johnson, Judith. "The Truth about Writer's Block." *The Huffington Post.* HuffPost News,

25 July 2011. Web. 11 Nov. 2011.

King, Jr., Martin Luther. "I Have a Dream." Speech. March on Washington for Jobs and

Freedom. Lincoln Memorial, Washington, D.C. 28 Aug. 1963. *Americanrhetoric.*

com. Michael E. Eidenmuller. n.d. Web. 12 Nov. 2011.

Lincoln, Abraham. "Gettysburg Address." Speech. Dedication of the Soldiers' National

Cemetary. Gettysburg, Pennsylvania 19 Nov. 1863. *Ourdocuments.gov.* n.d. Web.

15 Nov. 2011.

McArdle, Megan. "Anatomy of a Fake Quotation." *The Atlantic* 2 May 2011. Print.

McGrath, Charles. "The Lexicon." *NYTimes.com* 8 Sept. 2011. Web. 9 Sept. 2011.

Meyers, Justin. "How to Make a Kindle Cover from a Hollowed Out Hardback Book."

Wonder How To. n.p., March 2011. Web. 12 Nov. 2011.

Neil, Dan. "BMW 1M: Miniature, Mighty and Miles of Fun." *The Wall Street Journal*

3 Sept. 2011. Print.

Obama, Barack. "Remarks by the President on Osama bin Laden." Speech. Address to the Nation that Osama bin Laden is dead. The White House, Washington, D.C. 1 May 2011. *The White House Blog*. Macon Phillips. 2 May 2011. Web. 29 Sept. 2011.

Rosen, Jeffrey. "The Web Means the End of Forgetting." *The New York Times* 25 July 2010: MM30. Print.

Schalet, Amy. "The Sleepover Question." *The New York Times* 23 July 2011: SR9. Print.

Scham, Sam. "Top Ten Distractions for Writers, or Any Job Really." *Yahoo*.com 12 Aug. 2008. Web. 12 Nov. 2011.

Shemtob, Zachary, and David Lat. "Executions Should Be Televised." *The New York Times* 31 July 2011: SR4. Print.

Skinner, E. Benjamin. "People for Sale." *Foreign Policy*. March–April 2008. Print.

Thornburgh, Nathan. "Violent Rhetoric and Arizona Politics." Editorial. *Time* 9 Jan. 2011. Print.

Wright, Don. "Obama Grammarian Cartoon." *International Herald Tribune* 20 January 2009. Print.

Wynn, Craig. "Take a Leap Into Writing." Student essay. Used by permission.

Young, Neil. "Let's Roll." *Are You Passionate?* Reprise Records, 2002. CD.

Zuniga, Janine. "San Ysidro Shooting Survivor Lives His Dream of Being a Cop." *San Diego Union-Tribune* 18 July 2004. Print.

Index

Signs

A Grammar Handbook

by Allison D. Smith

APPROPRIATE WORD CHOICE

11a   Check for exactness and clarity

1. Be precise

Make every word and phrase count by making your point in the fewest possible words.

Wordy:

→ In point of fact, in language, a code is a sign or rule that allows you to change a piece of information into another sign, form, or representation, and this new sign, form, or representation does not necessarily have to be of the same system.

Concise:

→ A code is a sign that changes information into another sign, sometimes not in the same system.

2. Use specific, concrete words

Student writers often are asked to give their opinions about literature, films, or music. Using vague descriptors such as *good, bad, great, best, greatest,* and *worst* weakens writing. Make descriptions stronger by using specific, concrete words.

Vague:

➜ *The Old Man and the Sea* is the best novel.

Specific:

➜ In *The Old Man and the Sea*, Ernest Hemingway depicts the accurate and heart-wrenching life of a fisherman.

In addition, be sure to use concrete words, instead of vague or abstract ones, to make a description the strongest it can be. This would be a good time to check a thesaurus (see Chapter 14).

Using specific, concrete words	
Instead of this...	**Try this...**
blue	azure, cobalt, navy, sea blue, turquoise
car	Ford Escort, Toyota Camry, Volkswagen Beetle
friend	school acquaintance, close friend, movie pal
house	home, abode, igloo, apartment, student dormitories
hungry	famished, ravenous, starving
piece of literature	short story, poem, novel, play
river	Danube, Mississippi, Nile
the city	Austin, Los Angeles, Nashville, New York

When searching for a more specific or concrete word, be careful not to just let your computer thesaurus make an automatic replacement. For instance, if you just automatically substitute a more specific word for *blue*, you might end up with a problematic sentence, as shown below.

➜ I wanted to buy the blue car.

Automatic substitute from thesaurus➜ I wanted to buy the depressed car.

Effective substitute from thesaurus➜ I wanted to buy the navy car.

3. Delete empty words and phrase

It is not the number of words you use, but the exactness of the words that demonstrates writing maturity. Using empty phrases or expletives, such as *there/it + be*, may be grammatically correct, but you can be more concise by just dropping them.

Wordy:

➔ There were only three sailors on *The Enterprise* who knew semaphore signs.

Concise:

➔ Only three sailors on *The Enterprise* knew semaphore signs.

If your instructor assigns a first-person essay, be sure that you do not overuse the empty phrases that can sometimes go along with this type of writing. Some instructors call these empty phrases "weasel words" because they can make your writing sound non-authoritative. By dropping these empty phrases or weasel words, you can present your views with more authority.

Wordy:

➔ In my opinion, I think that learning Morse code is difficult.

Concise:

➔ Learning Morse code is difficult.

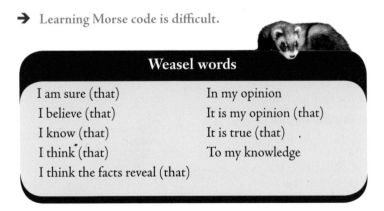

Weasel words

I am sure (that)	In my opinion
I believe (that)	It is my opinion (that)
I know (that)	It is true (that)
I think (that)	To my knowledge
I think the facts reveal (that)	

4. Replace wordy prepositional phrases with more concise adverbs

Wordy descriptions sometimes fill up a lot of space but do not say anything important or necessary. This type of wordiness usually includes unnecessary prepositional phrases that can be deleted without changing any real meaning.

Wordy:

→ In this day and age in the event that a boat has trouble in the water, semaphores or Morse code can be used to signal for help.

Concise:

→ When in trouble, boaters can use semaphores or Morse code to signal for help.

Using adverbs for conciseness	
Replace these prepositional phrases	**with these adverbs**
at all times	always
at that point in time	then
at the present time	now, today
at this moment	now, today
beyond a shadow of a doubt	certainly, surely
due to the fact that	because
for the purpose of	for
in order to	to
in point of fact	undoubtedly, clearly
in spite of the fact that	although
in the event that	if, when
in the final analysis	finally
in this day and age	today
in view of the fact that	because
it is clear that	clearly
it is obvious that	obviously

it is my opinion that	(drop completely)
there is no question that	unquestionably, certainly
without a doubt	undoubtedly

5. Describe exactly who, what, when, where, why, and how

Vague descriptions or empty words contribute nothing to the meaning of the sentence or the description you are trying to give. Rephrase these vague descriptions into specific words. Once you have identified the specifics (who, what, when, where, why, how), do not repeat the same information.

Wordy:

➜ When on the water and not in close contact with other boats, boaters can use Morse code, but when on the water and in eye view of another boat, boaters can use semaphores.

Concise:

➜ Boaters can use semaphores when close to another boat and Morse code when farther than eye view.

6. Use figurative language when appropriate

Using words in an imaginative or creative way, rather than in the literal sense, is figurative language. The most common figures of speech are metaphors (a comparison of dissimilar things) and similes (a comparison of dissimilar things using *like* or *as*).

Simile➜ The boat glided on the water like a pelican in flight.

Metaphor➜ Morse code is the Model T of communication.

However, be careful about being too flowery with descriptions. Flowery language is writing that often contains too many adjectives, adverbs, or words that you have looked up in a thesaurus and used incorrectly.

Flowery:

→ The old faded scarlet dinghy sashayed on the cool, fresh, and blue water like a storm-tossed pelican in dangerous flight.

Concise:

→ The old red dinghy bounced on the water.

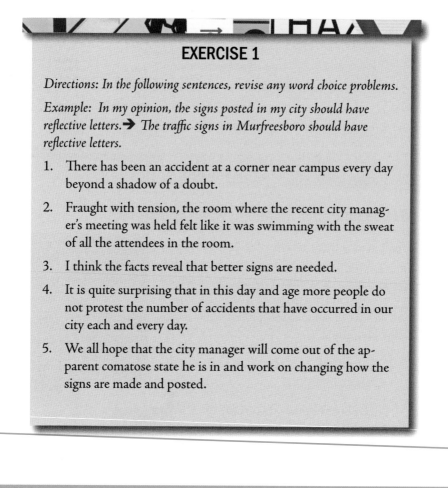

EXERCISE 1

Directions: In the following sentences, revise any word choice problems.

Example: In my opinion, the signs posted in my city should have reflective letters. → *The traffic signs in Murfreesboro should have reflective letters.*

1. There has been an accident at a corner near campus every day beyond a shadow of a doubt.

2. Fraught with tension, the room where the recent city manager's meeting was held felt like it was swimming with the sweat of all the attendees in the room.

3. I think the facts reveal that better signs are needed.

4. It is quite surprising that in this day and age more people do not protest the number of accidents that have occurred in our city each and every day.

5. We all hope that the city manager will come out of the apparent comatose state he is in and work on changing how the signs are made and posted.

11b   Check for completeness

The words we use in conversations often have clear references in the environment or context around us. However, in academic and professional writing, some conversational words need to be replaced for full clarity and transparency.

Deictic or pointing words, such as *here, there, this,* and *that,* that are frequently used in spoken language need clear antecedents or full descriptions in writing.

Unclear reference:

→ When traveling by sea, be sure to take that manual.

Clear reference:

→ When traveling by sea, be sure to take the semaphore manual.

Intensifiers, such as *so, such,* and *too,* that are used in speech to mean "very" or "exceptionally" usually need an extra phrase or clause to describe **why** something is being intensified.

Unclear reference:

→ Morse code is so out of date.

Clear reference:

→ Morse code, which was created in the early 1840s, is so out of date that it is rarely used anymore.

When comparing two or more things in academic writing, be sure to provide both parts of the comparison.

Unclear reference:

→ Semaphore codes are even older.

Clear and full reference:

→ Semaphore codes, created in the early 1800s, are even older than Morse code, which was first used in the 1840s.

11c   Check for tired, stale, or unnatural language

Descriptive language that is innovative can quickly capture the reader's attention and interest. Note the difference between the following two sentences.

Simple➔ The boat floated out to sea.

Descriptive➔ The rowboat drifted two miles off shore.

However, as writers, we need to be careful not to get so caught up in our description that we borrow the overused expressions of others. As a rule, it is best to stay away from clichés and idioms that have lost their original innovativeness.

Some clichés to avoid

after all is said and done	easier said than done
beat around the bush	face the music
believe it or not	fish out of water
best foot forward	flat as a pancake
better late than never	food for thought
calm before the storm	grin and bear it
cart before the horse	in a nutshell
chalk up a victory	in one ear and out the other
come through with flying colors	in the nick of time
crying shame	last but not least
don't rock the boat	more than meets the eye
drop in the bucket	raining cats and dogs

Overused idiom/cliché:

➔ I felt like I was *out to sea* as I learned Morse code.

Straightforward description:

➔ Morse code was difficult to learn.

If you are asked as a writer to be creative and innovative in your expressions, such as when you write a narrative or descriptive essay, stay away from clichés, and use some creativity of your own.

Innovative/creative description:

→ Morse code was as difficult to learn as snowboarding on a mountain of Jell-O.

Jargon, the language used by a particular profession or a group of people, is usually too technical to be natural for an academic essay. Reword techno-speak into more straightforward descriptions.

Jargon:

→ Morse code is a type of character encoding that uses rhythmic language and telegraphic information to transmit a given communication.

Straightforward description:

→ Morse code uses dots and dashes to send out messages.

DID YOU KNOW?

William Shakespeare is credited with the first usage of around 2,000 words in the English language. He is also responsible for some of the most well-known idioms, some of which are now clichés: *neither rhyme nor reason, in my mind's eye, I must be cruel only to be kind, dead as a door-nail, it was Greek to me, love is blind, pomp and circumstance, a good riddance,* and *I have been in such a pickle.*

11d Check for appropriate levels of formality

What is Academic English? For some instructors, this term refers to good grammar and formal style. For others, it refers to having students be constructive critics and clear writers. Whatever it means, most instructors will expect you to use a style that is more formal than your conversational English but not to the point where your writing sounds stilted and pretentious. Remember that formality depends on the audience and purpose of the writing assignment; if you are unsure about what is expected of you, ask your instructor.

Informal language, in the form of slang or colloquial language, is usually not part of your academic writing, unless you are writing a narrative that uses dialogue. Even though some slang words (such as *jazz* or *mob*) can become part of the broader standard language, most slang is considered too localized and too informal for academic writing.

Slang description:

- → That boat was too cool.
- → That boat was wicked.
- → That boat was tight.
- → That boat was dope.

Academic description:

- → *The Enterprise,* a new addition to the fleet, has innovative engines that are less harmful to the environment.

Colloquial language, relaxed or casual speech used across many speakers, is also not usually part of academic writing. Words or expressions such as *a lot, gonna,* and *wanna* are too informal for essay writing.

Colloquial description:

- → The boaters wanna learn how to use semaphores in case of emergency.

Academic description:

→ The boaters want to learn how to use semaphores in case of emergency.

Doublespeak or doubletalk are words or expressions that are used to hide or distort the truth, such as using *protective custody* instead of *imprisonment* or *pre-hostility* instead of *peace*. In argumentative essays, using doublespeak can sound cagey or shifty.

Doublespeak description:

→ State employees now have job flexibility.

Academic description:

→ State employees now have a lack of job security because they are only employed week to week.

Be careful that when you are more formal in your writing, you do not go too far and sound pretentious, sometimes referred to as writing *gobbledygook*. This can happen if you use a thesaurus without considering the context or formality of the essay or letter you are writing. Also, be sure to use American English spelling, rather than British English.

Pretentious:

→ When I finalized my perusal of the optimal methodology to acquire the semaphore signals, I ascertained that it was more effortless to gain knowledge of Morse code.

Academic:

→ Learning Morse code was easier than learning semaphore signs.

Pretentious words

Instead of...	Try...
aficionado	fan
ascertain	find out
commence	begin
conviviality	friendliness
desist	stop
imbroglio	mess
instantiate	support
finalize	finish, complete
impact	affect
jejune	boring, childish
lugubrious	gloomy
methodology	method
nadir	lowest point
optimal	best
peruse	look at, read
potentiate	improve effectiveness
utilize	use

DID YOU KNOW?

British and American English, though mutually intelligible, have a number of distinct differences. Aside from pronunciation and vocabulary, spelling is often very different. We can thank Noah Webster (writer of the eponymous dictionary) for standardizing many American spellings, such as dropping the *u* from words like *colour* and *labour*, ending words with *−er* instead of *−re* (*center/centre*), and replacing *−ce* endings with *−se* (*offense*, *suspense*) to name a few examples. Not all of Webster's spelling reforms were accepted, though—*medicin*, *soop*, and *tung* never caught on.

11e Check for sexist and offensive language

Use language that gives equal value and respect for all people and places.

1. Use appropriate words for gender

Give equal treatment to each gender; do not privilege either. Also, be sure not to use the generic *he* for all writing occasions. Try rephrasing singular subjects to plural ones; this allows you to switch from the singular pronoun (she or he) to a plural one (they).

Possible sexist language:

➔ The sailor learned Morse Code in his training.

Inclusive language:

➔ Sailors learn Morse Code in training.

Do not assume that one gender cannot do a particular type of work or gender role, as in *the male nurse, the female astronaut, faculty wives,* and *both men and their wives.*

Sexist language:

➔ The stewardess learned Morse code in training.

Inclusive language:

➔ The flight attendant learned Morse code in training.

Sexist language:

➔ The sailors brought their wives and kids to the dock party.

Inclusive language:

➔ The sailors brought their families to the dock party.

Here are some substitutions that you might consider when writing about job titles.

Recommended terms for job titles

Instead of...	Try...
barman, barmaid	bartender
businessman	businessperson, executive, manager, staff person
chairman	chair, presiding officer, moderator
congressman	member of Congress, representative, senator
comedienne	comedian
fireman	firefighter
mailman	letter carrier, mail carrier, postal worker
salesman	salesperson, sales representative
sculptress	sculptor
steward, stewardess	flight attendant
usherette	usher
waiter, waitress	server

2. Use appropriate words for age

In academic writing, use non-offensive terms when referring to the age of a person.

Recommended terms for age

Instead of...	Try...
kids (to age 18)	children
kids (college students)	students, young adults, adults, men, women
elderly, old man, old woman	senior citizens, older adults

3. Use appropriate words for ethnicity or race

Be sure to use terms that are non-discriminatory and non-offensive when referring to the ethnic backgrounds or races of people. If unsure, you can check for acceptable general or specific terms in a current dictionary.

Acceptable terms for ethnicity or race

General Terms for People in the United States	Specific Terms for People in the United States
African American, Black	
American Indian, Native American	Alaska Native, Cherokee, Hopi, Navajo
Anglo-American, White American, White	French American, Irish American, Polish American
Arab American	Egyptian American, Lebanese American
Asian American	Chinese American, Japanese American, Korean American, Thai American
Hispanic, Hispanic American, Latino/a	Mexican American, Puerto Rican
Pacific Islander American, Native Hawaiian	

4. Use appropriate words for disability or illness

The current preference in referring to people with disabilities or illnesses is to put the *person* first. For example, refer to *a person with disabilities* or *a person who is differently abled* rather than *a disabled person*.

Recommended terms for disability or illness

Instead of this...	Try this...
AIDS victim	a person with AIDS
blind person, visually impaired person	a person with a visual impairment
deaf person	a person with a hearing impairment
dumb person	a person with speech impairment
handicapped person, disabled person	a person with disabilities
neurotic person	a person with a psychological disability
quadriplegics	a person who is quadriplegic

5. Use appropriate words for geographical areas

Because social and political boundaries may change, you can use *a person from (place name)* when referring to someone and her place of origin or residence and rarely be wrong. Definitely, stay away from any derogatory terms for a person's origin. The terms that are most frequently seen as problematic include the following.

Recommended terms for geographical areas	
Instead of...	**Try this...**
American	person from the United States, U.S. citizen
Arab	Egyptian, Iraqi, Saudi Arabian, Yemeni
English, Irish (from Northern Ireland), Welsh	British, person from the United Kingdom, U.K. citizen
Oriental	Asian, Asian American, Japanese, Korean, Chinese
Polish	Pole, person from Poland

EXERCISE 2

Directions: The following summary of a news event contains 12 words that are not appropriate for the more standardized language used for summarizing. Change these words to more appropriately reflect the summary writing you might do in a writing course.

Two kids have been taken into custody by the cops in connection with a recent string of vandalism in the area. The kids are accused of vandalizing stop signs in commemoration of the latest volume of the Harry Potter film franchise, *Harry Potter and the Half-Blood Prince,* by writing the name of evil wizard Voldemort on dozens of stop signs. Fanatics of the series might appreciate the vandals' urging to "STOP Voldemort," but the authorities were less entertained by the trick, which will cost the county $50 per devastated sign. The cops gave a statement warning would-be vandals that vandalism will not be tolerated, no matter how harmless or humorous vandalism may seem.

http://www.wisn.com/news/20061083/detail.html

Chapter 12

COMMONLY CONFUSED OR MISSPELLED WORDS

We can trace why words become commonly confused back to one thing—spelling. English spelling comes from a set of conventions or rules that have been agreed upon by dictionary editors. Since English has been a language for around 1600 years, how some words are spelled has changed many times. Regardless of these historic changes and how they often make it difficult to figure out a standardized alphabetic form for many sounds, most English words now have fixed spellings that can be looked up in dictionaries at any time.

Since using good spelling is usually considered a sign that a writer is educated, it is a good idea to work on improving your spelling, no matter how good you are at it. One way to improve your spelling is to read more, keeping a spelling list or journal in which you write down and practice new words. Another way is to own your own college dictionary, using it to look up the spellings and definitions of words you have trouble spelling. Since computerized dictionaries often lead you to use words you may not understand, be sure not only to use the dictionary provided with your word processor, but to use print dictionaries as well. For more specific help in using your dictionary, see Chapter 13.

DID YOU KNOW?

Ever wonder why English spelling is so un-predictable? English has a long history of foreign influence, which not only accounts for many of the unusual spellings, but also often indicates the origin of the word. For example, the words *doubt* and *debt* original-ly entered English from French influence, but misguided linguists added the silent *b* hundreds of years ago to both words to re-flect the words' Latin origins (*dubitare* and *debitum*, respectively). While these alterations might make spelling and pronunciation frustrating (especially for non-native speakers), they reveal the rich history of English.

12a   Check for words that are always separate

A common spelling error is to run together words that should be writ-ten as two. The following phrases should always be written as separate words.

→   a lot, all right, even if, even though, going to, in fact, just as, no one, of course

12b   Check for words that can be written together or apart

The spelling of some words depends on the meaning you intend. For example, *already* means "previously" and *all ready* means "to be prepared." First, decide upon the meaning, and then choose the correct form by consulting your dictionary.

Different spacing, different meaning

One word	Two words
already	all ready
altogether	all together
always	all ways
anybody	any body
anyone	any one
anyway	any way
awhile	a while
everybody	every body
everyday	every day
everyone	every one
however	how ever
into	in to
maybe	may be
nobody	no body
somebody	some body
someone	some one
whatever	what ever
whoever	who ever

12c ### Check for words that are pronounced the same or similarly

In English, we have many homophones—words that are pronounced the same but have different meanings. Homophones use different spellings, and since this is what distinguishes the meaning, you need to use your dictionary to find the correct word. Here is a list of the most commonly misspelled homophones.

Most commonly misspelled homophones

it's (it is or it has)	its (possessive)
you're (you are)	your (possessive)
they're (they are)	their (possessive), there (place)
who's (who is or who has)	whose (possessive)

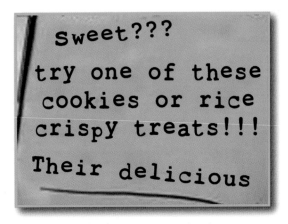

What's the problem with this sign
at a bake sale?

Here are some other commonly confused or misspelled words.
Learning these will help you become a proficient speller and editor.

Other commonly confused words

A	A
a	an
*alot (ungrammatical)	a lot
accept	except
access	excess
adapt	adopt
adverse	averse
advice	advise
affect	effect
agree to	agree with

aisle	isle
allude	elude
allusion	illusion
already	all ready
alright	all right
altar	alter
altogether	all together
among	amongst between
amoral	immoral
amount	number
and/or	and or
angry at	angry with
annual	biannual semiannual biennial perennial
ant	aunt
ante-	anti-
anybody	any body
anyone	any one
anymore	any more
anyway	anyways
assistance	assistants
assure	ensure insure
ate	eight
awhile	a while
B	**B**
backup	back up
bad	badly poorly
bare	bear

base	bass
be	bee
beach	beech
because of	due to
being as	being that
berry	bury
berth	birth
beside	besides
between	among amongst
blew	blue
board	bored
brake	break
bring	take
breadth	breath
breath	breathe
business	busyness
by	bye buy
C	**C**
can	may
canvas	canvass
capital	capitol
cell	sell
censor	censure
cent	sent scent
cereal	serial
chord	cord
chose	choose
climactic	climatic
coarse	course
compare to	compare with
complement	compliment

conscience	conscious
consequently	subsequently
continual	continuous
could have	could of
counsel	council
criteria	criterion
D	**D**
dairy	diary
data	datum
dear	deer
decent	descent
desert	dessert
device	devise
dew	due
die	dye
different from	different than
disinterred	uninterested
discreet	discrete
do not	don't
dual	duel
due to	because of
dying	dyeing
E	**E**
effect	affect
elicit	illicit
elude	allude
emigrate from	immigrate to
eminent	imminent
ensure	insure
everyone	every one
except	accept
explicit	implicit

F	F
faint	feint
fair	fare
farther	further
fewer	less
firstly	first
flour	flower
for	fore four
former	latter
formally	formerly
further	farther
G	**G**
good	well
gorilla	guerilla
grate	great
H	**H**
hair	hare
hanged	hung
he/she	he or she
heal	heel
healthful	healthy
hear	here
heard	herd
higher	hire
his/her	her or her
hole	whole
hostel	hostile
hung	hanged
I	**I**
idle	idol
if	whether
illusion	allusion

immigrate	emigrate
immoral	amoral
implicit	explicit
imply	infer
in	into
ingenious	ingenuous
insure	assure ensure
in regard to	in regards to
*irregardless (ungrammatical)	regardless
it's	its
K	**K**
knew	new
know	no
L	**L**
later	latter
lay	lie
lead	led
learn	teach
leave	let
led	lead
lend	borrow loan
less	fewer
lie	lay
like	as as if
literally	figuratively
loose	lose loss
lots	lots of
M	**M**
made	maid

mail	male
main	mane
may	can
maybe	may be
maze	maize
meat	meet
medal	metal, meddle
media	medium
miner	minor
moral	morale
N	**N**
number	amount
O	**O**
oar	ore
of	off
OK	O.K. okay
off	off of
one	won
P	**P**
pain	pane
pair	pear, pare
passed	past
patients	patience
peace	piece
peak	peek, pique
peer	pier
percent	per cent percentage
personal	personnel
phenomena	phenomenon
plain	plane

pore	pour poor
precede	proceed
pretty	rather quite
principal	principle
proceed	precede
Q	**Q**
quiet	quite
quote	quotation
R	**R**
rain	reign, rein
raise	rays
real	very really
respectfully	respectively
right	write wright rite
rise	raise
role	roll
S	**S**
sail	sale
scene	seen
scent	sent, cent
seed	cede
seem	seam
set	sit
shall	will
should of	should have
sight	cite site
should have	should of
sit	set

site	cite
	sight
sole	soul
some	sum
somebody	some body
someone	some one
sometime	some time
	sometimes
so	very
stationary	stationery
steal	steel
suppose to	supposed to
sure	surely
T	**T**
take	bring
taught	taut
team	teem
than	then
that	which
their	there
	they're
*theirselves (ungrammatical)	themselves
there	their
	they're
thorough	through
threw	through
tide	tied
to	too
	two
toward	towards
U	**U**
*most unique (ungrammatical)	unique
*use to (ungrammatical)	used to

V	V
vain	vane vein
W	**W**
waist	waste
wait	weight
wait for	wait on
wander	wonder
ware	wear where
way	weigh
way	ways
weather	whether
well	good
were	where, wear
which	that who
while	whereas
who	which that
who	whom
who's	whose
wood	would
would have	would of
Y	**Y**
your	you're

EXERCISE 1

Directions: Correct any problems with commonly confused or misspelled words.

Who would of thought that a simple hike threw the woods would result in a classic emblem of Americana? Beginning in the mid 19th century, people from all over started coming too Lookout Mountain near Chattanooga, Tennessee too see "Rock City" and experience it's natural rock formations. In the 1920s, a businessman named Garnet Carter began developing Lookout Mountain into a residential neighborhood called Fairyland, but his wife had other plans. Freida Carter began exploring Rock City—now her property—and turning it into an elaborate rock garden. Recognizing the potential profit of his wife's ornate garden, Garnet opened Rock City to the public in 1932. Business was slow, however, so Garnet had to find a way to entice visitors to there garden with more advertising then they currently had. Garnet hired Clark Byers to paint farmers' barns for free as long as the phrase "See Rock City" was added. Farmers from Michigan to Texas excepted the offer, and the iconic black and white signs on red barns became part of are American landscape. The advertisements had—and continue to have—a significant effect on the Carters' business; every year, over half a million people see the sites of Rock City, likely having past many of the famous signs on there way to Lookout Mountain.

http://www.seerockcity.com/pages/Our-Story/

Chapter 13

USING THE DICTIONARY

> Language is not an abstract construction of the learned, or of dictionary makers, but is something arising out of the work, needs, ties, joys, affections, tastes, of long generations of humanity, and has its bases broad and low, close to the ground.
> – Noah Webster

Dictionaries are invaluable tools for writers, in that they provide the correct spellings of words, give guidance about accurate meanings, and offer other information essential for effective writing. Every writer should have a personal copy of a collegiate or abridged dictionary, such as *Merriam-Webster's Collegiate Dictionary*, at hand for help with content development and editing. In your school or local library, you will find unabridged dictionaries, such as *The Oxford English Dictionary* or *Webster's Third New International Dictionary of the English Language* (available in print, on CD-ROM, or through your university library's portal), which give complete coverage of English words, including sample sentences and interesting information about word origins. When using dictionaries online, be sure to use one that is reputable, such as the Merriam-Webster online dictionary or American Heritage online dictionary.

Merriam-Webster   http://www.merriam-webster.com

American Heritage   http://dictionary.reference.com

When you are writing on a specialized topic, such as idioms or literature, you can also find specialized dictionaries in your local or school library that focus exclusively on that topic. Visit the OWL (Online Writing

Lab) at Purdue University for more information on how to choose and evaluate dictionaries.

Online Writing Lab
http://owl.english.purdue.edu/owl/resource/738/02/

Helpful hint

The spell checker in your word-processing program may be helpful to a certain extent when you are concerned about the spelling of a word; however, a dictionary not only will help you with spelling, it will also help you expand those 50,000 or so words that you are now using.

DID YOU KNOW?

The *Oxford English Dictionary* (OED) is considered by many to be the greatest dictionary of the English language. Since its inception in 1857, the OED has attempted to record the meaning and origin of every word in the English language by including the quotation where the word first appeared. Originally published in installments, the first edition took over 70 years to complete. The second edition, published in 1989, is 20 volumes, spanning 21,730 pages and including 291,500 entries. It would take 60 years for one person to proofread the text.

What's the problem with this sign?

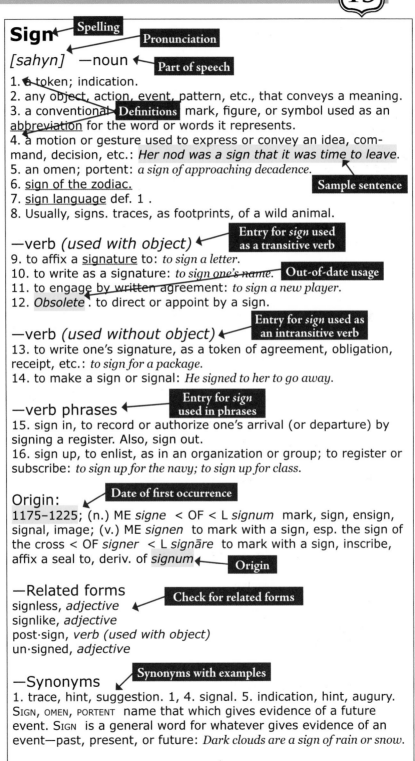

Sign — Spelling

Pronunciation

[sahyn] —noun ← Part of speech

1. a token; indication.
2. any object, action, event, pattern, etc., that conveys a meaning.
3. a conventional — Definitions — mark, figure, or symbol used as an abbreviation for the word or words it represents.
4. a motion or gesture used to express or convey an idea, command, decision, etc.: *Her nod was a sign that it was time to leave.*
5. an omen; portent: *a sign of approaching decadence.*
6. sign of the zodiac.   Sample sentence
7. sign language def. 1 .
8. Usually, signs. traces, as footprints, of a wild animal.

—verb *(used with object)* ←   Entry for *sign* used as a transitive verb
9. to affix a signature to: *to sign a letter.*
10. to write as a signature: *to sign one's name.*   Out-of-date usage
11. to engage by written agreement: *to sign a new player.*
12. *Obsolete* . to direct or appoint by a sign.

—verb *(used without object)* ←   Entry for *sign* used as an intransitive verb
13. to write one's signature, as a token of agreement, obligation, receipt, etc.: *to sign for a package.*
14. to make a sign or signal: *He signed to her to go away.*

—verb phrases ←   Entry for *sign* used in phrases
15. sign in, to record or authorize one's arrival (or departure) by signing a register. Also, sign out.
16. sign up, to enlist, as in an organization or group; to register or subscribe: *to sign up for the navy; to sign up for class.*

Origin: Date of first occurrence
1175–1225; (n.) ME *signe* < OF < L *signum* mark, sign, ensign, signal, image; (v.) ME *signen* to mark with a sign, esp. the sign of the cross < OF *signer* < L *signāre* to mark with a sign, inscribe, affix a seal to, deriv. of *signum* ←   Origin

—Related forms
signless, *adjective*   Check for related forms
signlike, *adjective*
post·sign, *verb (used with object)*
un·signed, *adjective*

—Synonyms   Synonyms with examples
1. trace, hint, suggestion. 1, 4. signal. 5. indication, hint, augury.
SIGN, OMEN, PORTENT name that which gives evidence of a future event. SIGN is a general word for whatever gives evidence of an event—past, present, or future: *Dark clouds are a sign of rain or snow.*

EXERCISE 1

Directions: Use your dictionary to correct any misspelled words in this paragraph.

The song "The Sign" by Ace of Base tells the storey of a woman's realization that she must end an unhealthy, dificult relationship with a loser in order to live a better life. Though the listner does not know what specificly "the sign" is, the singer makes it clear that her new life, unrecognizible to her ex ("you would hardly recognize me") is infinately better than it was in that relationship. With her epifany, the singer realized that not only was her ex "not the one for [her]," but her ex was definately not going to change for the good. "No one's going to drag you up to get into the light where you belong," she says, suggesting that although she sees potential in her ex, no one is willing—or capable—to make him live in "the light."

However, she questions whether or not potential for good even exists: "But where do you belong?" she asks, unsure of this person's ability to live a signifcant existence. She knows, though, that her ex was unable to "bring [her] joy." Whatever the sign was that she recieved, she makes it clear that she is "happy now" having "left [her ex] all alone."

USING AND OVERUSING THE THESAURUS

When you use a dictionary, you usually know at least a little bit about the word you are looking up. With a thesaurus, you usually know a general definition but need to find a specific word that will fit the topic and context about which you are writing. Be sure to review all the synonyms that are offered as a substitute for the general word you look up; you need to consider the synonyms in the context of your essay or writing, and then choose the one that fits.

Helpful hint

The thesaurus that came with your word processor may be helpful, but just clicking on the first synonym it offers may harm, rather than help, your writing. Use a thesaurus in conjunction with a dictionary, and you will be able to correctly choose the appropriate word for the context.

Sign

When using a thesaurus, find the ENTRY and DEFINITION before you look at the synonyms. On this page, there are two noun entries.

Main Entry | sign

Part of Speech: | noun — Part of speech

Definition: | indication, evidence — Definition

Synonyms: | assurance, augury, auspice, badge, beacon, bell, caution, clue, divination, flag, foreknowledge, foreshadowing, forewarning, gesture, giveaway, handwriting on wall, herald, hint, light, manifestation, mark, nod, note, omen, precursor, prediction, premonition, presage, proof, signal, suggestion, symbol, symptom, token, trace, vestige, warning, wave, whistle, wink

Use synonyms that are already familiar to you, or be sure to look them up in a dictionary to use them appropriately.

Main Entry | sign

Part of Speech: | noun — Noun usage with a different definition

Definition: | document with information; symbol

Synonyms: | badge, board, character, cipher, crest, device, emblem, ensign, guidepost, insignia, logo, mark, notice, placard, proof, representation, signboard, signpost

Part of Speech: | verb — Verb usage

Definition: | write name

Synonyms: | acknowledge, authorize, autograph, confirm, endorse, initial, ink, inscribe, put John Hancock on, put John Henry on, set one's hand to, signature, witness

Phrasal synonyms

Part of Speech: | verb

Definition: | motion to another

Synonyms: | beckon, express, flag, gesticulate, gesture, indicate, motion, signal, signalize, signify, use sign language, wave

Be sure to know the full definition and appropriate context for an unfamiliar word before using it.

Part of Speech: | noun, verb

Related Adjectives: | armorial, characteristic, connotative, curiological, demonstrative, diagnostic, emblematic, indelible, indicated, indicating, indicative, indicatory, individual, jolloped, known by, marked, pantomimic, pathognomonic, pointed, recognizable by, representative, symbolic, symptomatic, typical

EXERCISE 1

Directions: This student apparently overused the thesaurus as he was writing this letter to his instructor. See if you can help him out by replacing inappropriate words with more appropriate ones.

Dear Professor Walker,

I'm very sorry that I was absent for the eighth time this semester. As I was driving back to school yesterday (I'm from out of state), I missed my egress off the interstate because a tempest had blown down several road signs, including the one directing me to university grounds. Since I'm novel to the area, I didn't apprehend that I had missed anything until I had driven three hours out of my way. By the time I figured out that something was erroneous, it was late at night and I was too weary to continue driving. I called home to ask what I should do, and my patriarch told me to discontinue for the night and find my way back in the morning, causing me to miss your 8:00 a.m. Monday class. I'm sure you'll concur that my safety was much more momentous than your English class, so I'll assume that you will not castigate me for another absence. Also, I was hoping I might have an extension on the essay that was due on Monday; I was planning to write it Sunday night when I got back to my dorm, but obviously I was at the hotel and stressed out. I did, however, inscribe a letter to the Tennessee Department of Transportation expressing my frustration over their neglect to replace the missing signs, which I'll be happy to show you as attestation of the incident. Thank you for understanding, and I promise I'll be in class for the residual ten weeks of the semester.

Sincerely,

Dan Johnson

THE COMMA

Commas are one of the most frequently used punctuation marks. Unfortunately, commas are also the most frequently misused punctuation mark. Having a reference tool available is always a good idea when you are not sure about how a comma rule applies to your sentence, but the abundance of comma rules can sometimes be frustrating. In this chapter, you will find a few ways to help you use comma rules more effectively.

In this section, comma rules are presented in the order of frequently used sentence-level comma rules followed by less frequently used rules. In addition to this useful set-up, you will also find a laminated one-page QUICK EDITING ROADMAP inside your copy of this handbook. Using up-to-date research on college writing, I have developed this guide as a quick reference to the sentence-level rules that confuse writers the most. Half of the rules included on the QUICK EDITING ROADMAP are comma rules.

15a Set off introductory words, phrases, and clauses

1. Set off introductory words and phrases

Commas are often used to set off introductory words and phrases. If the word or phrase includes a verb, a comma should always be used to separate the word or phrase from the main sentence.

→ Shocked, Alex put out his cigarette when he saw the new No Smoking sign.

→ Frustrated by the new sign, Alex put out his cigarette.

If the introductory word is a single preposition or adverb, you may omit the comma.

→ Yesterday the guests grumbled about the new sign.

If the introductory prepositional phrase is short (usually viewed as being five words or fewer), you may also omit the comma.

→ Below the stage the guests grumbled about the new sign.

Helpful hint

If you are unsure about punctuating an introductory word, phrase, or clause, use a comma. The presence of a comma, rather than its absence, is always a good choice.

→ Yesterday, the guests grumbled about the new sign.

→ Below the stage, the guests grumbled about the new sign.

2. Set off introductory clauses

Always use a comma after an introductory clause. The use of a verb in any kind of introductory word, phrase, or clause is the clue to always using a comma.

→ Since he had recently quit smoking, Alex was happy to see the new No Smoking sign.

→ Although Chris was unhappy about the new sign, Alex was quite content.

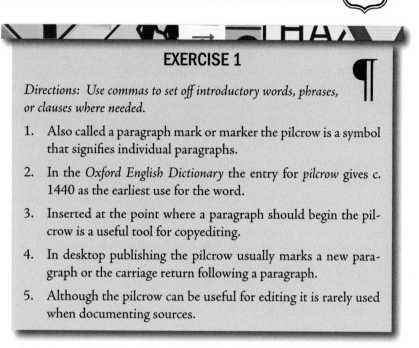

EXERCISE 1

Directions: Use commas to set off introductory words, phrases, or clauses where needed.

1. Also called a paragraph mark or marker the pilcrow is a symbol that signifies individual paragraphs.

2. In the *Oxford English Dictionary* the entry for *pilcrow* gives c. 1440 as the earliest use for the word.

3. Inserted at the point where a paragraph should begin the pilcrow is a useful tool for copyediting.

4. In desktop publishing the pilcrow usually marks a new paragraph or the carriage return following a paragraph.

5. Although the pilcrow can be useful for editing it is rarely used when documenting sources.

15b   Combine independent clauses in compound sentences

A comma is used between two independent clauses that are joined by a coordinating conjunction, such as any of the FANBOYS—*for, and, nor, but, or, yet, so.*

> Independent clause/simple sentence➜Chris was unhappy about the new sign.

> Independent clause/simple sentence➜Alex was quite content about the new sign.

> Compound sentence➜ Chris was unhappy about the new sign, but Alex was quite content.

Be sure that the clauses on each side of the comma + conjunction are independent. A comma is never used between conjoined noun phrases or conjoined verb phrases.

Misused comma➤ Chris, and Alex had a terrible argument outside the building.

OK➤Chris and Alex had a terrible argument outside the building.

Misused comma➤Chris was unhappy about the sign, and left campus early.

OK➤ Chris was unhappy about the sign and left campus early.

You can sometimes omit the comma when the two clauses are short—this is not always acceptable to all instructors or editors, though. You will always be correct if you include it.

➤ Chris was unhappy and he left.

➤ Chris was unhappy, and he left.

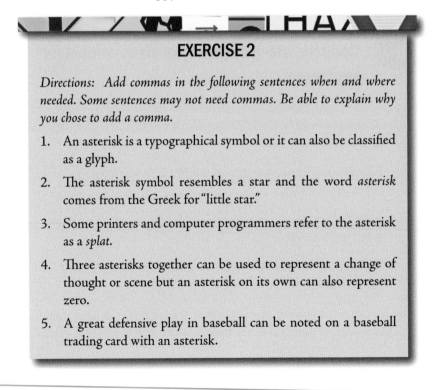

EXERCISE 2

Directions: Add commas in the following sentences when and where needed. Some sentences may not need commas. Be able to explain why you chose to add a comma.

1. An asterisk is a typographical symbol or it can also be classified as a glyph.

2. The asterisk symbol resembles a star and the word *asterisk* comes from the Greek for "little star."

3. Some printers and computer programmers refer to the asterisk as a *splat*.

4. Three asterisks together can be used to represent a change of thought or scene but an asterisk on its own can also represent zero.

5. A great defensive play in baseball can be noted on a baseball trading card with an asterisk.

15c   Separate items in a series

Commas are used to separate words, phrases, or clauses in a series. A series contains at least three items that are parallel with each other (e.g., three nouns or three phrases).

➜ Chris, Alex, and Max spent three hours arguing about the new signs around campus.

➜ I saw the three musketeers—Chris, Alex, and Max—outside the building.

➜ Chris talked, cajoled, and yelled as he tried to convince the administrators.

➜ As I left the building, Max was taking down the sign, yelling at some strangers, and jumping up and down.

If the items in a series that you are connecting already have commas, use semi-colons to separate them.

➜ When the campus police arrived, they wanted to ticket Chris, who began the argument; Alex, who escalated the argument; and Max, who threw the first punch.

15d   Set off non-essential elements

Commas can be used to enclose non-essential information that is included in a sentence. To be non-essential, the information needs to be unnecessary for a reader to understand the central meaning of the sentence.

1. Relative clauses

Relative clauses can be essential or non-essential when it comes to understanding the main meaning of the full sentence. Relative clauses that are not necessary are non-restrictive and need to be set off by commas.

➜ Chris and Alex, who were in my English class, were arguing violently.

In the above sentence, the information about which class Chris and Alex were in is non-essential to the meaning of the independent clause.

If a relative clause is essential to the full meaning of the sentence, it is restrictive and should not have any commas around it.

→   The audience that was closest to Chris and Alex was getting violent as well.

In the sentence above, the relative clause ("that was closest to Chris and Alex") is essential information. It was just the audience closest to Chris and Alex who were getting violent, not those in the audience farther away.

Using *that* for non-essential relative clauses and a comma plus a relative pronoun, such as *which* or *who*, for essential relative clauses is a way that some editors and writers help distinguish between non-essential and essential sentence elements. If you are required to follow MLA (Modern Language Association) or APA (American Psychological Association) guidelines, follow this convention. However, even MLA acknowledges that some writers do not follow this convention, so it's a good idea to check with your instructor about this grammar rule that is in flux.

Remember, though, that punctuation works together with meaning. Two sentences that look almost the same can use different punctuation due to the meaning the writer has in mind.

Non-restrictive relative clause→ Tennessee, which is a beautiful state, has all the signs of a bad economy.

Restrictive relative clause→ I like the Tennessee that is a beautiful state and not the one that has signs of a bad economy.

In the first sentence above, the main idea of the sentence can be understood without the relative clause *which is a beautiful state*. This makes the relative clause non-essential, requiring commas. In the second sentence, the main idea of the sentence can only be understood with the two relative clauses *that is a beautiful state* and *that has signs of a bad economy* included. This makes the two relative clauses essential, thus requiring no commas.

2. Participial phrases

Participial phrases are verb phrases that describe nouns. They take commas wherever they occur—at the beginning of the sentence, in the middle of the sentence, or at the end of the sentence.

Sentence with participial phrase➔
The Hollywood sign, first built in
1923, was restored in 1978 with
money from Gene Autry, Alice Cooper, and others.

Sentence with participial phrase➔ The Hollywood sign,
located in Griffith Park and not Hollywood, was restored in
1978 with money from Gene Autry, Alice Cooper, and others.

3. Appositives

Appositives are nouns, noun phrases, and noun clauses that rename
nouns. The same restrictive/non-restrictive comma rule that applies to
relative clauses applies to appositives (see 15d for more information on
restrictive and non-restrictive elements).

Sentence with non-restrictive appositive➔ The Hollywood
sign, a national monument, was restored in 1978 with money
from Gene Autry, Alice Cooper, and others.

Sentence with restrictive appositive➔ The musician Alice
Cooper helped fund the restoration of the Hollywood sign.

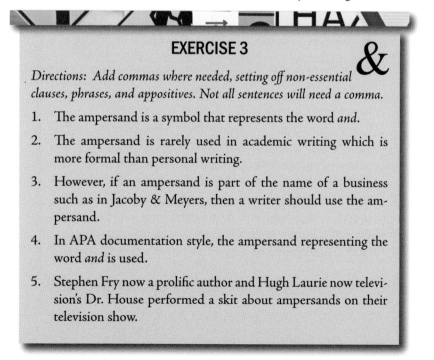

EXERCISE 3 &

*Directions: Add commas where needed, setting off non-essential
clauses, phrases, and appositives. Not all sentences will need a comma.*

1. The ampersand is a symbol that represents the word *and*.

2. The ampersand is rarely used in academic writing which is
   more formal than personal writing.

3. However, if an ampersand is part of the name of a business
   such as in Jacoby & Meyers, then a writer should use the ampersand.

4. In APA documentation style, the ampersand representing the
   word *and* is used.

5. Stephen Fry now a prolific author and Hugh Laurie now television's Dr. House performed a skit about ampersands on their
   television show.

15e   Separate coordinate adjectives

A comma is used to separate coordinate adjectives. Adjectives are considered coordinate when they directly and equally modify a noun phrase. One test to see whether you are using coordinate adjectives is to reverse their order—if the original modification relationship exists, you have coordinate adjectives. Another test to see whether you are using coordinate adjectives is to place an *and* between the two adjectives—once again, if the original meaning exists, you have coordinate adjectives.

→ Sam and Alex saw the dull, unappealing billboard for the movie and changed their minds about seeing it.

→ Sam and Alex saw the unappealing, dull billboard for the movie and changed their minds about seeing it.

DID YOU KNOW?

"Put a comma where you pause." Have you ever been told to punctuate based upon how a sentence is spoken? While you'll get in trouble if you follow this advice too much, it's not entirely misguided. Punctuation marks were originally intended to aid orators when reading a text aloud, and only in the past 100 or so years has punctuation become standardized. The comma can be traced back to the 3rd century BCE when Aristophanes of Byzantium invented a system of dots to separate verse; different groupings of dots represented different types of breaths needed to complete the reading of part of a text. Although the word comma comes from the Greek *komma* ("something cut off"), the shape of today's comma was standardized in the 16th century when the original comma—the diagonal slash (/)—dropped to the bottom of the line and curved.

15f   Set off interrupters

1. Transitions

When an adverbial conjunction (also called a conjunctive adverb) appears in the middle of a sentence, it is separated off from the main sentence with commas.

→ The Hollywood sign, *moreover*, does not include any of the original letters.

→ Alice Cooper, *however*, donated money for the renovation in honor of Groucho Marx.

Adverbial conjunctions can also be used to connect two independent clauses when the adverbial conjunction is enclosed by a semi-colon and a comma. Since adverbial conjunctions function as both transitions and as compound sentence connectors, it is wise to always double check the punctuation that you use with an adverbial conjunction.

Adverbial conjunctions

Addition → moreover, furthermore, likewise, finally, additionally, also, incidentally

Contrast → however, nevertheless, in contrast, on the contrary, nonetheless, otherwise, on the other hand, in comparison, conversely, instead

Comparison → similarly, likewise

Exemplification → for example, for instance

Intensification → indeed, in fact, moreover, still, certainly

Result → therefore, thus, consequently, as a result, finally, then, accordingly, hence, subsequently, undoubtedly

Time → meanwhile, then, next, finally, still, now

2. Interjections

A comma is used to mark or enclose a weak exclamation or interjection, separating it from the rest of the sentence. An interjection can come at the beginning, in the middle, or at the end of a sentence.

→ For goodness sake, the instruction book about traffic signs is over 20 pages long.

→ The instruction book about traffic signs is over 20 pages long, for goodness sake.

→ I do not understand, for goodness sake, why that book about traffic signs is so long.

3. Direct address

A comma is used to mark or enclose a noun phrase that is used as a direct address. When you use a noun phrase that names the person or persons being spoken to, you are using the form of a direct address.

→ "Sam, did you see the billboard for *Terminator: Salvation?*"

→ "Did you see the billboard for *Terminator: Salvation*, Sam?"

→ "I thought the billboard for *Jumper* was good, Sam, but did you see the one for *Terminator: Salvation?*"

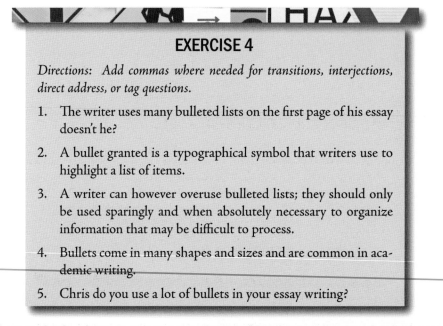

EXERCISE 4

Directions: Add commas where needed for transitions, interjections, direct address, or tag questions.

1. The writer uses many bulleted lists on the first page of his essay doesn't he?

2. A bullet granted is a typographical symbol that writers use to highlight a list of items.

3. A writer can however overuse bulleted lists; they should only be used sparingly and when absolutely necessary to organize information that may be difficult to process.

4. Bullets come in many shapes and sizes and are common in academic writing.

5. Chris do you use a lot of bullets in your essay writing?

4. Tag questions

Commas are also used to mark tags, which are added to the end of a sentence to question whether the statement that precedes the tag is accurate or not.

→ The poster for *Sherlock Holmes* made the main character look somewhat dastardly, didn't it?

→ It has been a long time since we have had a modern Sherlock Holmes, hasn't it?

15g   Set off quotations or dialogue

Commas are used to set off a speaker's words from the rest of the sentence.

→ Chris complained, "That book is over 20 pages long."

→ "That book is over 20 pages long," Chris complained.

→ "That book," Chris complained, "is over 20 pages long."

Commas are not used with indirect quotations or speech.

→ Chris complained that the book was too long.

Commas are not used after an exclamation point or question mark.

→ "That book is too long!" complained Chris.

→ "How long is that book on traffic signs?" asked Chris with a frown on his face.

15h   Set off geographic locations

Commas are used to set off items in an address or in the name of a place.

→ Please send any comments about the new sign to Department of Signage, Box 50, Fairbanks, Alaska 99701.

→ Murfreesboro, Tennessee, is near Nashville.

→ Be sure to check out the new sign at The Stone's River Mall, Murfreesboro, Tennessee.

A comma is never used between the name of a state and a Zip Code.

→ You should send your card and return postage to the Department of Signage, Box 50, Fairbanks, AK 99701.

15i   Set off dates

Commas are used to set off items in a date. Use commas between the day and month, the date and year, and the year and the rest of the sentence.

→ The smoking signs were changed on Monday, January 1, 2010, when the new law took effect.

A comma is never used between the date and month or the month and year when the date is written in inverted order.

→ The smoking signs were changed on Monday, 1 January 2010, when the new law took effect.

A comma is never used when only the month and year are given.

→ The smoking signs were changed in January 2010.

15j   Set off titles

A comma is used to set off a person's title or degree.

→ Dr. Watson had a sign outside his front door that said John H. Watson, M.D.

→ Juliet Freestone, PhD, noted expert on Sherlock Holmes, will speak at the library today.

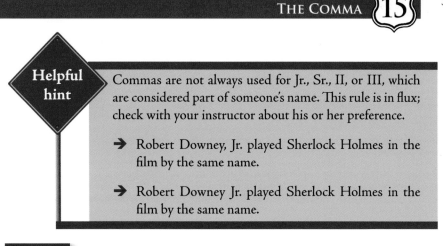

Helpful hint

Commas are not always used for Jr., Sr., II, or III, which are considered part of someone's name. This rule is in flux; check with your instructor about his or her preference.

➔ Robert Downey, Jr. played Sherlock Holmes in the film by the same name.

➔ Robert Downey Jr. played Sherlock Holmes in the film by the same name.

15k   Set off numbers

When numbers are longer than four digits, use commas to separate them, placing a comma every three numbers starting from the right.

➔ 1,000

➔ 1,000,000

➔ 1,000,000,000

Do not use commas in the above way when writing years, telephone numbers, street addresses, or zip codes.

15l   Prevent confusion

Most grammar handbooks will tell you to use commas to prevent confusion or for clarity. These might be the kinds of examples shared with you.

➔ What Chris did, did affect all of us.

➔ It was the sign she had waited for, for years.

However, if you find yourself needing to use a comma to avoid confusion, you probably need to revise the entire sentence.

➔ What Chris did that day affected all of us.

➔ She had waited for years for the sign.

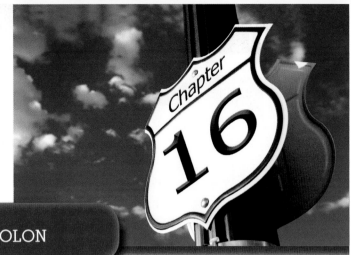

THE SEMI-COLON

A semi-colon connects phrases or clauses that are closely linked in meaning. Using a semi-colon is limited to three situations.

16a Connect independent clauses

Semi-colons can connect two independent clauses (or simple sentences) to form a compound sentence.

> Simple sentence/independent clause➔ The Chinese zodiac uses twelve animals to represent human qualities.

> Simple sentence/independent clause➔ The Chinese zodiac runs on a twelve-year cycle.

> Compound sentence➔ The Chinese zodiac uses twelve animals to represent human qualities; it also runs on a twelve-year cycle.

16b Use with adverbial conjunctions or transitional phrases to connect clauses

Two simple sentences can be connected with an adverbial conjunction (also known as a conjunctive adverb) when a semi-colon is used to the left of the adverbial conjunction and a comma to the right of it. See 15f for a list of adverbial conjunctions.

Transitional phrases

after all	in contrast
as a matter of fact	in fact
as a result	in like manner
at any rate	in other words
at the same time	in the meantime
equally important	on one hand
even so	on the contrary
for example	on the other hand
for instance	to illustrate
in addition	while this may be true
in conclusion	

➔ The Chinese zodiac uses twelve animals to represent human qualities; furthermore, it runs on a twelve-year cycle.

➔ The Chinese zodiac uses twelve animals to represent human qualities; in fact, it runs on a twelve-year cycle.

16c   Separate groups that contain commas

If the items in a series that you are connecting already have commas, use semi-colons to separate them.

➔ The Chinese zodiac uses twelve animals, such as the boar and the snake, to represent human qualities; runs on a twelve-year cycle; and is widely used throughout Asia, not just in China.

Chinese zodiac

EXERCISE 1

Directions: Revise these sentences, adding semi-colons where needed. Not all sentences will need semi-colons.

1. Bob Berner first introduced the backslash to computer programming in the 1960s it is sometimes called a *slosh*.

2. The backslash is a typographical mark furthermore it is an ASCII character.

3. The backslash is also used to separate the directory and file parts of a Web site address.

4. The backslash, a typographical mark, is used in computing to indicate that whatever follows should be treated differently or specially it is used in mathematics to indicate a set difference and it is used with the forward slash in linguistics to indicate phonemes.

5. Asian programmers can use other characters that are treated exactly as the backslash consequently this can cause some confusion.

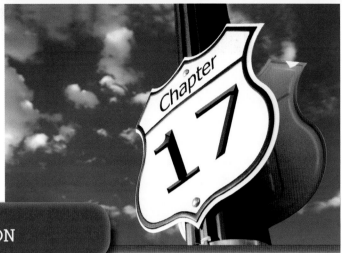

THE COLON

A colon has a variety of uses, but its overall function is to connect elements while still keeping them slightly separated from each other.

MLA guidelines suggest using one space after a colon; however, the MLA also allows for two spaces if this strategy is used consistently. APA guidelines require one space after a colon.

According to the MLA, the first letter of the word that follows a colon should be in lower case, unless that word is one that is normally capitalized or is part of a rule, principle, or quotation. However, according to the APA, the first letter of the sentence following a colon should be in upper case if the sentence is an independent clause. Since the rule for using capitalization with a colon can change across documentation styles, it is a good idea to ask your instructor for clarification about which style she or he prefers.

17a   Connect independent clauses

A colon is used to connect two independent clauses (or simple sentences) when the clause to the left of the colon is of a general or abstract nature and the clause to the right gives more specific information.

→ The Chinese zodiac uses twelve animals and runs on a twelve-year cycle: the animals represent different qualities of human nature, such as calmness or righteousness.

17b Add emphasis

Colons can be used to emphasize words, phrases, or clauses.

➔　When I first studied the Chinese zodiac, I could not believe my sign: the pig.

17c Introduce a series or list

A colon is used to introduce a list or a series of words or phrases. As you can see in the sentence below, on the left side of the colon is an independent clause.

➔　The Chinese zodiac also describes its animal signs with four elements: fire, metal, water, and wood.

Colons should not follow phrases like *such as, for example, includes,* or *including.* In fact, no punctuation should be used after these phrases when giving a list.

Okay ➔ The Chinese zodiac has signs such as roosters, snakes, and boars.

17d Introduce a quotation or saying

A colon should be used to introduce a quotation or saying when it is a complete sentence.

➔　I have a Chinese proverb by which I live: "When you only have two pennies left in the world, buy a loaf of bread with one and a lily with the other."

17e Use for salutations in formal letters

In a formal business letter, the colon is commonly used in the salutation. A comma can be used for personal letters.

➔　Dear Judge Smith:

17f   Connect numbers

Colons are used for connecting numbers in a variety of ways.

1. Connect ratios

→ The ratio of sunny days to snow days is 45:1.

2. Connect chapters and verses of holy texts

→ Ezra 6:18

→ Job 29:4

→ Qur'an 3:3

→ Vedanta-sutra 4:1:12

3. Connect hours, minutes, and seconds

→ 11:05:01

→ 3:13 a.m.

→ 7:03 p.m.

17g   Connect titles and subtitles

→ *The Chinese Zodiac: Twelve Personalities Represented by Animals*

17h   Separate geographical location and publisher name in bibliographic entries

→ Southlake, TX: Fountainhead, 2010.

EXERCISE 1

Directions: Add colons where needed in the following sentences. Not all sentences may need a colon.

1. The English word *colon* came to English through two languages that influenced many English words Greek and Latin.

2. The colon was introduced to English in the 1600s early British printers, such as William Caxton, embraced its use.

3. Be sure to use a colon when writing any of these types of elements a ratio, a scriptural verse, or a subtitle.

4. How colons are used in different ways is discussed in *Girl Talk Complete Guide to IM Lingo, Emoticons, and More!*

5. While trying to use commas accurately, the author was upset by the variations in MLA and APA rules "Why is it that so many different styles exist?"

Chapter 18

THE PERIOD, EXCLAMATION POINT, AND QUESTION MARK

Choosing end punctuation is easy if you know the type and function of the sentence you are writing. Writers use declarative sentences to give information, imperative sentences to give instructions or commands, interrogative sentences to obtain information, and exclamatory sentences to express emotion.

Declarative sentence or statement➜ The Chinese zodiac has four elements.

Imperative sentence or command➜Tell me which zodiac sign I am.

Interrogative sentence or question➜How many Chinese zodiac signs are there?

Exclamatory sentence or exclamation➜ You're a Boar! Really!

18a   Use a period to end a sentence or separate initials or abbreviations

> No iron can pierce the heart with such force as a period put just at the right place.
>
> –Isaac Babel

1. End a sentence

A period ends a declarative sentence that gives information, makes a statement, or gives a mild command.

> Gives information➜ In the Chinese zodiac, different animals not only rule each year, different ones rule each day.

> Makes a statement➜ The Chinese zodiac is fascinating, especially when it is compared to our Western zodiac.

> Gives a mild command➜Learn the animals and elements of the Chinese zodiac for the quiz tomorrow.

2. Separate initials or abbreviations

Periods are placed after an initial or an abbreviation.

➜ Ms. Smith, Mr. Smith, Mrs. Smith, Dr. Allison D. Smith, Adam D. Smith, Jr., Sen. Thomas P. Smith, Prof. Adam Smith, Rev. Smith

Using periods for the above list is always correct. Some other initials or abbreviations can take a period or not. This is something you will need to check with your instructor or with the specific style guidelines you are using, such as Modern Language Association (MLA) or American Psychological Association (APA). For instance, both MLA and APA suggest not using periods or spaces in abbreviations composed only of capital letters, but some instructors prefer that students use periods.

The following abbreviations can appear with or without periods.

➜ BA, BS, MA, PhD

➜ GP, LPN, MBA, MD, RN

➜ BC, BCE, AD, CE, AM, PM

States can often be abbreviated in a variety of ways, including some forms that take periods. For instance, *PA* or *Penn.* can be used for the state of Pennsylvania. However, in formal writing, it is not commonly accepted that states be abbreviated in any way except in complete addresses.

18b   Emphasize with an exclamation point

An exclamation mark is used at the end of an exclamatory sentence to express a strong feeling or to give emphasis.

➔ This is the last time I will comment. Stop asking me!

➔ Imagine! The foundation of astrology goes back thousands of years.

> Cut out all those exclamation marks. An exclamation mark is like laughing at your own jokes.
> —F. Scott Fitzgerald

18c   End a direct question, show uncertainty, or embed a short question with a question mark

1. End a direct question

A question mark is used at the end of a direct question or interrogative.

➔ Are there any similarities between the Chinese zodiac and Western astrology?

Helpful hint

A question mark is never used for an indirect question.

➔ Molly asked why I used Chinese zodiac examples.

2. Show uncertainty

A question mark can also be used to show uncertainty about a fact or piece of information. When used this way, the question mark should be placed within parentheses.

➔ Western astrology began in the 2nd century AD (?).

Western zodiac

3. Embed a short question within the middle of a sentence

A short question can be embedded within a longer sentence in three ways: within parentheses, enclosed by dashes, or just within the sentence itself.

→ Western astrology began in the 2nd century AD (is this similar to Chinese astrology?) and has twelve signs.

→ Western astrology began in the 2nd century AD—is this similar to Chinese astrology?—and has twelve signs.

→ When she asked the question, why are Western and Chinese zodiacs so similar? at the lecture, the speaker gave her a point-by-point answer.

Helpful hint

Although embedding questions within longer sentences is grammatical, it is rarely done and often questioned. A writer might want to revise these types of sentences into something that is more common.

EXERCISE 1

Directions: Fill in the blanks with the correct punctuation mark: period (.), exclamation point (!), or question mark (?).

1. Have you ever gotten lost reading something that is poorly written___

2. Punctuation marks are like tiny road signs for the reader___

3. Also referred to as a full stop, the period tells the reader that a complete thought, or sentence, has come to an end___

4. Although periods are the most common way to end a sentence, did you know that there are two other ways to do this___

5. The exclamation point is sometimes overused by excited students___ Be careful___

The Apostrophe

The apostrophe is used in a variety of situations and is one of the most complicated punctuation marks to use. Unless you know for sure that the way you use it is always correct, it is a good idea to double check its use during your editing sessions or revise your sentence to avoid it.

19a   Mark omissions when parts of words are removed

An apostrophe is used to show that one or more letters have been omitted. For instance, use an apostrophe to show in *I'm* that the *a* has been deleted.

1. Mark contractions when parts of words are removed

→ I'm, you're, he's, she's, it's, they're, we're

→ I hadn't, you haven't

→ I can't, I couldn't, you won't, you wouldn't, they'll, they shouldn't

2. Mark numbers when parts of numbers are removed

→ in the year '95

3. Mark words used to represent oral language

When using unusual or informal spellings to represent oral language, you can use apostrophes to mark contractions.

→ a-walkin', trekin', y'all

DID YOU KNOW?

You ain't ever gonna believe this! *Ain't* is, in fact, a word. This "improper" word is a contraction of *am* (from the verb *to be*) and *not*—similar in construction to *isn't* and *aren't*. Grammatically, it should follow a first person pronoun (*I*), but it is often used in informal speech following any noun. But watch out! *Ain't* ain't acceptable in formal English.

19b   Form plurals

The MLA recommends that an apostrophe along with an *−s* be used to create the plural of abbreviations that include lowercase letters, uppercase letters, or both.

→ A's, B's, C's, D's, E's

→ PhD's, Mind your P's and Q's!

However, many instructors prefer that no apostrophe be used at all.

→ As, Bs, Cs, Ds, Es

→ PhDs, Mind your Ps and Qs

Some instructors may prefer that you italicize the letter and use regular font style for the *−s* ending.

→ *A*s, *B*s, *C*s, *D*s, *E*s

It is best to check with your instructor on how he or she wants you to format letters.

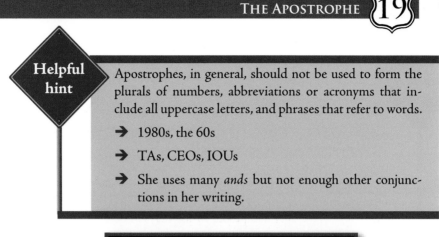

Apostrophes, in general, should not be used to form the plurals of numbers, abbreviations or acronyms that include all uppercase letters, and phrases that refer to words.

➔ 1980s, the 60s

➔ TAs, CEOs, IOUs

➔ She uses many *ands* but not enough other conjunctions in her writing.

How would you edit this sign?

19c Form possessives

An apostrophe is used in various ways to form possessives. Knowing the difference between singular nouns, indefinite pronouns, and plural nouns will help you use the apostrophe correctly.

1. Form singular possessives

A. Singular nouns

An apostrophe and −*s* can be added to most singular nouns and acronyms to form the possessive.

➔ Sam's book, the student's pen, the new sign's message

➔ the CEO's email, MLA's style guide

> **Helpful hint**
>
> In the past, several apostrophe rules were dependent on what letter ended the singular noun. However, *The MLA Handbook for Writers of Research Papers* now recommends always using an apostrophe and −*s* at the end of any singular noun. If your instructor wants you to use another style guide for your research and writing, you will need to check how this rule is handled in that system.
>
> ➜ Giles's plan, the boss's idea, Ms. Jones's books

B. PERSONAL PRONOUNS

Personal pronouns do not take an apostrophe since they already show possession.

➜ my, your, yours, his, her, hers, its, our, ours, their, theirs

C. INDEFINITE PRONOUNS

An apostrophe and an −*s* is used at the end of an indefinite pronoun to show possession.

➜ anyone's, anybody's, everyone's, everybody's, someone's, somebody's

2. Mark plural possessives

Plural nouns that do not end in −*s* take an apostrophe plus an −*s* to form the possessive. Plural nouns that end in −*s* only take the apostrophe.

➜ the children's song, the geese's honk, the data's collection

➜ the cats' meows, the judges' decision, the zodiacs' signs, the Smiths' house , the Joneses' cat

3. Form possessive compound nouns

When a sentence includes conjoined nouns, the type of ownership or possession determines how to use the apostrophe. If each noun has separate ownership, each noun is marked by the possessive. If the nouns have ownership together, only the last noun is made possessive by using the apostrophe.

> Separate ownership➔Sam's and Alex's zodiac signs are not compatible.

> Joint ownership ➔Jack and Jill's pail fell down the hill.

19d Form compounds

An apostrophe and −*s* is placed at the end of a compound word when signaling possession.

➔ my mother-in-law's sign, mother-of-pearl's color

An apostrophe and −*s* can be placed at the end of a plural compound word, or the possession can be signaled with an *of* phrase.

➔ my brothers-in-law's zodiac signs

➔ the zodiac signs of my brothers-in-law

Foodmaster carry's the finest quality of beef product of the United States, Canada, and Mexico

http://jeffreyhill.typepad.com/english/2008/11/ apostrophe-catastrophes.html

What is wrong with the sign in this picture?

EXERCISE 1

Directions: Add the missing apostrophes to the following paragraph.

I cant believe how lucky I was to land the latest client for my advertising company. Its not that I doubted my abilities, but this client has been particularly picky in choosing an advertising firm to represent it. Since its such an established company, the boards decision to reinvent themselves with a new logo could launch them into future success or signal the end of their heyday. Its a delicate situation to be sure, and Im excited for the challenge. I already have an idea in mind, and its success could land me a significant promotion if all goes to plan. Though I cant disclose specific details, Ill just say that the clients former business focus was on an outdated technology. Now that theyve adapted to modern technological advances, my job is to bring their image up to date as well. Ive handled similar situations with other outdated companies images with success, so Im confident that I'll be able to pull this off. I cant wait to see my familys reaction when I tell them about this great news!

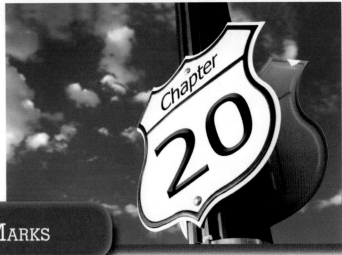

QUOTATION MARKS

Quotation marks are used in a variety of situations as described below. Generally, when a quotation mark falls at the end of a clause or sentence, place periods and commas inside the quotation mark.

→ My instructor assigned us a new story entitled "Signs and Symbols."

→ When I read "Signs and Symbols," I was reminded of a story from my childhood.

When you use MLA style for in-text citations, the period follows the citation in parentheses.

→ Margaret Jones, in her essay on sign language, says that "anyone who really wants to learn sign language can do so relatively easily" (101).

20a Signal titles of short works

Quotation marks are used to enclose the titles of short works, including poems, short stories, lectures, book chapters, song titles, magazine articles, newspaper articles, encyclopedia entries, and television/radio episodes.

→ "Pedestrians Not Permitted on this Highway" – a poem by Jackson H. Day

→ "Signs and Symbols" – a short story by Vladimir Nabokov

→ "The Signs of Life" – a lecture by Augustus D. Waller, MD

→ "Signs Inconjunct" – a book chapter by Ptolemy

→ "Signs" – a song by Five Man Electrical Band

→ "Swine Flu Myth: The Symptoms Are Like Regular Flu" – a magazine article

→ "CDC: Swine Flu Outbreak Signs Encouraging" – a newspaper article

→ "Sign Language (Communications)" – an encyclopedia entry

→ "Born Under a Bad Sign" – episode from television's *Supernatural*

Helpful hint

To highlight the title of a larger or longer work, use italics. Thus, you should italicize the titles of poetry collections, short story collections, anthologies, books, albums/CDs, magazines, newspapers, encyclopedias, television series, and radio series.

20b   Set off a direct quotation

Quotation marks are also used to set off direct quotations.

→ "The thunderstorm last night was the first sign of spring," said the ABC weatherman.

→ Albert Einstein said, "The true sign of intelligence is not knowledge but imagination."

20c   Set off dialogue in prose

Quotation marks are used to set off dialogue. Be sure to use a separate paragraph for each speaker, and use quotation marks around everything each person says.

→ from *Signs* (2002 film):
"What kind of a machine bends a stalk of corn without breaking it?" asked Officer Caroline.

Graham responded, "It can't be by hand; it's too perfect."

DID YOU KNOW?

Quotation marks were first used in printing during the middle of the 16th century. Up to the 18th century, some printers would repeat the quotation mark at the beginning of every line in a long quotation. When printers stopped this repetition of the quotation mark at the beginning of every line, the empty left margin was left behind, giving the modern form of the indented block quotation.

20d   Share a few lines of poetry

Quotation marks are used when quoting four or fewer lines of poetry. Be sure to enclose all material from the poem in quotation marks, and use a slash—with a space on each side of the slash—to show where the original line was divided. When quoting material from a source, be sure to give the documentation information.

→ I cannot help but compare my visit to the lines of one of my favorite poems by Jackson H. Day called "Wesley Theological Seminary: No Thoroughfare": "O you who see this sign, pray it may go/And all it represents; and later, lo/This path can be the broadest thoroughfare" (II.4-6).

20e   Share personal thoughts

→ During the visit, I could not help but compare my reception to the metaphor of a favorite poem: "I wish these people would think about how they could create the broadest of thoroughfares."

20f   Signal something being discussed, defined, or used in an unusual or ironic manner

→ I never thought there were so many sentences with the word "sign" in them.

→ Joe has been "signing off" to his girlfriend lately, meaning that he has been showing off.

→ At the bar, when Joe said his "sign" meant he was open for business, I had to laugh.

Helpful hint

When you want to place a quotation within a quotation, use single quotation marks within double quotation marks.

→ "What would you suggest I do when I'm feeling frustrated at being left out of things?" Mark asked his friend, the 60s fan.

→ His friend replied, "I'd go and listen to 'Signs' by the Five Man Electrical Band."

What's wrong with this sign?

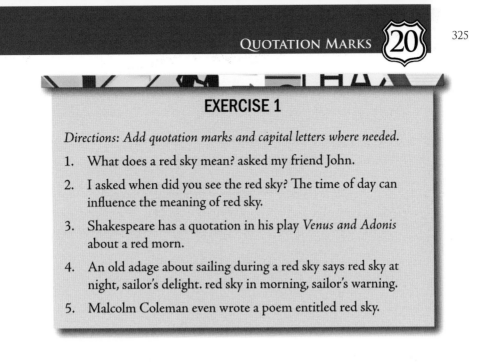

EXERCISE 1

Directions: Add quotation marks and capital letters where needed.

1. What does a red sky mean? asked my friend John.

2. I asked when did you see the red sky? The time of day can influence the meaning of red sky.

3. Shakespeare has a quotation in his play *Venus and Adonis* about a red morn.

4. An old adage about sailing during a red sky says red sky at night, sailor's delight. red sky in morning, sailor's warning.

5. Malcolm Coleman even wrote a poem entitled red sky.

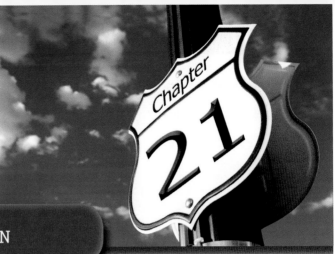

THE HYPHEN

Helpful hint

A hyphen is not a dash; a hyphen is one keyboard stroke. A dash equals two hyphens, without spacing before or after. See Chapter 22 for when to use a dash.

21a — Join words to make compound adjectives

A hyphen is used to join two adjectives into a compound adjective before a noun. Do not use a hyphen between the two adjectives when they follow a verb and are not in front of a noun to describe it.

→ freeze-dried coffee, red-light district, well-lighted sign, carry-on luggage

→ She can't tolerate coffee that is freeze dried.

21b — Connect prefixes and suffixes to root words

1. Join certain prefixes (*all-*, *ex-*, *half-*, and *self-*) to a root word

→ all-inclusive, ex-husband, half-back, self-starter

2. Link a single letter to a noun or participle

A hyphen can also be used to join single letters to a noun or participle.

→   X-ray, y-axis, U-turn, G-rated

DID YOU KNOW?

In 2007, the sixth edition of the *Shorter Oxford English Dictionary* removed the hyphens from over 16,000 words, including *crybaby*, *toolbar*, *ice cream*, and *chickpea*.

21c   Join words to make compound numbers

A hyphen is used to join compound numbers from *twenty-one* to *ninety-nine*.

→   twenty-one, thirty-two, forty-three, forty-four

Attention Dog Guardians:
Dogs are restricted from Main Areas, Beaches & must be leashed on trails. Please pick up after your dogs. Thank-you.

Attention Dogs:
Grrrr, Bark, Woof Good Dog.

Storrs Pond Recreation Area Management

What's wrong with this sign?

21d   Join numbers

Hyphens are used to join the numerator and denominator in a fraction. They are also used to give a person's life span or a score.

→   one-fourth, two-thirds, four-fifths

→   Edward Minor Gallaudet (1837-1917) was the founder and first president of a university for the deaf.

→   In last night's bowling championship, Smith beat Jones 222-219.

21e   Prevent confusion

A hyphen should be used to avoid awkward spelling or confusion when using a prefix or suffix.

→   pre-eminent, re-educate, anti-infective

→   The football player will re-sign. vs. The football player will resign.

EXERCISE 1

Directions: Add a hyphen where necessary.

1. My motherinlaw's Xray was the first sign of her health crisis.

2. The recreation or remodeling of a piece of art can cause controversy.

3. *Signs* is a hairraising film from beginning to end, even though the audience does not know what is truly happening until halfway through.

4. Although M. Night Shyamalan is best known for *The Sixth Sense*, *Signs* is also a well known film.

5. Both *The Sixth Sense* and *Signs* are truly all American films.

Photo from: crackdmuskegonnewz.blogspot.com: "Hyphen-Nation."

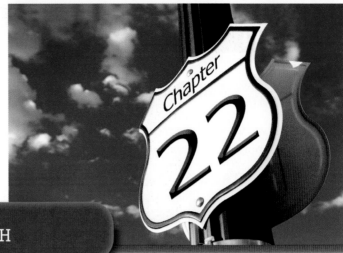

THE DASH

A dash is two strokes of the hyphen key without spacing before or after. Dashes are used in a variety of ways as seen below. Be sure, though, that you need to use a dash and not a hyphen. See Chapter 21 for rules on hyphen use.

22a   Highlight introductory material

A dash can be used to highlight introductory material. Usually, the clause that follows the dash will give further explanation about the introductory material.

→ A pig or a boar—those are the two names for my Chinese zodiac sign.

22b   Set off parenthetical, explanatory, or contrasted material

→ I cannot accept either name—a pig or boar—for my Chinese zodiac sign.

→ Chinese zodiac signs—based on animals and natural elements—describe general qualities of a person's nature.

→ I'd much rather be a dragon—not a pig—for my Chinese zodiac sign.

22c Add emphasis

Dashes can be used instead of commas when you want to add emphasis to something.

→ I still can't believe what my Chinese zodiac sign is—a pig or boar!

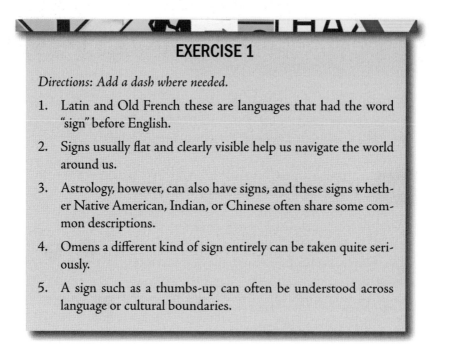

EXERCISE 1

Directions: Add a dash where needed.

1. Latin and Old French these are languages that had the word "sign" before English.

2. Signs usually flat and clearly visible help us navigate the world around us.

3. Astrology, however, can also have signs, and these signs whether Native American, Indian, or Chinese often share some common descriptions.

4. Omens a different kind of sign entirely can be taken quite seriously.

5. A sign such as a thumbs-up can often be understood across language or cultural boundaries.

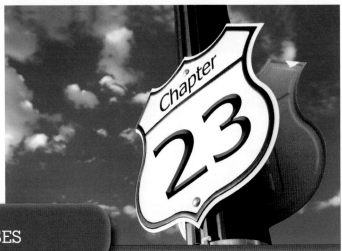

Chapter 23

PARENTHESES

A parenthesis (the singular form of "parentheses") is a type of bracket. A dash is more commonly used nowadays in formal writing although parentheses and dashes basically have the same function.

23a   Enclose explanatory, minor, or secondary information

Parentheses are used to add material that might interrupt the flow of the sentence. The added information is considered secondary or minor to the main idea of the sentence.

➜   In the Chinese zodiac, a person with the boar (a pig) sign is honest, sociable, and hard-working.

23b   Enclose in-text citations

Parentheses are also used to enclose in-text citations when you need to document your source(s).

MLA in-text citation➜ Williams theorizes that the overlap in different systems of astrology is due to "the inherent relationship between travel and storytelling" (234).

APA in-text citation➜ Although astrology systems around the world may differ, some overlap is possible due to how stories and travel go together (Williams, 234).

Helpful hint

You can embed parenthetical elements within other elements; however, this is not common in formal writing. Use different types of brackets to set off both elements in this case.

➜ Astrology (whether it is Indian [from India] or Chinese) usually is based in some way on nature.

23c Enclose numbers or letters in outlines

Parentheses can be used at different levels of outlines to enclose numbers or letters.

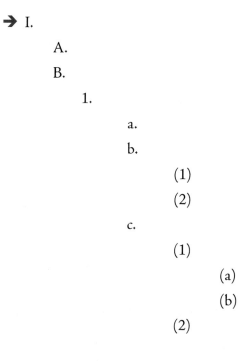

➜ I.

   A.

   B.

     1.

       a.

       b.

         (1)

         (2)

       c.

         (1)

           (a)

           (b)

         (2)

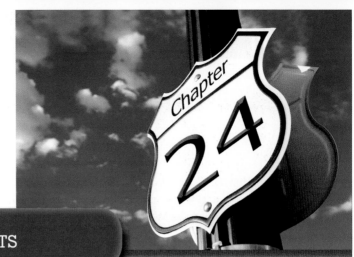

BRACKETS

24a Use square brackets to signal corrections or errors

1. Signal editorial correction

Square brackets are usually used to signal that an editorial correction or clarification has been made within a quotation.

→ "The inherent relationship between [the Chinese and Western] systems of astrology is due to exploration and storytelling" (Williams 234).

2. Signal editorial error

Square brackets that are placed around the word *sic* ("as such" in Latin) signal that an editorial error was made by the original writer or speaker.

→ "The inherent relationship between [*sic*] the three systems of astrology is due to exploration and storytelling" (Williams 234).

> **Helpful hint**
> You can avoid using square brackets by being selective in choosing what you use as quoted material. If you can summarize or paraphrase, instead of quoting, a section that lacks clarity or has a typographical error, do so.

24b   Use angle brackets to signal Web addresses

Angle brackets (< >) are used to signal Web addresses and separate them unmistakably from the rest of the sentence.

Angle brackets also allow for the end punctuation to fall outside the brackets, thus not creating any confusion about whether the end punctuation is part of the Web address.

→   To learn more about Chinese astrology, visit <http://chinesezodiac.com>.

THE SLASH

The slash (/) is often called the forward slash to distinguish it from the backslash (\) used in Web addresses. It is also sometimes called the diagonal or the oblique.

25a Quote lines of poetry

When quoting more than one line of poetry, the slash (or diagonal) is used to show where each line of poetry ends. Be sure to place a space on each side of the slash.

→ I cannot help but compare my visit to the lines of a favorite poem by Jackson H. Day called "Wesley Theological Seminary: No Thoroughfare": "O you who see this sign, pray it may go / And all it represents; and later, lo / This path can be the broadest thoroughfare" (II.4-6).

25b Show a choice

A slash can also be used between two words to show that either choice is available or acceptable.

→ the in/out door, the up/down button

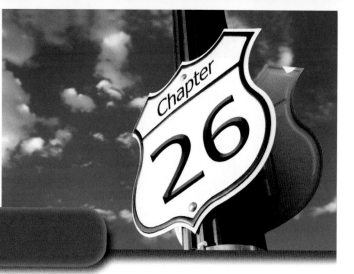

Ellipses

26a   Signal omissions

Ellipses (or ellipsis points) consist of three periods that are spaced equally apart. They are used in quotations to indicate that words have been omitted. If the omission occurs at the end of a sentence, put the ellipses after the period that is at the end of the sentence.

> Original➜ "My attitude towards punctuation is that it ought to be as conventional as possible. The game of golf would lose a good deal if croquet mallets and billiard cues were allowed on the putting green. You ought to be able to show that you can do it a good deal better than anyone else with the regular tools before you have a license to bring in your own improvements."
>
> –Ernest Hemingway

> Quotation➜ "My attitude towards punctuation is that it ought to be as conventional as possible. . . . You ought to be able to show that you can do it a good deal better than anyone else . . . before you have a license to bring in your own improvements."

When quoting poetry, use a line of ellipsis points to signal that you have dropped a line or more of the poem.

GIVE ME A SIGN

By Linda R. O'Connell
2008

Give me a sign
of any kind
at all.

That tells me we share
the same soul.

. . . .

And walk with me
forever.

Until the moonlight is not required.

For this love
within our hearts,

Would light the world
on fire.

26b   Signal a pause or hesitation

Ellipses can also be used to signal a pause or hesitation.

→ I wish . . . that punctuation was as conventional as possible,
just as Hemingway describes it.

CAPITALIZATION

27a Indicate the first word

1. Indicate the first word in a sentence

Capitalization is used for the first word in every sentence.

→ Traffic signs are sometimes difficult to understand.

2. Indicate the first word in a quotation

Capitalization is also used to indicate the first word in a quotation.

→ My brother told the police officer, "But the sign was covered by a tree branch."

3. Indicate the first word inside parentheses

Capitalization is used when a full sentence is placed within parentheses. If the parenthetical statement is inserted into another sentence, do not capitalize.

→ My brother told the officer that the sign was covered by a tree branch. (However, it wasn't.)

→ My brother told the officer (from our father's precinct) that the sign was covered by a tree branch.

→ My brother told the officer (the officer was from our father's precinct) that the sign was covered by a tree branch.

4. Indicate the first word in a sentence following a colon

Capitalization after a colon is optional; however, capitalize the first word after a colon if you want to emphasize the sentence.

→ My brother has had several tickets: he has been caught driving with a broken headlight, driving too fast in a school zone, and not stopping for a pedestrian in the crosswalk.

→ The police officer voided the ticket: He was from our father's precinct.

27b   Indicate proper nouns and proper adjectives

Capitalization is used to indicate proper nouns and proper adjectives.

1. Indicate proper nouns

Proper nouns name specific people, places, things, or ideas. For more information on proper nouns, see 2b.

People→Abigail Breslin, Joaquin Phoenix, Aunt Joan, Uncle Ralph, Senator Jones, Reverend Smith, Dr. Black, Chief Johnson, Professor White

Places→ Europe, Australia, Alaska, Washington, D.C., the South, the Northeast, the Mississippi River, the Grand Canyon, New York City, United States

Organizations, governmental institutions, and academic institutions→Federal Bureau of Investigation, Department of Labor, the United Nations, Long Beach City College, Harvard University

Abbreviations of titles and organizations→ AAA, FBI, MD, MLA, PhD, UN, UCLA

Monuments and buildings→ the Washington Monument, the Willis Tower, the Taj Mahal, the Eiffel Tower

Languages➔ Chinese, English, Arabic, Swahili, Spanish, French, Japanese, Russian, Mandarin, American Sign Language

Races➔ American Indian, Alaskan Native, Pacific Islander, African American, Black, White, Asian

Nationalities➔Spanish, Ethiopian, Arabic, Chinese, South African, Greek, American

Religions and religious terms➔ Buddhism, Islam, Christianity, Judaism, Shinto, Protestant, Catholic, Baptist, Buddha, Mohammed, God, Jesus, Moses, Talmud, Bible, Koran, Allah, Jehovah, Genesis

Course titles➔ English 101, Biology 1001, French 300, English Composition 101, Modern War Ethics, An Introduction to Computer History

Days and months➔ January, March, May, Sunday, Tuesday, Thursday

2. Indicate proper adjectives

Capitalization is also used for proper adjectives, which are usually derived from proper nouns and can be found inside a proper noun phrase.

➔ Chinese food, English language, Spanish eyes

27c Indicate titles and subtitles

Capitalization is used for titles of books, stories, plays, poems, songs, articles, films, newspapers, magazines, works of art, musical compositions, and photographs. Always capitalize the first word in the title, no matter the type of word. Also, if using MLA (Modern Language Association) style, capitalize all other words in the title or subtitle except for articles (*a, an, the*), conjunctions (*for, and, nor, but, or, yet, so*), and short prepositions (*in, on, for, to*). If using another style, such as from the APA (American Psychological Association), be sure to check specific guidelines.

Books➔ *The World According to Garp*
Books with subtitles➔*Chinese Astrology: Exploring the Eastern Zodiac*

Short stories➔ "Everyday Use"

Plays➔ *Hamlet*

Poems➔ "Casey at Bat"

Songs➔ "Rudolph, the Red-Nosed Reindeer"

Articles➔ "Fifty Ways to Avoid the Flu"

Films➔ *Moulin Rouge*

Newspapers➔ *The New York Times*

Magazines and journals➔ *Vogue, English Journal*

Works of art➔ *Starry Night*

Musical compositions➔ *Romeo et Juliette*

Photographs➔ *The Kiss*

Vessels➔ *Spruce Goose, Queen Mary*

VJ Day, The Kiss, New York 1945
Gelatin Silver by Alfred Eisenstaedt
© Time Inc.

27d   Indicate acronyms

Acronyms are made up of the first letter of each word in a phrase. For instance, *FBI* is the acronym for "Federal Bureau of Investigation." Acronyms are usually capitalized except for those that have become regular words such as *scuba*, *laser*, and *radar*.

Acronyms ➔CBS, CEO, CIA, FAQ, SAT, USA, WGN

DID YOU KNOW?

The official name for the Roman Empire, long before the Christian era, was SPQR, an acronym that means *Senatus Populusque Romanus* or "the Senate and the People of Rome."

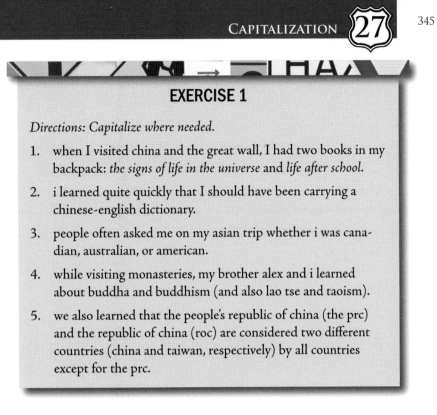

EXERCISE 1

Directions: Capitalize where needed.

1. when I visited china and the great wall, I had two books in my backpack: *the signs of life in the universe* and *life after school*.

2. i learned quite quickly that I should have been carrying a chinese-english dictionary.

3. people often asked me on my asian trip whether i was canadian, australian, or american.

4. while visiting monasteries, my brother alex and i learned about buddha and buddhism (and also lao tse and taoism).

5. we also learned that the people's republic of china (the prc) and the republic of china (roc) are considered two different countries (china and taiwan, respectively) by all countries except for the prc.

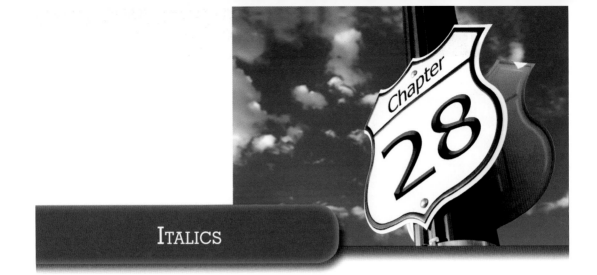

Italics are used to emphasize special words, phrases, or clauses. If you are writing by hand or are unable to use italics, you can underline the items that should be in italics.

28a   Highlight titles

1. Highlight titles of longer works

To highlight the title of a larger or longer work, use italics. Thus, you should italicize the titles of poetry or short story collections, anthologies, books, albums/CDs, magazines, newspapers, encyclopedias, television series, and radio series.

- ➔ *Signs of Life: A Book of Visual Poetry* by John Ecko
- ➔ *Vital Signs: International Short Stories on Aging* by Dorothy Sennett and Anne Czarniecki
- ➔ *The Signs of Language Revisited: An Anthology in Honor of Ursula Bellugi and Edward Klima* – edited by Karen Emmorey and Harlan L. Lane
- ➔ *Lonely Planet Signspotting* – a book by Doug Lansky
- ➔ *The Sign* – a CD by Ace of Base
- ➔ *Vital Signs* – a magazine
- ➔ *Encyclopedia Britannica* – an encyclopedia
- ➔ *Sign of the Times* – a television series
- ➔ *The Bob and Tom Radio Show* – a radio series

> **Helpful hint**
>
> Quotation marks are used to enclose the titles of short works, including poems, short stories, lectures, book chapters, song titles, magazine articles, newspaper articles, encyclopedia entries, and television/radio episodes.
>
> ➔ "Signs and Wonder" is episode 7.9 of *The X-Files*.
>
> For information on using quotation marks, see Chapter 20.

2. Highlight legal cases

Italics are used to highlight the titles of legal cases.

➔ *Roe v. Wade, Brown v. Board of Education of Topeka, State v. Scopes*

3. Identify naval and air ships

Italics are used to identify naval crafts, aircraft, and spacecraft.

➔ *Nimitz, Titanic, Queen Mary*

➔ *Spruce Goose, Spirit of St. Louis, Lockheed Vega, Air Force One*

➔ *Challenger, Atlantis, Enterprise, Sputnik, Explorer*

28b　Highlight special letters, words, phrases, or clauses

Italics are used to highlight special letters, words, phrases, and clauses.

1. Highlight non-English words

Italics are used when you write a non-English word or phrase. If the word or phrase is used multiple times, use italics only the first time it is used.

French phrase for "joy of living"➜ Every time I see Karen, I drink in her *joie de vivre*.

Japanese word for "special singing and dancing"➜ My favorite part of Japanese night was the *kabuki* theater.

Arabic phrase for "have a safe journey"➜ As he left me on the trail, the guide wished me, "*Bissalama*."

The English language has borrowed heavily from other languages for centuries, and some of these words are now considered part of English. For these types of everyday words, you do not use italics.

➜ soy (Japanese), glasnost (Russian), banana (Wolof), Kwanzaa (Swahili), cider (Hebrew)

DID YOU KNOW?

In 1973, a survey (by Thomas Finkenstaedt and Dieter Wolff) of about 80,000 words found in the *Shorter Oxford Dictionary* (3rd edition) showed that 28.3% of the English words were borrowed from French, 28.24% from Latin, 25% from Germanic languages (including Old and Middle English), and 5.32% from Greek. All other languages contributed less than 1% of the borrowed words (with 3.28% deriving from proper names and 4.03% of the word origins being unknown).

2. Highlight referenced or discussed letters, words, phrases, and clauses

You also use italics to highlight words that you are discussing, defining, or using in a special way.

➜ Words with the letters *SK* at the beginning are usually of Scandinavian origin.

➜ I had no idea that the word *banana* came from the African language Wolof.

➡ *Leviathan* had the original meaning of "sea monster" but now refers to anything of an unusual size.

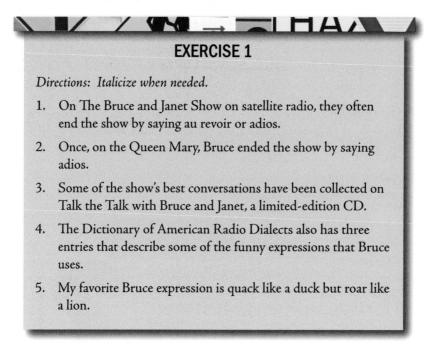

EXERCISE 1

Directions: Italicize when needed.

1. On The Bruce and Janet Show on satellite radio, they often end the show by saying au revoir or adios.

2. Once, on the Queen Mary, Bruce ended the show by saying adios.

3. Some of the show's best conversations have been collected on Talk the Talk with Bruce and Janet, a limited-edition CD.

4. The Dictionary of American Radio Dialects also has three entries that describe some of the funny expressions that Bruce uses.

5. My favorite Bruce expression is quack like a duck but roar like a lion.

The Simple Sentence

29a   The simple sentence

A simple sentence contains a subject and main verb combination, either or both of which may be conjoined. There are two kinds of clauses: independent and dependent. An independent clause, sometimes called a main clause, can stand alone as a simple, but complete, sentence. A dependent clause—with its own subject and verb—can never stand alone and is never part of a simple sentence.

Independent clause/simple sentence➔ Sam saw the stop sign.

Conjoined noun phrase➔ Sam and Chris saw the stop sign.

Conjoined verb phrase➔ Sam saw the stop sign and braked the car at the same time.

An independent clause can be modified in a variety of ways and still be a simple sentence. Most often, simple sentences are modified with either participial verb phrases, which are verb phrases that do not include an auxiliary, or prepositional phrases (see 6c3).

➔   **Driving down Elm Street,**
Participial VP

Sam saw the stop sign.
Independent Clause

➔　Stopped at the corner, **Sam saw the stop sign.**
　　　Participial VP　　　　　　　Independent Clause

➔　**Sam saw the stop sign** at the corner.
　　Independent Clause　　　Prep Phrase

Simple sentences can be modified by participial phrases and prepositional phrases at the same time.

➔　**Driving down Elm Street,**
　　　Participial VP
　　Sam saw the stop sign at the corner.
　　Independent Clause　　　Prep Phrase

Multiple prepositional phrases can also be used in the same simple sentence.

➔　**Sam saw the stop sign** at the corner　of Elm and Sixth.
　　Independent Clause　Prep Phrase　　　Prep Phrase

As you may have already noticed, participial phrases that appear at the beginning of the sentence always have a comma that separates the phrase from the independent clause. In fact, all phrases or clauses that contain a verb and occur at the beginning of a sentence should be separated from the main clause by a comma.

When you write a sentence that has a prepositional phrase at the beginning, you have the option of including a comma or not; however, if the introductory prepositional phrase is five words or longer, it usually takes a comma.

OK➔　In spring the stop sign at Elm and Sixth is covered with a tree branch.

OK➔　In spring, the stop sign at Elm and Sixth is covered with a tree branch.

OK➔　At the corner of Elm and Sixth, the stop sign is covered with a tree branch.

29b   **Check for common errors with the simple sentence**

1. Check for overuse of simple sentences

Simple sentences are often used for effect or emphasis and should be used sparingly. Be sure that you do not overuse simple sentences, so when you are ready to use them for emphasis, they can stand out from the more complex sentences around them. See how the addition of a simple sentence in the combination below stands out against the more complex sentence that precedes it.

→   Our city manager says that there are no funds available to cut the overgrown tree branch on Elm and Sixth; however, there were enough funds for her recent junket to Las Vegas. She needs to stop irrelevant spending now.

2. Check for fragments

Be sure that simple sentences have both a subject and predicate. If one or the other is missing, you have created a common sentence error—the fragment.

Fragment (missing a subject)→ Leaving the party with his friends in the blue car.

OK→ Sam left the party with his friends in the blue car.

OK→ Leaving the party early, Sam went with his friends in the blue car.

Fragment (missing a predicate)→ My neighbor Sam and his friends, along with many of the people at the party.

OK→ My neighbor Sam and his friends, along with many of the people at the party, were in the backyard.

Sentences that give directions or a command have an understood subject (*you*), so even though a subject may not appear explicitly in the sentence, the implied subject makes the sentence an independent clause and not a fragment.

→   (You should) Go east on Elm, and then turn on Sixth.

3. Check for parallelism

When conjoining multiple instances of the same type of word class or phrase, be sure that they are in parallel form.

> Not parallel➔ Sam ran quickly to the sign at the corner, returned just as quickly, and singing all the while.

> OK➔ Sam ran quickly to the sign at the corner, returned just as quickly, and sang all the while.

EXERCISE 1

Directions: Revise any fragments below into full sentences.

Example: Many people have had accidents at the tree-covered stop sign. For instance, my neighbor John.➔ Many people, including my neighbor John, have had accidents at the tree-covered stop sign.

1. Nothing has been done to fix the problem. No tree work. No sign moving.

2. I like to visit my friends on Elm Street. Who have a pool and a hot tub.

3. My friends' daughter had an accident at the stop sign at Sixth and Elm. Not seeing the sign.

4. The city manager needs to take the accidents seriously. Along with other city officials losing more funds due to court cases.

5. Running for office to fix the small problems of our city, including the overgrown trees that are blocking traffic signs.

Chapter 30

THE COMPOUND SENTENCE

30a   The compound sentence

One way to add variety to your writing is to use coordination to join some of your simple sentences together. When you coordinate or combine together two simple sentences (also known as two independent clauses), you create a compound sentence.

→ The signs for American Sign Language were originally based

Independent Clause

on French, and **the signs for Signed English were originally**

Independent Clause

based on English.

You can choose from four options to create compound sentences, and the option you choose determines the punctuation you will use.

> **Helpful hint**
>
> The compound sentence includes the combination of two full sentences, not two subjects, two verbs, or two verb phrases. For instance, the following sentences are not compound sentences, just simple sentences.
>
> Compound subjects→ Mary and the new professor left the classroom early.
>
> Compound verbs→ Mary laughed and cried at the same time.
>
> Compound verb phrases→ Mary laughed at the joke and cried at the picture at the same time.

30b   Use appropriate punctuation for the compound sentence

1. Punctuating a compound sentence—Option 1: Using a comma + conjunction

Notice that the two independent clauses on the previous page are joined together with a comma and a conjunction (*and*). Independent clauses can be joined in a variety of acceptable ways, and using a comma plus a coordinating conjunction is one of the most popular.

The conjunctions that you can use to join together two independent clauses can be remembered by using the mnemonic device FANBOYS, in which each letter represents one conjunction.

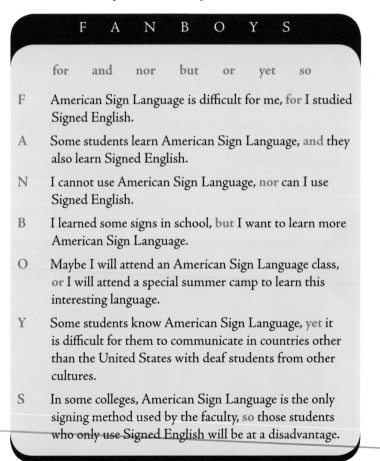

F A N B O Y S

for   and   nor   but   or   yet   so

F   American Sign Language is difficult for me, for I studied Signed English.

A   Some students learn American Sign Language, and they also learn Signed English.

N   I cannot use American Sign Language, nor can I use Signed English.

B   I learned some signs in school, but I want to learn more American Sign Language.

O   Maybe I will attend an American Sign Language class, or I will attend a special summer camp to learn this interesting language.

Y   Some students know American Sign Language, yet it is difficult for them to communicate in countries other than the United States with deaf students from other cultures.

S   In some colleges, American Sign Language is the only signing method used by the faculty, so those students who only use Signed English will be at a disadvantage.

2. Punctuating a compound sentence—Option 2: Using a semi-colon

A semi-colon can be used to connect two independent clauses. When you use a semi-colon in this way, you suggest to the reader that the two connected clauses are related in some way.

American Sign Language

→ Some students learn American Sign Language; **they can also**
　　　　Independent Clause
learn Signed English.
Independent Clause

3. Punctuating a compound sentence—Option 3: Using a semi-colon + adverbial conjunction

Another way to connect two independent clauses is with a semi-colon plus an adverbial conjunction (sometimes called a conjunctive adverb). Note that a comma follows the adverbial conjunction.

→ Some students attend a school that requires American Sign
　　　　Independent Clause
Language; therefore, knowing Signed English is not enough.
　　　　　　Independent Clause

You can use the acronym THIN TIC to help you remember some common adverbial conjunctions.

T　therefore

H　however

I　in fact

N　nevertheless

T　thus

I　indeed

C　consequently

Adverbial conjunctions signify relationships such as result, cause, contrast, or condition. Be sure to signal the appropriate relationship with the adverbial conjunction you use.

Result/cause ➔ I learned Signed English in elementary school; therefore, I had problems understanding some American Sign Language signs later on.

Contrast ➔ American Sign Language is popular at Gallaudet University; however, English is used alongside ASL.

Condition/intensification ➔ American Sign Language and English are popular at Gallaudet University; indeed, many students use both.

Other than the common THIN TIC adverbial conjunctions, there are other adverbial conjunctions that can be used to connect two independent clauses and signify particular relationships. Here is a list to help you make appropriate choices.

Addition ➔ moreover, furthermore, likewise, finally, additionally, also, incidentally, further, similarly, in addition

Contrast ➔ however, nevertheless, in contrast, on the contrary, nonetheless, otherwise, on the other hand, in comparison, conversely, instead

Comparison ➔ similarly, likewise, at the same time, comparatively

Exemplification ➔ for example, for instance, namely, that is

Intensification ➔ indeed, in fact, moreover, still, certainly, notably, undoubtedly

Result ➔therefore, thus, consequently, as a result, finally, hence, then, accordingly, henceforth, subsequently, undoubtedly, in fact

Time ➔ meanwhile, then, next, finally, still, now, thereafter

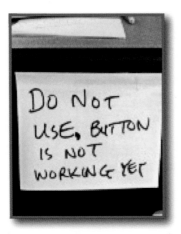

This image of a note placed on an information desk shows a compound sentence that is missing the appropriate punctuation. How could you fix the punctuation problem?

4. Punctuating a compound sentence—Option 4: Using a colon

Although not as common as the first three methods of joining two independent clauses together, you can also use a colon if the clause following the colon defines or elaborates the clause before the colon.

→ American Sign Language and Signed English are different in
 Independent Clause
 one important way: **many linguists consider American Sign**
 Independent Clause
 Language a full and complete language and Signed English
 not.

Since both independent clauses are connected in meaning and since the second independent clause elaborates on the first, giving more information about why, a colon can be used.

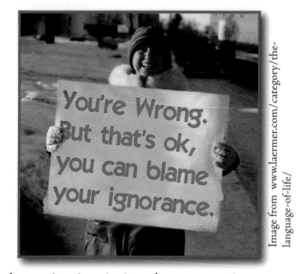

Image from www.laermer.com/category/the-language-of-life/

The above sign is missing the appropriate punctuation—how ironic! How would you edit this sign to make it grammatically correct?

30c   Common sentence errors with the compound sentence

1. Use a variety of punctuation, conjunctions, and adverbial conjunctions

Be careful when you decide how to join compound sentences. Combining sentences in the same way each time or in a way that creates an obviously consistent pattern will negatively impact your writing. It is best to use a variety of punctuation, conjunctions, and adverbial conjunctions.

2. Check for comma splices

Mistakenly joining two independent clauses together with only a comma creates one of the most frequent sentence errors that writers make. You can fix a comma splice by using one of the four options given above.

Comma splice➜ Some American students learn Signed English as children, they learn American Sign Language as adults.

OK➜ Some American students learn Signed English as children, and they learn American Sign Language as adults.

OK➜ Some American students learn Signed English as children; they then learn American Sign Language as adults.

OK➜ Some American students learn Signed English as children; then, they learn American Sign Language as adults.

3. Check for run-on or fused sentences

If you fail to join two independent clauses together with the appropriate punctuation, you can create another common sentence problem—the run-on or fused sentence.

Run-on/fused sentence➜ My third-grade teacher taught us some signs they were Signed English.

OK➜ My third-grade teacher taught us some signs, yet I don't know many now.

OK➜ My third-grade teacher taught us some signs; they were Signed English.

EXERCISE 1

Directions: The following paragraph contains five comma splices. Correct the errors by turning the comma splices into compound sentences.

I've never been one for believing in astrological signs, I couldn't really even tell you what my sign, Scorpio, actually means. But every now and then, I'll run across a daily horoscope chart, curiosity gets the better of me. One day in particular, my horoscope said to be careful in business dealings and avoid conflict. I had been having a disagreement with one of my clients, who was threatening to give her business to our biggest competitor, immediately that situation came to mind as I read the horoscope over my morning breakfast. I walked into the office later that morning, my secretary informed me that the client was waiting on me—and not happy. I quickly made up an excuse and left the office, remembering what was in store for Scorpios that day. Come to find out, the client's anger was not directed at me, but because she wasted her time coming to the office that morning, she decided to take her business elsewhere. My decision to avoid the conflict altogether resulted in my losing this client and significant income for my company, needless to say, I try to avoid horoscopes now.

Citation = http://news.bbc.co.uk/2/hi/uk_news/magazine/7292252.stm

EXERCISE 2

Directions: The following paragraph contains five run-on sentences. Correct them by adding the appropriate punctuation.

Who would have guessed that a simple piece of fruit would become synonymous with innovative technology well this is exactly what has happened with the symbol for Apple, Inc. With the increasing international popularity of the iPhone, Apple's logo is becoming one of the most recognizable symbols in business and technology today. The trademark silhouette of an apple missing a bite has been around practically since the company's inception although the company's earliest logo features a sketch of Isaac Newton sitting under the apple tree. Apple co-founder Steve Jobs hired Rob Janoff in 1976 to redesign the company's logo and the iconic rainbow apple design was born this version of Apple's apple remained in use until a redesign of the Macintosh operating system and computer hardware in 1998 warranted a monochrome makeover. Two more versions of the symbol would follow: an aqua theme in 2001 and the current glass theme unveiled in 2003, both of which gave the trademark a three dimensional, textured appearance though it's already an internationally recognized symbol, the Apple logo will only become even more common as the company continues to expand.

Chapter 31

THE COMPLEX SENTENCE

31a   The complex sentence

Another way to add variety to your writing is to use subordination and modification to create complex sentences. A complex sentence consists of a simple sentence (also known as an independent clause) plus one or more dependent clauses.

Dependent clauses, like independent clauses, contain a subject and predicate; however, whereas independent clauses can stand alone, dependent clauses are dependent or subordinate to an independent clause and must be attached to that independent clause to form a complete sentence. You can track most dependent clauses back to their independent counterparts, as in the set of sentences below.

Independent clause➔ Each letter in our alphabet is a sign.

Independent clause➔ Each letter in our alphabet gives us information about our language's history and sound system.

Complex sentence➔ Because each letter in our alphabet is a
                            Dependent Clause
sign, it gives us information about our language's history and
sound system.   Independent Clause

Note that the dependent clause above includes the subordinator "because" at the beginning of the clause. A dependent clause usually begins with a subordinator—also called a subordinating conjunction—or a relative pronoun. A subordinator or relative pronoun gives information about the relationship between the independent and dependent clause.

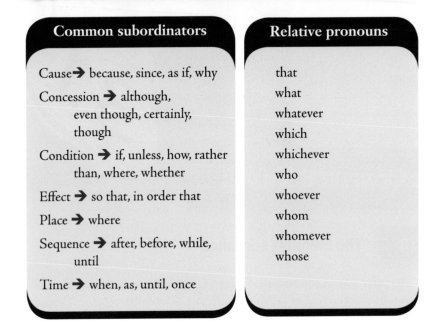

Common subordinators	Relative pronouns
Cause➜ because, since, as if, why	that
Concession ➜ although, even though, certainly, though	what
	whatever
	which
Condition ➜ if, unless, how, rather than, where, whether	whichever
	who
Effect ➜ so that, in order that	whoever
Place ➜ where	whom
Sequence ➜ after, before, while, until	whomever
	whose
Time ➜ when, as, until, once	

<table>
</table>

31b   Dependent clauses

Dependent clauses can be nominal (used like nouns), adjectival (used like adjectives), or adverbial (used like adverbs). This means that dependent clauses can be used as subjects, objects, or modifiers. Although it is sometimes difficult to distinguish which type of dependent clause is being used, it is a good idea to learn the different clause types because your choice of punctuation depends on how a clause is being used.

31c   Noun (or nominal) clauses

Dependent noun clauses can function as subjects, direct objects, subject complements, objects of prepositions, or appositives. Since these types of clauses are dependent or subordinate, they are always attached to an independent clause or a critical part of an independent clause. Noun clauses usually begin with a relative pronoun or with one of these subordinators: when, where, how, why or whether. There are two types of noun clauses: nominal relative clauses and appositive clauses.

1. Nominal relative clauses

Nominal relative clauses take the place of a subject, direct object, or an object of a preposition. A good way to see whether you are using a nominal relative clause is to see if you can substitute a pronoun (*it, she, he*) for the clause in question.

> In place of a subject ➔ What sound a letter makes is complicated.
> Dependent Clause/
> Nominal Relative Clause

> In place of a direct object ➔ For new language learners, it is sometimes difficult to know which letter represents a particular sound.
> Dependent Clause/
> Nominal Relative Clause

> In place of a subject complement ➔ This alphabet disconnection is why many linguists suggest changing our alphabet.
> Dependent Clause/Nominal Relative Clause

> In place of an object of the preposition ➔ Many linguists theorize about when the alphabet will become more transparent.
> Dependent Clause/Nominal Relative Clause

2. Appositive clauses

Appositive clauses follow nouns that are general or abstract in nature, such as a theory, reason, fact, or story. The appositive clause begins with a "that" and provides more information about the abstract noun.

> The alphabet disconnection theory that letters do not clearly
> Dependent Clause/
> match sounds is widely known by linguists.
> Appositive Clause

It is important to be able to distinguish these dependent clauses as noun clauses because neither one of these dependent noun clauses requires a comma. Putting a comma around these clauses to highlight them or separate them in some way from the independent clause is a comma error.

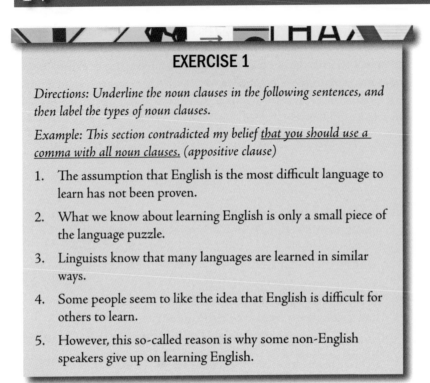

EXERCISE 1

Directions: Underline the noun clauses in the following sentences, and then label the types of noun clauses.

Example: This section contradicted my belief <u>that you should use a comma with all noun clauses.</u> *(appositive clause)*

1. The assumption that English is the most difficult language to learn has not been proven.

2. What we know about learning English is only a small piece of the language puzzle.

3. Linguists know that many languages are learned in similar ways.

4. Some people seem to like the idea that English is difficult for others to learn.

5. However, this so-called reason is why some non-English speakers give up on learning English.

31d   Adjective (or adjectival) clauses

Adjective clauses, another type of dependent or subordinate clause, modify noun phrases, which can be made up of either nouns or pronouns. There are two types of adjective clauses: the comparative clause and the relative clause.

1. Comparative clauses

Comparative clauses compare two noun phrases and use the phrase *as XXX as* to make the comparison, where *XXX* is filled in with an adjective. The clause to the left of the *as XXX as* phrase is the beginning of the independent clause, and the clause to the right of the *as XXX as* phrase is the dependent clause.

→ That sign is as uninformative as the one I saw at the zoo last week.   Dependent Clause

→ She is as tall as the sign is.
     Dependent Clause

2. Relative clauses

Relative clauses, the most common type of dependent clause, are used to modify or give more information about the noun phrase to the clause's left. These clauses usually begin with a relative pronoun, such as that, which, who, whom, or whose.

→ Highway signs that are funny often defeat the purpose of their warning.   Relative Clause

→ The student who is signing for the deaf audience is obviously
                                Relative Clause
still learning American Sign Language.

→ The highway workers whose job it was to paint the new sign forgot the paint.   Relative Clause

Relative pronouns can sometimes be dropped if they can be understood to be part of the relative clause.

→ The signs [that] the highway workers need to paint are the
                                Relative Clause
ones [that] taggers have covered with graffiti.
                        Relative Clause

Relative clauses can be essential or necessary for the full meaning of the sentence to be understood, or they can be non-essential. An essential relative clause is described as a restrictive relative clause. Restrictive relative clauses never take commas around the clause.

→ Highway signs that are covered in mud
                Restrictive Relative Clause
can cause accidents.

In the sentence above, **ALL** highway signs do not cause accidents; only highway signs that are covered in mud can cause them. Thus, the relative clause is essential to understand the meaning of the full sentence.

→ The architect **who designed the building** has a plaque with his
Restrictive Relative Clause
name on it near the front.

Likewise, in the sentence above, it is only the architect who designed the building who has a plaque, not just any architect. Therefore, this relative clause is also essential to the sentence.

A relative clause that is not essential to understand the full meaning of the sentence is described as a non-restrictive relative clause. Non-restrictive relative clauses always take commas around the clause.

→ The signs along Route 66, **which are often stolen,** classify
Non-Restrictive Relative Clause
it as a national monument.

In the sentence above, the relative clause is not essential for us to understand the meaning of the main sentence. In the relative clause, we get extra or non-essential information. With or without the relative clause, we still understand that the signs along Route 66 label it as a national monument.

→ The architect, **who wore a seersucker suit to the ceremony,** was
Non-Restrictive Relative Clause
awarded a plaque.

Likewise, in the above sentence, the relative clause is not essential. Whether he wore a seersucker or wool suit is not important; the architect would still have been awarded the plaque either way.

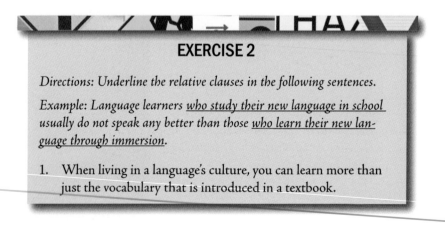

EXERCISE 2

Directions: Underline the relative clauses in the following sentences.

Example: Language learners <u>who study their new language in school</u> usually do not speak any better than those <u>who learn their new language through immersion</u>.

1. When living in a language's culture, you can learn more than just the vocabulary that is introduced in a textbook.

2. Many language learners who live outside their native country find themselves learning new vocabulary from another language quickly.

3. The younger that a language learner is, the more chance she has of learning a new language.

4. Language textbooks, which are often published by a variety of publishers, can only get you so far into your new language.

5. It is a good idea to stay as long as you can in the country of the language that you are learning.

31e   Adverb (or adverbial) clauses

Adverbial clauses begin with a subordinator (sometimes called a subordinating conjunction) and usually give information about cause/reason, concession, condition, effect, place, sequence, and time. The clauses do this by answering the questions *when? where? why? how? how frequently?* and *in what manner?* Adverbial clauses are always dependent or subordinate to the main or independent clause.

Common subordinators

Cause➔ because, since, as if, why

Concession ➔ although, even though, certainly, though

Condition ➔ if, unless, how, rather than, where, whether

Effect ➔ so that, in order that

Place ➔ where

Sequence ➔ after, before, while, until

Time ➔ when, as, until, once

➜ **Because she was caught with the freeway sign in her car,** she
　　　　　　　　Adverbial (Dependent) Clause
was arrested for theft.

Notice that the adverbial clause above gives the reason why the woman was arrested, thus giving information about cause.

Adverbial clauses can function like adverbs, moving to various points in a sentence. When an adverbial clause is at the beginning of the sentence, use a comma to separate it off from the main or independent clause.

➜ **Because the highway trooper watched him**
　　　　　　Adverbial Clause
closely, the driver followed the detour sign.

When an adverbial clause appears in the middle of a sentence, you should also set it off by placing commas around the adverbial clause.

➜ The driver, **because the highway trooper**
　　　　　　Adverbial Clause
watched him closely, followed the detour sign.

However, when an adverbial clause appears at the end of a sentence, it usually does not take a comma.

➜ The driver followed the detour sign **because the highway**
　　　　　　　　　　Adverbial Clause
trooper watched him closely.

EXERCISE 3

Directions: Underline the adverbial clauses in the following sentences, and circle the subordinator.

Example: You usually do not need a travel guide <u>when you travel in your own neighborhood.</u>

1. When you travel to a foreign country, it is a good idea to bring a travel guide.

2. Although travel guides can be helpful, they cannot get you out of complicated situations.

3. If you do find yourself with a serious problem in a foreign country, you should check if there is an embassy located near you.

4. Finding an embassy is a good idea, so that you feel more secure when dealing with the problem.

5. While embassy employees can usually help you with serious problems, they cannot provide a translator for you for everyday use.

31f — Common sentence errors with the complex sentence

1. Check for fragments

Dependent clauses do not express a complete thought, and they need to be attached to an independent clause to be grammatically complete. Because dependent clauses are clauses, they contain a subject and a full verb, a fact that sometimes leads a writer to use a dependent clause as a complete sentence. When dependent clauses are presented as a full sentence, they are fragments.

Fragment➜ Because the highway trooper watched him closely.
　　　　　　　　　　Dependent Clause

OK➜ The driver took the detour because the highway trooper watched him closely.
　　　　　　　　　　　　　　　　Dependent Clause

Fragment➜ When she saw the tornado.
　　　　　　　　　Dependent Clause

OK➜ When she saw the tornado, she took it as a sign to take cover.
cover.　　　　Dependent Clause

EXERCISE 4

Directions: Identify six fragments in the following paragraph, and change them into grammatically correct sentences.

Our office was chosen to design the latest advertising campaign. For an internationally known sporting goods company. They've specifically requested a series of promotional billboards. Which will be displayed along highways in major cities. Because of the company's high profile. Our focus and dedication to the project is of the utmost importance, and we've also been told to keep the details of the project a secret. This advertising campaign will bring a significant amount of revenue to our relatively small company, so my boss has told me. That he will be creating a new administrative position. Will be filled by an internal promotion. The promotion, however, will be contingent upon the success of this latest campaign. With this information, the office is dedicated to not only satisfying our client, but also excelling in this project. To ensure our boss promotes one of the many qualified, hard-working employees in the office.

Source= http://news.bbc.co.uk/2/hi/uk_news/magazine/7292252.stm

2. Check for unnecessary commas

A noun clause can replace a subject, direct object, subject complement, or object of a preposition. When using a noun clause to replace these items, avoid placing an unnecessary comma between the noun clause and the rest of the sentence.

Extra comma➔ What I like about Saturdays, is seeing all the
           Dependent Noun Clause
yard sale signs in my neighborhood.

OK➔ What I like about Saturdays is seeing all the yard sale
           Dependent Noun Clause
signs in my neighborhood.

3. Check for restrictive or non-restrictive punctuation

Be sure to use the correct punctuation for relative clauses. When they provide essential information, they are restrictive and should not have commas. When relative clauses provide non-essential or extra information, they are non-restrictive and should always be separated from the rest of the sentence with commas.

> Extra commas➜ The protester, who had the derogatory sign, was removed from the lecture.   Restrictive Relative Clause

> OK➜ The protester who had the derogatory sign was removed from the lecture.   Restrictive Relative Clause

In the above example, the relative clause gives necessary information—the reason the protester was removed from the lecture. Therefore, the relative clause is restrictive and does not take commas.

> Missing commas➜ M. Night Shyamalan who directed *Sixth*
> Non-Restrictive
> *Sense* and *Signs* has not won an Academy Award.
> Relative Clause

> OK➜ M. Night Shyamalan, who directed *Sixth Sense* and
> Non-Restrictive Relative Clause
> *Signs,* has not won an Academy Award.

In the example above, the information that Shyamalan directed the movies *Sixth Sense* and *Signs* is not essential to the main point that he has not won an Academy Award. Thus, the relative clause is non-restrictive and needs to have commas surrounding it.

4. Check for adverbial clause punctuation

When including an adverbial clause in your writing, be sure to use the appropriate punctuation. If the clause appears at the beginning of the sentence, use a comma between it and the independent clause. If the adverbial clause appears in the middle of the sentence, surround the clause with commas. And, finally, if the adverbial clause appears at the end of the sentence, do not separate the dependent adverbial clause and the independent clause.

Missing comma➜ **As I left the movie** I saw a sign advertising
Dependent Clause

next week's feature.

OK➜ **As I left the movie,** I saw a sign advertising next week's
Dependent Clause

feature.

Extra comma➜ I saw a sign advertising next week's feature, as I
left the movie.
Dependent Clause

OK➜ I saw a sign advertising next week's feature **as I left the
movie.** Dependent
Clause

Chapter 32

THE COMPOUND-COMPLEX SENTENCE

32a   The compound-complex sentence

A compound-complex sentence is made up of two or more simple sentences or independent clauses (this is the compound part) and one or more subordinate or dependent clauses (this is the complex part).

➜ While she waited for a sign from the employees, **other shop-**
                Dependent Clause
pers sneaked into the toy store, and they were the ones fortu-
        Independent Clause
nate enough to find the most popular toy for Christmas.
                Independent Clause

When you punctuate a compound-complex sentence, you use the rules for both compound and complex sentences. For instance, in the above sentence, the dependent adverbial clause appears at the beginning of the sentence; thus, it needs a comma between it and the independent clause. In addition, the combination of a comma and coordinating conjunction is used to join together the two independent clauses.

EXERCISE 1

Directions: Label the sentence type (simple, compound, complex, compound-complex) for each sentence in this paragraph.

_____It is often difficult to figure out where a language actually begins.

_____The problem is that historical records only date back so far.

_____There are usually no recordings of early language; we can only guess at their initial sounds and words.

_____Historical documents that include symbols, characters, and drawings can help.

_____Language changes quickly, and that also complicates investigating the beginnings.

_____For instance, English dictionaries add and delete words during each publication period.

_____Words that may be slang today can be common words in a decade.

_____Languages rarely add new conjunctions, subordinators, or prepositions; however, they do add new nouns, verbs, and adjectives quite frequently.

_____It is a historical linguist's job to analyze the history of languages.

_____Even though this task can be frustrating at times, it can also be quite rewarding.

DID YOU KNOW?

How old is English? While this isn't an easy question to answer, Old English, a language that would look and sound foreign to modern English speakers, is thought to have been established when Germanic tribes, most notably the Anglo-Saxons, arrived to the British Isles in 449 CE. Not until the twelfth or thirteenth century had English evolved to the point that it would be intelligible to modern speakers.

32b Common sentence errors with the compound-complex sentence

Pay attention to the common sentence errors for both compound and complex sentences, and you will be successful in punctuating a compound-complex sentence.

1. Check for run-on or fused sentences

Run-on/fused sentence➜ Students who use both American Sign Language and Signed English understand that some of the signs are the same and this makes it easier for them to learn both.

OK➜ Students who use both American Sign Language and Signed English understand that some of the signs are the same, and this makes it easier for them to learn both.

2. Check for comma splices

Comma splice➜ Students who use both American Sign Language and Signed English understand that some of the signs are the same, this makes it easier for them to learn both.

OK➜ Students who use both American Sign Language and Signed English understand that some of the signs are the same, and this makes it easier for them to learn both.

3. Check for fragments

Fragment➜ Students who use both American Sign Language and Signed English understand that some of the signs.

OK➜ Students who use both American Sign Language and Signed English understand that some of the signs are the same, and this makes it easier for them to learn both.

Chapter 33

SENTENCE FOCUS

Be sure that all your sentences are focused on the main idea of your paragraph, essay, or document. In addition, check that the sentence style you use helps each idea flow from sentence to sentence.

33a   Use transitions

You can use transitions to connect from one sentence to the next, creating a flow of ideas that all support the main idea. Transitions can also help clarify meanings by highlighting relationships between words, phrases, or sentences. Writing without transitions often sounds disjointed and rambling, but be sure that the transitions you use fit the relationship you are trying to describe.

→ The Chinese zodiac has twelve signs; similarly, so does Western astrology.

→ As previously mentioned, I am frustrated that my Chinese zodiac sign is the boar.

Transitions

Addition ➔ moreover, furthermore, besides, likewise, also, too, finally, second, third, last, additionally

Cause ➔ since, because

Comparison ➔ similarly, likewise

Concession ➔ although, though, despite

Condition ➔ unless, provided that, if

Contrast ➔ but, yet, however, nevertheless, in contrast, on the contrary, nonetheless, whereas, even though, although, otherwise, on the other hand

Exception ➔ except

Exemplification ➔ for example, for instance

Intensification ➔ indeed, in fact

Place ➔ where, here, near, beyond

Purpose ➔ (in order) to, to this end

Repetition ➔ in other words, as I have said, as previously mentioned, as stated above

Result ➔ therefore, thus, consequently, as a result, hence

Summary ➔ in conclusion, in short, all in all, overall, finally

Time ➔ when, after, before, until, as long as, meanwhile, while, immediately, soon, afterward, then, henceforth

33b   Emphasize key ideas

1. Use sentence order for emphasis

When you use a sentence that includes a list or series, be sure to use an order that is consistent. Listing items from most important to least important, or vice versa, will help you emphasize key ideas.

Poor order ➔ Before completing the sign project, we will need to check with these levels of government: city, national, regional, and county.

OK➔ Before completing the sign project, we will need to check with these levels of government: city, county, regional, and national.

2. Use end-focus for emphasis

In English, it is normal to arrange sentences so that the most important information comes at the end of the sentence. This type of end-focus allows you to organize general knowledge—information that is obvious or already known to the reader—at the beginning of a sentence and lead up to the most important or emphasized information at the end.

End-focus➔ Before the sign project can be completed, we will need to get approval from the governor's office.

3. Use front-focus for emphasis

You can also place a sentence element in an abnormal position—usually at the front of the sentence—to make the element more emphatic. This type of front-focus is used effectively if you know the regular patterns of English sentences (see Chapter 35).

Front-focus➔ Red paint they used rarely for the signs, so using it at the governor's mansion allowed the signs to stand out.

4. Reorder negative adverbials for emphasis

Placing a negative adverbial at the beginning of a sentence places an emphasis on that part of the sentence.

Fronting a negative adverbial➔ Never have I seen such a paint color on a government sign!

5. Use parenthetic expressions

Parenthetic expressions, which are enclosed by punctuation, place an emphasis on the previous sentence element.

Parenthetic expression➜ At the governor's mansion, for example, they used red paint.

Parenthetic expression➜ Red paint, of course, will grab pedestrian attention.

EXERCISE 1

Directions: Rewrite the following sentences, so the underlined part is placed in a different and more emphatic position.

1. They are painting the governor's mansion <u>on a state holiday</u>.

2. The paint used on the mansion is <u>similar to the paint used on the state prison</u>.

3. <u>Tourists were visiting</u> while they painted the building.

4. I would call the paint color <u>dull gray</u>.

5. The paint project costs the state <u>over two million dollars</u>.

33c   Be clear

1. Avoid tangents

To keep your sentence on topic, avoid tangents or irrelevant information.

Lack of focus➜ I am frustrated that my Chinese zodiac sign is the boar, which by the way is also the sign for Arnold Schwarzenegger and Ronald Reagan, because I see myself more of a dragon.

OK➜ I am frustrated that my Chinese zodiac sign is the boar because I see myself more as a dragon.

2. Rephrase ambiguous expressions

Watch out for misplaced expressions that cause ambiguity. Place modifiers effectively in sentences, so the meaning you want to give is clear. Check out how the following ambiguous sentence can be rewritten to show its two different meanings.

> Ambiguous sentence➔ Writing clearly is important.
> Meaning #1➔ It is important to write clearly.
> Meaning #2➔ It is clear that writing is important.

Ambiguity can occur with conjoined noun phrases that have adjectives placed in an ambiguous position.

> Ambiguous sentence➔ The gray foyer and hallway were being painted next.
> Meaning #1➔ The gray foyer and gray hallway were being painted next.
> Meaning #2➔ The hallway (not gray) and the gray foyer were being painted next.

Be sure that any adjective that is used to describe the first noun in a conjoined noun phrase is placed in a position that allows for clear understanding.

3. Make sentence elements parallel

Make sure that your sentence meanings are clear by using parallel sentence elements. Combined or coordinated sentence elements should be similar in type. Notice the lack of parallelism in the sentence below. The *and* is used to join a full clause and a noun phrase. To fix the problem, you need to use either two full clauses or two noun phrases. The second sentence below is parallel and uses two full clauses.

> Lack of parallelism➔ They discontinued the painting because the results did not satisfy the governor and a lack of funding.
>   Independent Clause   NP

> Parallel➔ They discontinued the painting because the results did not satisfy the governor and there was a lack of funding.
>   Independent Clause   Independent Clause

33d Show confidence

When you write, show that you know the topic well by using authority in your phrasing. Stay away from what some teachers and editors call *weasel words*, such as *I think, I believe, I know, I think I know*. See **11a** for more information on how not to "weasel."

> Non-authoritative sentence➜ I think that I know why the Chinese zodiac has twelve signs and four elements.

> OK➜ The Chinese zodiac has twelve signs, based on the months, and four elements, based on the seasons.

EXERCISE 2

Directions: Each of the following sentences has a clarity problem; rewrite them so their meanings are clear.

1. A letter requesting that the governor stop the painting of the mansion and choose another paint color was sent.

2. Although the governor only saw three letters, he knew there was a problem.

3. The color of the atrium, the color of the foyer, and the driveway concrete color did not match.

4. The angry governor and secretary both called the painters' office.

5. The governor wanted the painters, groundskeepers, and the painting supervisors to all be on the same page.

SENTENCE FUNCTIONS

In English, there are four sentence functions that serve different purposes. Writers use declarative sentences to give information, imperative sentences to give instructions or commands, interrogative sentences to obtain information, and exclamatory sentences to express emotion. In academic writing, you will probably use more declarative sentences than any other. However, if you are writing a narrative or descriptive essay or a piece of creative writing, you will want to use sentences with a variety of functions since that will most closely replicate real life.

34a   Use declarative sentences to give information

Use declarative sentences that end with a period for statements that give information. Declarative sentences are the most common type of sentence function in English.

Declarative sentence➜ The Chinese zodiac has five elements.

34b   Use imperative sentences to give commands

Imperative sentences usually do not have a subject; they are used to give instructions or commands.

Imperative sentence➜ Tell me what zodiac sign I am.

Imperative sentence➜ Do not tell me that you forgot the answer.

Imperatives can also take the form of *let* plus a subject.

Imperative sentence➔ Let's talk about the Chinese zodiac.

The imperative sentence can include *you* or a third person subject, but these types of subjects are not used very often.

Imperative sentence➔ You should tell me the answer now.

Imperative sentence➔ The guilty party should stand up now.

Imperative sentences can also add a noun phrase that directly addresses the subject of the sentence.

➔You, tell me the answer now.

➔Those students at the back, tell me the answer now.

34c　Use interrogative sentences to ask questions

To ask questions, use one of the six types of interrogative sentences, including yes/no questions, wh-questions, declarative questions, alternative questions, tag questions, and rhetorical questions.

A yes/no question begins with a verb and can be answered with a *yes* or *no* but can also be answered with other information as well.

Yes/No question➔ Should we mention that the Chinese zodiac is different from other zodiacs?

A wh-question starts with an interrogative word or phrase, usually *who*, *what*, *where*, *when*, *why*, or *how*.

Wh-question➔ How many Chinese zodiac signs are there?

A declarative question is in the form of a declarative sentence but asks a question. These types of questions take the declarative form but usually end with a question mark.

Declarative question➔ The Chinese zodiac has five elements?

Alternative questions give a choice or choices.

Alternative question➔ Do you prefer to be called a boar or a pig?

Tag questions can attach to declarative or interrogative sentences, making the sentences into questions. If the sentence part is negative, the tag will be positive, and vice versa.

Tag question➜ You're a boar, aren't you?

Tag question➜ Tell me your sign, won't you?

Rhetorical questions are basically equal to forceful declarative statements. You do not reply to a rhetorical question.

Rhetorical question➜ Who could be happy being called a *pig*?

34d   Use exclamatory sentences to show surprise

Exclamatory sentences (sometimes called exclamatives) show surprise and end with an exclamation mark. They can begin with *what* or *how*.

Exclamatory sentence➜ What a strange name that is!

Exclamatory sentence➜ How strange that is!

These types of sentences can also look like a forceful declarative statement.

Exclamatory sentence➜ You're a Boar! Really!

EXERCISE 1

Directions: Take the declarative sentence given, and revise it into the type of sentence given in the parentheses.

Example: In medicine, signs are different than symptoms. (yes/no question) → Did you know that in medicine signs are different than symptoms?

1. A symptom is reported by a patient, and a sign is found by a doctor. (alternative question)

2. Fatigue is considered a symptom. (exclamatory sentence)

3. In an examination, a doctor looks for clinical signs. (declarative question)

4. Doctors make hypotheses, and they use signs to support their hypotheses. (Wh-question)

5. Reddening of the hands is considered a sign. (imperative sentence)

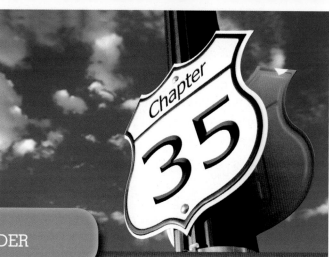

SENTENCE ORDER

35a   Vary basic sentence order

In English, there are seven basic sentence orders for declarative sentences, influenced by different types of verbs and the elements that work with those verbs. Becoming familiar with these basic sentence orders will help you revise your writing if you find yourself frequently writing the same pattern or order. For more in-depth discussion of the word classes that form these patterns, see Section I.

1. Subject + intransitive verb

A sentence that includes an intransitive verb does not need anything to follow the verb for the sentence to be complete. However, the intransitive verb **can** be followed by an adverb or other optional elements, such as a prepositional phrase, and other optional elements can occur in other places in the sentence.

→   Money talks.
       S   V

→   Money talks loudly.

→   Sometimes, money talks loudly.

→   Sometimes, money talks loudly in a bad economy.

→   Sometimes, in a bad economy, money talks loudly.

Notice that all of the sentences above have the same basic sentence order with the subject and intransitive verb at the center of the sentence.

Even though these sentences might appear different to you, they have the same underlying pattern, and as such, if you write most of your sentences using this same pattern, your prose style will take on a monotonous rhythm.

2. Subject + transitive verb + direct object

A sentence that has a subject, transitive verb, and direct object is the most frequently used English sentence order. The transitive verb requires a noun or noun phrase as its direct object. A noun that comes after a direct object answers one of these questions: What? Whom? (What did the highway workers clean? Whom did John see?) Just like any other sentence pattern, this one can take optional elements, such as adverbs or prepositional phrases.

➔ The highway workers **cleaned** the sign.
         S   V   DO

➔ Yesterday, the highway workers cleaned the sign.

➔ Yesterday, the highway workers cleaned the sign vigorously.

3. Subject + transitive verb + indirect object + direct object

Some transitive verbs require both a direct object and an indirect object. There is a simple way to tell the difference between an indirect object and a direct object. Direct objects answer one of these questions: What? or Whom? Indirect objects answer one of these questions: To what? To whom? For what? For whom?

➔ The foreman **gave Chris** the work order.
        S   V   IO   DO

Gave what? the work order

To whom? Chris

You can also add optional elements to this type of sentence order.

➔ At the beginning of the shift, the foreman gave Chris the lost work order.

4. Subject + transitive verb + direct object + object complement

A small number of transitive verbs—such as *declare, call, name*—require a direct object and object complement. The object complement is a necessary element in this type of sentence; it describes the direct object. Remember that a direct object answers one of these questions: Whom? What? An object complement can be either a noun phrase or an adjective phrase.

> → Sarah **called me a novice.**
>   S   V   DO NP

Whom did Sarah call a novice? me

> → Sarah **called me lazy.**
>   S   V   DO Adj

Whom did Sarah call lazy? me

Just like with any other sentence pattern, you can add other optional elements, but you still have the same sentence pattern.

> → When I could not do the ASL sign for *water,* Sarah called me a novice.

5. Subject + transitive verb + direct object + adverbial complement

Some transitive verbs—such as *place, put*—require both a direct object and an adverbial complement. An adverbial complement is the name for a prepositional phrase that gives information about when, where, why, and how.

> → Alex **put the sign on the door.**
>   S   V   DO   Adv

You can also lengthen this type of sentence pattern with optional elements.

> → Yesterday morning, Alex put the sign on the door with the red stripes.

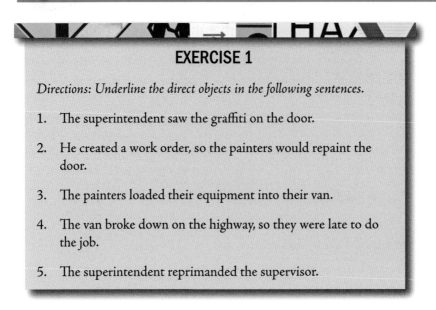

EXERCISE 1

Directions: Underline the direct objects in the following sentences.

1. The superintendent saw the graffiti on the door.

2. He created a work order, so the painters would repaint the door.

3. The painters loaded their equipment into their van.

4. The van broke down on the highway, so they were late to do the job.

5. The superintendent reprimanded the supervisor.

6. Subject + linking verb + subject complement

A common sentence pattern includes a subject, linking verb, and subject complement. Linking verbs are verbs that describe a state of being: *be, appear, seem, taste, sound.* The linking verb, if you think in terms of math, functions as an equal sign, and the subject complement renames (noun phrase) or describes (adjective phrase).

➔ A changing traffic signal **is a sign.**
     S   V NP

➔ A changing traffic signal **is frustrating.**
     S   V Adj

Optional elements can also be added to this type of sentence.

➔ In the spring, a sound like a train engine is a sign.

➔ A sound like a train engine is scary, especially in the spring.

➔ A sound like a train engine is scary, especially when a tornado warning has sounded.

7. Subject + linking verb + adverbial complement

A linking verb can also take an adverbial complement. The adverbial complement—usually a prepositional phrase—is required for this type of sentence to be complete.

➔ The warning signs are on the back wall.
      S   V   Prep Ph

DID YOU KNOW?

You might think that sentences in all languages are structured the same as many English sentences: begin with a subject, add a verb, and end with an object (e.g., *Sam drank the water*). But not all languages are subject-verb-object (SVO) languages. Many are SOV (e.g., *Sam the water drank*), including Japanese and Persian. There are even a few languages with VOS, OVS, and OSV word orders; Fijian, for example, has a VOS word order: *Drank the water Sam.*

35b   Vary sentence openings

You can vary sentence openings to help your writing not take on a dull or boring sentence rhythm.

1. Add introductory words, phrases, and clauses

Adding in optional introductory words, phrases, or clauses can also lengthen your sentences, a sign of a more sophisticated and complex writing style.

Sample of dull or boring sentence rhythm➔ The Hollywood sign is a national monument. The Hollywood sign is in Griffith Park in Los Angeles. The sign is 45 feet tall, and it has white letters. It was created as an advertisement in 1923.

Add a transitional/introductory word➜ The Hollywood sign is a national monument. However, it is located in Griffith Park and not Hollywood.

Add an introductory verb phrase➜ Located in Griffith Park, the Hollywood sign is a national monument.

Add an introductory prepositional phrase➜ In Griffith Park, the Hollywood sign is a national monument.

Add an introductory clause➜ Although the Hollywood sign was first created as an advertisement in 1923, it is now a national monument.

EXERCISE 2

Directions: Join the pairs of sentences together by using introductory words, phrases, or clauses.

Example: The Hollywood sign was created in 1923. The Hollywood sign is a national monument. ➜ *Created in 1923, the Hollywood sign is a national monument.*

1. The Welcome to Las Vegas sign is a historic landmark. The Welcome to Las Vegas sign is on the U.S. National Register of Historic Places.

2. The Welcome to Las Vegas sign is a historic landmark. It was funded and erected in May 1959.

3. The sign is in the town of Paradise. The sign is roughly four miles away from the city limits of Las Vegas.

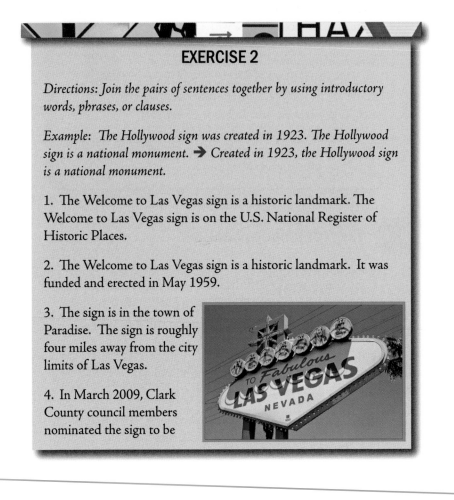

4. In March 2009, Clark County council members nominated the sign to be

placed on the U.S. National Register of Historic Places. On May 1, 2009, the sign was placed on the U.S. National Register of Historic Places.

5. The sign is 25 feet tall. The sign is a classic roadside pole design.

2. Avoid *subject-itis*

When you use the same sentence pattern or order, your sentences can start to look like they all have the same beginning. Some teachers and editors call this *subject-itis*, labeling it as a sentence disease. Check out this group of sentences that all begin with a subject.

> The Hollywood sign is a national monument. The Hollywood sign is in Griffith Park in Los Angeles. The sign is 45 feet tall, and it has white letters. It was created as an advertisement in 1923.

One of the ways you can cure *subject-itis* is by using introductory words, phrases, or clauses. Another way is to do some sentence combining, joining some of the sentences together to form compound or complex sentences.

> Add an introductory verb phrase➜ Standing 45 feet tall with white letters, the Hollywood sign is a national monument located in Griffith Park in Los Angeles.

> Join sentences together➜ The Hollywood sign is a national monument located in Griffith Park in Los Angeles; its white letters stand 45 feet tall.

> Add an introductory verb phrase➜ Created as an advertisement in 1923, the Hollywood sign is a national monument located in Griffith Park; its white letters stand 45 feet tall.

Helpful hint

Subject-itis can quickly turn into *I-itis* (with every sentence beginning with an *I*) when you write a first-person narrative. Be especially careful of this type of repetition when using the first-person for narratives or other types of academic writing.

35c   Fix misplaced modifiers

Modifiers can be used to add information to sentences, but they can sometimes cause problems as well if not placed in the correct position in the sentence.

1. Check for misleading or misplaced modifiers

If a modifier is misplaced, it can cause confusion or even give an unwanted meaning to a sentence. There are three main types of misleading or misplaced modifiers: squinting, limiting, and disruptive.

Squinting modifiers are words or phrases that can refer to more than one word or phrase in the sentence. Revise the sentence so the modifier is placed directly where it refers to only a single word or phrase.

> Squinting modifier➜ The girl in my English class is in the corner with the protest sign.

Is the girl in the corner? Is the protest sign in the corner? Are they both in the corner? Place the modifier where its meaning cannot be misleading.

> OK➜ The girl with the protest sign is in the corner; I know her from English class.

Limiting modifiers, such as *almost, even, just, merely,* and *only,* usually give information about how many or how often. Be careful where you place these modifiers since poor placement can cause ambiguity.

Limiting modifier poorly placed ➔ We almost had 30 signs painted by the end of the day.

How can you *almost have* something? The *almost* is modifying how many signs were done by the end of the day, so this limiting modifier needs to be next to the phrase it modifies.

OK➔ We had almost 30 signs painted by the end of the day.

Disruptive modifiers are any type of modifiers that come in the middle of a phrase or sentence, **and** their position allows them to disrupt that same phrase or sentence. Some disruptive modifiers can be grammatically correct and still be disruptive. Be sure that modifying phrases or clauses do not become long and winding paths that lead the reader off the main point.

Disruptive modifier ➔ We had 30 signs—ten blue ones, five yellow ones, five red ones, three green ones, three purple ones, three orange ones, and one black one—that needed to be painted by the end of the day.

OK➔ We had to paint 30 signs by the end of the day; they included ten blue ones, five yellow ones, five red ones, three green ones, three purple ones, three orange ones, and one black one.

Splitting a verb infinitive (*to* + *verb*) with a modifier is also disruptive. Although some instructors and editors accept split infinitives, many do not; it will always be fine to rework a split infinite.

Split infinitive➔ The foreman warned us to carefully place the signs in the truck.

OK➔ The foreman warned us to place the signs carefully in the truck.

Helpful hint

Some split infinitives are part of our culture; fixing them might cause confusion and comment.

➔ On *Star Trek*, the captain and crew want to boldly go where no one has gone before.

2. Check for dangling modifiers

Dangling modifiers are verbals (to + verb, verb + *–ing*, or verb + *–en/ –ed*) placed either at the beginning or end of the sentence and has the verbal modifying the wrong word.

> Dangling modifier ➜ **Having been painted**, we put the signs into the delivery truck.

The dangling modifier (*having been painted*) appears to modify *we*, but it should modify *the signs*. You can fix a dangling modifier in a variety of ways, including moving the word being modified into the correct position or rewording the entire sentence.

> OK➜ **Having been painted**, the signs were put into the delivery truck.

> OK➜ The **painted** signs were put into the truck.

> OK➜ We put the **painted** signs into the truck.

Participial verb phrases (with *–ing* or *–ed*) endings are often at the beginning of a dangling modifier.

> Dangling modifier ➜ **Left on their own**, the signs were put into the truck by the kids.

> OK➜ The kids, **left on their own**, put the signs into the truck.

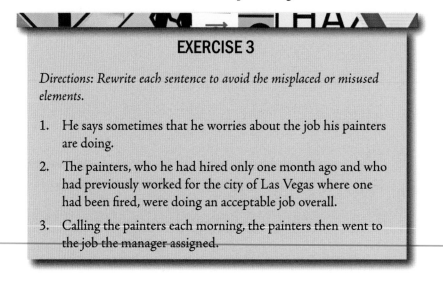

EXERCISE 3

Directions: Rewrite each sentence to avoid the misplaced or misused elements.

1. He says sometimes that he worries about the job his painters are doing.

2. The painters, who he had hired only one month ago and who had previously worked for the city of Las Vegas where one had been fired, were doing an acceptable job overall.

3. Calling the painters each morning, the painters then went to the job the manager assigned.

4. The painters sometimes left their equipment at the job site which sometimes included brushes and paint.

5. The manager wants his painting crew to only do good work.

35d Check direct v. indirect speech

Direct speech is highlighted with quotation marks. Indirect quotations or speech do not take quotation marks. When you use an indirect quotation or indirect speech, be sure to change the order of the sentence, if necessary, and use the correct punctuation.

Direct quotation➜ The manager said, "Put the signs in the truck."

Indirect quotation➜ The manager said to put the signs in the truck.

Direct question➜ Did you put the signs in the truck?

Indirect question➜ He asked if the signs had been put in the truck.

35e Check for empty phrases and clauses

Even though sentences that begin with *it* or *there* + *be* are grammatically correct, they use extra words or empty phrases that sometimes can be easily removed if the sentence is rephrased.

1. Check for empty *it*

Empty phrase ➜ It had taken three hours for the students to paint the signs.

OK➜ The students took three hours to paint the signs.

2. Check for empty *there*

Empty phrase ➜ There were three signs that the students forgot to paint.

OK➜ The students forgot to paint three signs.

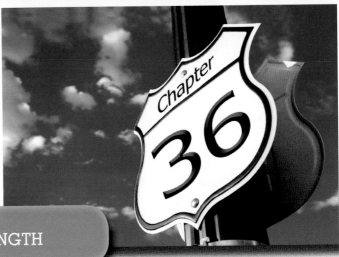

SENTENCE LENGTH

A variety of sentences with a mixture of sentence lengths is a sign of a mature, sophisticated writing style. Becoming familiar with how to shorten or lengthen sentences will help you revise when your sentences are too choppy, too repetitive, or too underdeveloped.

36a   Check for choppy sentences

Nothing is wrong with a short simple sentence every once in a while; however, many short simple sentences in a row can create a dull and repetitive rhythm that is uncomfortable for the reader. Consider the following sentences.

> → The Hollywood sign is a national monument. The Hollywood sign is in Griffith Park in Los Angeles. The sign is 45 feet tall. It has white letters. It was created as an advertisement in 1923.

What can you do to rephrase these short and choppy sentences that have the same simple-subject-predicate rhythm? You can join some of the sentences together by using coordinating conjunctions (*for, and, nor, but, or, yet, so*) and creating some compound sentences.

> Compound sentences → The Hollywood sign is a national monument, and it is located in Griffith Park in Los Angeles. The sign is 45 feet tall, and it has white letters. It was created as an advertisement in 1923.

What do you notice about the above sentences? Does compounding make that dull and repetitive rhythm disappear? Probably not enough.

Plus, it was difficult to join the last sentence to the rest of the description. To improve even more, you can try combining more of the sentences by using complex sentences.

> Complex sentences➔ The Hollywood sign, which is located in Griffith Park in Los Angeles, is 45 feet tall with white letters. It was created as an advertisement in 1923.

Combining sentences by creating complex sentences helped cut out words and made the first sentence flow much better. However, we are still left with the last simple sentence that was difficult to combine. To improve even more, you can combine all the sentences using both complex and compound strategies.

> Compound and complex➔ The Hollywood sign, which is located in Griffith Park in Los Angeles, is 45 feet tall with white letters; it was created as an advertisement in 1923.

For more information on using sentence combining to create compound, complex, and compound-complex sentences, see Section IV.

Helpful hint

You can check the grade level of your writing by looking at the Flesch-Kincaid index. You can pull this up in Microsoft Word under the grammar checker and spell checker menu.

36b   Check for excessive coordination

When you use compound sentences to bring some variety to your writing, you are using a combining strategy that we use quite often in oral language. Be careful, though, that you do not overuse it in your writing since doing so will make your writing sound too conversational for academic writing.

> Too conversational ➔ The Hollywood sign is located in Griffith Park in Los Angeles, and it is 45 feet tall and has white letters, and it was created as an advertisement in 1923.

Use compound sentences sparingly, and mix them with complex sentences or compound-complex sentences to bring more intricacy to your writing.

OK➔ The Hollywood sign, which is located in Griffith Park in Los Angeles, is 45 feet tall with white letters; it was created as an advertisement in 1923.

36c Check for excessive subordination and modification

Creating complex sentences is done by using subordination and modification, and adding this complexity to your writing gives a more sophisticated style. However, be careful that you do not overuse subordination and modification to the point where it is difficult for the reader to understand what you are joining or describing.

Too complex➔ The Hollywood sign, which was created as an advertisement in 1923 and which is located in Griffith Park, which is in Los Angeles, is 45 feet tall with white letters.

OK➔ The Hollywood sign, which is located in the Griffith Park of Los Angeles, is 45 feet tall with white letters; it was created as an advertisement in 1923.

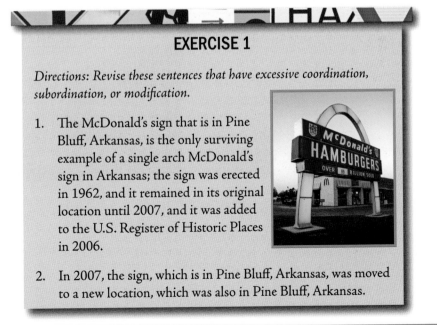

EXERCISE 1

Directions: Revise these sentences that have excessive coordination, subordination, or modification.

1. The McDonald's sign that is in Pine Bluff, Arkansas, is the only surviving example of a single arch McDonald's sign in Arkansas; the sign was erected in 1962, and it remained in its original location until 2007, and it was added to the U.S. Register of Historic Places in 2006.

2. In 2007, the sign, which is in Pine Bluff, Arkansas, was moved to a new location, which was also in Pine Bluff, Arkansas.

3. The Pine Bluff sign has many of the typical features of an early single arch McDonald's sign; it is back-lit; it has plastic panels in a metal frame; it has red advertising midway down the arch.

4. No one knows how many single arch McDonald's signs still exist, but there is one in Biloxi, Mississippi, and there is one in Lancaster, Pennsylvania, and there is one in Green Bay, Wisconsin, and there is one in Huntsville, Alabama.

5. The sign that is in Pine Bluff is the only single arch McDonald's sign that is on the U.S. Register of Historic Places, which is the United State's official list of buildings that are deemed worthy of preservation.

36d   Add descriptive words and phrases

You can enhance the descriptiveness of your sentences by adding modifiers in different places in the sentence.

1. Add descriptive nouns and noun phrases

Develop more descriptive noun phrases by adding pre-modifiers, such as adjectives, and post-modifiers, such as appositives, prepositional phrases, or relative clauses. Doing so will lengthen your sentences and show off your vocabulary.

Noun Phrase➜ the house

With pre-modifier➜ the **big blue** house
                  Adj Adj

With pre-modifier and post-modifier➜ the **big blue** house,
                  Adj Adj
a Colonial, which is sitting on the corner of Sixth and Elm.
Appositive   Relative Clause

You can also lengthen your sentences and show off your vocabulary by replacing simple nouns with words that carry more than a simple description.

> Simple noun➜ house

> Possible variations➜ abode, adobe, Colonial, domicile, dwelling, habitat, igloo

2. Add descriptive verbs

Your sentences can become more descriptive by changing out simple verbs for ones that fit the scene you are trying to set or describe. Remember, though, that your vocabulary should match the type of academic writing you are doing.

> Simple verb➜ go

> Possible variations➜ depart, exit, hit the road, make tracks, take leave

3. Add descriptive adjectives

Adjectives can be used in three different ways to add more description to a sentence. Showing that you have the facility to use all three types demonstrates a more sophisticated writing style.

A. ADJECTIVES AS PRE-MODIFIERS

An adjective or adjective phrase can be used to modify the noun that follows it.

> Adjective➜ the wet sign

> Conjoined adjective phrase➜ the wet and moldy sign

> Adjective phrase with modifying adverb➜ the extremely wet and moldy sign

B. ADJECTIVES AS POST-MODIFIERS

An adjective or adjective phrase can modify the noun it follows.

> Adjective➜ That problem, undoable, was the only one I did not complete.

Conjoined adjective phrase➔ The sign, wet and moldy, needs to be replaced.

Adjective phrase with modifying adverb➔ The sign, quite wet and moldy, needs to be replaced.

C. ADJECTIVES AS COMPLEMENTS

An adjective or adjective phrase can modify a subject as a subject complement, or it can modify a direct object as an object complement.

Subject complement/adjective➔ That problem is frustrating.

Subject complement/adjective phrase➔ That problem is quite frustrating.

Object complement/adjective➔ All the students called the problem undoable.

Object complement/adjective phrase➔ All the students called the problem frustratingly undoable.

4. Add descriptive adverbs

Adverbs or adverb phrases can be used to bring more description to your sentences by modifying verbs, adjectives, other adverbs, or even full sentences.

Modifying a verb➔ The Hollywood sign was created originally as an advertisement.

Modifying an adjective➔ The extremely tall Hollywood sign was created as an advertisement.

Modifying another adverb➔ The answer to the problem was quite frustratingly obvious after the teacher revealed it.

Modifying a sentence➔ The answer to the problem was frustrating; consequently, the students failed the test..

5. Add descriptive prepositional phrases

Prepositional phrases can be used to modify a variety of elements in a sentence. They can give optional adverbial-type information about time or place; they can give more detail to a noun phrase, adjective phrase, or adverbial phrase; or they can function as an adverbial complement.

Optional adverbial➔ In the spring, the Hollywood sign is cleaned.

Post-modifier to a noun➔ The Hollywood sign, in Griffith Park, is cleaned each spring.

Post-modifier to an adjective➔ Climbing to the Hollywood sign is supposed to be difficult for most people.

Post-modifier to an adverbial➔ The park ranger looked angrily at us when we started up the path to the Hollywood sign.

EXERCISE 2

Directions: Revise the following simple sentences by using the modifier type given in parentheses.

1. The Skipping Girl Vinegar sign is located on Victoria Street in Melbourne, Australia. (add descriptive adjective)

2. The sign is a painted metal structure. (add descriptive prepositional phrase)

3. The sign is also known as Little Audrey. (add descriptive noun phrase)

4. The sign was manufactured in 1936 to advertise vinegar. (add descriptive verb phrase)

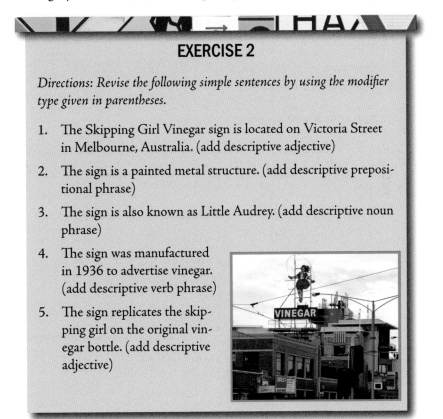

5. The sign replicates the skipping girl on the original vinegar bottle. (add descriptive adjective)